The Experience of Atheism

The Experience of Atheism

Phenomenology, Metaphysics and Religion

Edited by
Robyn Horner and Claude Romano

BLOOMSBURY ACADEMIC
LONDON • NEW YORK • OXFORD • NEW DELHI • SYDNEY

BLOOMSBURY ACADEMIC
Bloomsbury Publishing Plc
50 Bedford Square, London, WC1B 3DP, UK
1385 Broadway, New York, NY 10018, USA
29 Earlsfort Terrace, Dublin 2, Ireland

BLOOMSBURY, BLOOMSBURY ACADEMIC and the Diana logo are trademarks of
Bloomsbury Publishing Plc

First published in Great Britain 2021
This paperback edition published in 2023

Copyright © Robyn Horner and Claude Romano and Contributors 2021

Robyn Horner and Claude Romano have asserted their right under the Copyright,
Designs and Patents Act, 1988, to be identified as Editors of this work.

For legal purposes the Acknowledgments on p. x constitute an extension
of this copyright page.

Cover design by Charlotte Daniels
Cover image © Edwin Remsberg / Getty Images

All rights reserved. No part of this publication may be reproduced or transmitted in any
form or by any means, electronic or mechanical, including photocopying, recording,
or any information storage or retrieval system, without prior permission
in writing from the publishers.

Bloomsbury Publishing Plc does not have any control over, or responsibility for,
any third-party websites referred to or in this book. All internet addresses given in
this book were correct at the time of going to press. The author and publisher
regret any inconvenience caused if addresses have changed or sites have
ceased to exist, but can accept no responsibility for any such changes.

A catalogue record for this book is available from the British Library.

Library of Congress Cataloging-in-Publication Data

Names: Horner, Robyn, editor. | Romano, Claude, 1967– editor.
Title: The experience of atheism : phenomenology, metaphysics and religion /
edited by Robyn Horner and Claude Romano.
Description: London ; New York : Bloomsbury Academic, 2021. |
Includes bibliographical references and index. |
Identifiers: LCCN 2020055537 (print) | LCCN 2020055538 (ebook) |
ISBN 9781350167636 (hardback) | ISBN 9781350167643 (ebook) |
ISBN 9781350167650 (epub)
Subjects: LCSH: Atheism. | Experience. | Phenomenology.
Classification: LCC BL2710 .E97 2021 (print) | LCC BL2710 (ebook) | DDC 211/.8—dc23
LC record available at https://lccn.loc.gov/2020055537
LC ebook record available at https://lccn.loc.gov/2020055538

ISBN: HB: 978-1-3501-6763-6
PB: 978-1-3502-4557-0
ePDF: 978-1-3501-6764-3
eBook: 978-1-3501-6765-0

Typeset by RefineCatch Limited, Bungay, Suffolk

To find out more about our authors and books visit www.bloomsbury.com
and sign up for our newsletters.

Contents

List of Contributors		vi
Acknowledgments		x
1	Atheism, Faith, and Experience *Claude Romano and Robyn Horner*	1

Part One   The Experience of Atheism

2	Atheistic Experience *Jean-Luc Nancy*	19
3	Desire and Inertia *Jeffrey Bloechl*	27
4	No Gods, No Masters—Anarchism and Religious Experience *Catherine Malabou*	35
5	Nothingness against the Death of God—Mallarmé's Poetics after 1866 *Quentin Meillassoux*	43
6	There Is No Experience of Pure Atheism—Michel Serres and the Schema of Unbelief *Christopher Watkin*	61

Part Two   The Atheisms of Faith

7	Theism, Atheism, Anatheism *Richard Kearney*	79
8	Apocalypse or Revelation? *Emmanuel Falque*	87
9	Atheism and Critique *Anthony J. Steinbock*	103

Part Three   The Phenomenality of the Religious

10	The Death of God—Sartre against Heidegger *Philippe Cabestan*	123
11	Materialism, Social Construction, and Radical Empiricism—Debating the Status of "Experience" in the Study of Religion *Tamsin Jones*	135
12	Atheism, Religion, Experience (and Metaphysics?) *Patrick Masterson*	149
13	On Seeing Nothing—A Critique of Marion's Account of Religious Phenomenality *Christina M. Gschwandtner*	163
14	Doubling Metaphysics *Jean-Luc Marion*	181
Index		199

List of Contributors

Jacob Benjamins is a doctoral researcher at KU Leuven and Australian Catholic University. His research interests are in phenomenology of religion, the relationship between philosophy and theology, and political theology. He has published articles in *Research in Phenomenology*, *Literature and Theology*, *Political Theology*, and *Louvain Studies*. He is currently working on a phenomenology of creation's goodness and examining its consequences for understanding Christianity and culture.

Jeffrey Bloechl is Associate Professor of Philosophy at Boston College and an Honorary Research Fellow at the Australian Catholic University. His research is concentrated in the areas of phenomenology, philosophy and theology, philosophy and mysticism, and Freudian psychoanalysis. He is presently completing a monograph on the phenomenology of faith, hope, and love.

Philippe Cabestan is a professor of philosophy in *Classes préparatoires* (Paris) and Associate Member, Husserl Archives, Paris. His research is concentrated in the areas of phenomenology, existentialism, and psychopathology. He is President of the French School of Existential Analysis (Ecole Française de *Daseinsanalyse*) and Secretary of the European Association of Phenomenology and Psychopathology (EAPP). He is the author of *L'Être et la conscience: Recherches sur la psychologie et l'ontologie sartriennes* (Belgium: Ousia, 2004); *Qui suis-je? Sartre et la question du sujet* (Paris: Hermann, 2015), and *Tomber malade, devenir fou: Essai de phénoménologie existentielle* (Paris: Vrin, 2020). With Françoise Dastur, he authored *Daseinsanalyse. Phénoménologie et psychiatrie* (Paris: Vrin, 2011).

Emmanuel Falque is Professor and Emeritus Dean at the Faculty of Philosophy of the Catholic University of Paris. He is the founder of the International Network in Philosophy of Religion (INPR). He is a specialist in patristic and medieval philosophy, phenomenology, and philosophy of religion, and many of his works have been translated into English. For example, in patristic and medieval philosophy: *Saint Bonaventure and the Entrance of God into Theology* (New York: Franciscan Institute Publications, 2018), *God, The Flesh and the Other* (Evanston: Northwestern, 2015), and *The Book of Experience* (South Bend: Notre Dame, forthcoming). He also publishes in phenomenology, including *The Loving Struggle* (Lanham: Rowman and Littlefield, 2018), *Nothing to it* (Leuven: Leuven University Press, 2020), and in philosophy of religion, *The Metamorphosis of Finitude* (New York: Fordham, 2012), *The Wedding Feast of the Lamb* (New York: Fordham, 2016), and *The Guide to Gethsemane* (New York: Fordham, 2019).

Christina M. Gschwandtner is Professor of Philosophy at Fordham University, New York, where she teaches Continental Philosophy of Religion. She is author of *Reading Jean-Luc Marion: Exceeding Metaphysics* (Bloomington: Indiana University Press, 2007), *Postmodern Apologetics? Arguments about God in Contemporary Philosophy* (New York: Fordham, 2012), *Degrees of Givenness: On Saturation in Jean-Luc Marion* (Bloomington: Indiana University Press, 2014), *Marion and Theology* (Edinburgh: T&T Clark, 2016), and most recently *Welcoming Finitude: Toward a Phenomenology of Orthodox Liturgy* (New York: Fordham, 2019), besides many articles at the intersection of phenomenology and religion.

Robyn Horner is Associate Professor of Theology at Australian Catholic University, and a member of the University's Institute for Religion and Critical Inquiry. From 2010 to 2015, she held the position of Associate Dean (Learning and Teaching) in the Faculty of Theology and Philosophy. She is author of *Rethinking God as Gift* (New York: Fordham, 2001), *Jean-Luc Marion: A* Theo-*logical Introduction* (Farnham: Ashgate, 2005), and *Experience of God: The Event of Revelation* (forthcoming), as well as many shorter texts. Her research interests include fundamental theology, phenomenology, hermeneutics, and poststructuralism. She teaches in the areas of fundamental theology and the Enhancing Catholic School Identity Research.

Tamsin Jones is Associate Professor of Religious Studies at Trinity College, CT, where she teaches courses in the history of Christian thought, gender and religion, and the philosophy of religion. She is the author of *A Genealogy of Marion's Philosophy of Religion: Apparent Darkness* (Bloomington: Indiana University Press, 2011) as well as articles in the *Journal of Religion,* the *Journal of Theology and Sexuality, Political Theology, Journal of Religious and Cultural Theory,* and *Modern Theology*. She is currently working on the concept of "religious experience" as it is discussed in continental philosophy and against the backdrop of trauma theory.

Richard Kearney holds the Charles Seelig Chair in Philosophy at Boston College. He has published many works on the philosophy of narrative imagination and embodiment as well as the following works in the hermeneutics of religion—*Poetique du Possible, The God who May Be, Strangers Gods and Monsters, Anatheism,* and *Reimagining the Sacred*. He has also published two novels and a volume of poetry and is international director of the Guestbook Project, "Changing Stories, Changing Histories."

Catherine Malabou is Professor of Philosophy at the Centre for Research in Modern European Philosophy at Kingston University, UK, and a Distinguished Professor in the Department of Comparative Literature and European Languages and Studies at the University of California at Irvine where she regularly teaches in the Spring term. Her recent books include *Before Tomorrow: Epigenesis and Rationality,* trans. Carolyn Shread (Cambridge: Polity Press, 2016) and *Morphing Intelligence: From IQ to IA,* trans. Carolyn Shread (New York: Columbia, 2018). She is currently working on a new book project around anarchism and philosophy.

Jean-Luc Marion is Professor Emeritus of Philosophy at University of Paris IV (Sorbonne) and Andrew Thomas and Grace McNichols Greeley Professor of Catholic Studies and Professor of Theology and the Philosophy of Religion, Divinity School, University of Chicago. He is also Adjunct Professor of Philosophy at Australian Catholic University. In 2008 he was elected to the prestigious *Académie française*. He is the author of thirty-eight books, some of which have been translated into as many as eleven languages. His most famous works include *Dieu sans l'être* (*God without Being*), first published in 1982, and *Étant donné: Essai d'une phénoménologie de la donation* (*Being Given: Toward a Phenomenology of Givenness*), from 1997.

Patrick Masterson is President Emeritus and Professor Emeritus of Philosophy, University College Dublin. His other roles have included Vice-Chancellor, National University of Ireland (1987 and 1988) and President, European University Institute, Florence (1994–2002). He is the author of *Atheism and Alienation: A Study of the Philosophical Sources of Contemporary Atheism* (South Bend: Gill and MacMillan/Notre Dame Press, 1971), *The Sense of Creation* (Farnham: Ashgate, 2008), and *Approaching God: Between Phenomenology and Theology* (London: Bloomsbury, 2013). In his retirement, he writes novels and makes wine in the south of France.

Quentin Meillassoux is Associate Professor in Philosophy at University of Paris I (Panthéon-Sorbonne). He has published *Après la finitude. Essai sur la nécessité de la contingence* (Paris: Seuil, 2006) and *Le Nombre et la sirène. Un déchiffrage du Coup de Dés de Mallarmé* (Paris: Fayard, 2011). Both texts have been published in English: *After Finitude. An Essay on the Necessity of Contingency*, translated by Ray Brassier (London: Continuum, 2008) and *The Number and the Siren. A Decipherment of Mallarmé's Coup de Dés*, translated by Robin Mackay (Falmouth: Urbanomic, 2011).

Jean-Luc Nancy is Professor Emeritus of Philosophy at University of Strasbourg, France. He is the author of more than twenty monographs, many translated into multiple languages, in addition to a number of co-authored books. Some of his most well-known texts in English include *An Inoperative Community* (Minneapolis: University of Minnesota Press, 1991); *Being Singular Plural* (California: Stanford, 2000), *The Sense of the World* (Minneapolis: University of Minnesota Press, 2008), and the two-volume work with Fordham, *The Deconstruction of Christianity* (*Disenclosure*, 2009 and *Adoration*, 2012).

Claude Romano is Associate Professor of Philosophy at University of Paris IV (Sorbonne) and Distinguished Visiting Professor at Australian Catholic University. He also occupied the Gadamer Chair at Boston College in 2019–2020. He is the author of many books, especially in phenomenology, in history of philosophy and on the relations between philosophy and literature. Those translated into English are *Event and World* (New York: Fordham, 2009), *Event and Time* (New York: Fordham, 2013), *There is* (New York: Fordham, 2015), and *At the Heart of Reason* (Evnston: Northwestern, 2015). He recently published *Être soi-même. Une autre histoire de la philosophie* (Paris: Gallimard, 2018), *Les repères éblouissants. Renouveler la phénoménologie* (Paris: Presses universitaires de France, 2019), and *La liberté intérieure. Une esquisse* (Paris: Hermann, 2020). He is the 2020 winner of the Grand Prix de philosophie from the Académie Française for his entire work.

Anthony J. Steinbock is Professor of Philosophy at Stony Brook University, and Director of the Phenomenology Research Center. His works include *It's Not about the Gift: From Givenness to Loving* (Lanham: Rowman & Littlefield, 2018), *Limit-Phenomena and Phenomenology in Husserl* (Lanham: Rowman & Littlefield, 2017), *Moral Emotions: Reclaiming the Evidence of the Heart* (Evanston: Northwestern, 2014—winner of the 2015 Symposium Book Award), *Phenomenology and Mysticism: The Verticality of Religious Experience* (Bloomington: Indiana University Press, 2007/2009—winner of the 2009 Edward Goodwin Ballard Book Prize in Phenomenology), and *Home and Beyond: Generative Phenomenology after Husserl* (Evanston: Northwestern, 1995). He is the translator of Edmund Husserl, *Analyses Concerning Passive and Active Synthesis: Lectures on Transcendental Logic* (Dordrecht: Kluwer, 2001). He serves as editor-in-chief of the *Continental Philosophy Review* and as general editor of the Northwestern SPEP Series. His current book, *Knowing By Heart: Loving as Participation and Critique*, is forthcoming with Northwestern

University Press, 2021.

Christopher Watkin is a Senior Lecturer at Monash University, Melbourne, Australia, where he teaches across French and Literary Studies. His books include *Phenomenology or Deconstruction?* (Edinburgh: Edinburgh University Press, 2009), *Difficult Atheism* (Edinburgh: Edinburgh University Press, 2011), *French Philosophy Today* (Edinburgh: Edinburgh University Press, 2016), and *Michel Serres: Figures of Thought* (Edinburgh: Edinburgh University Press, 2020). Chris is currently working on a project interrogating the concepts of freedom and liberation in contemporary thought and society in the light of what has been called the Western "emancipation narrative." He blogs about philosophy and academic research at christopherwatkin.com, and you can find him on Twitter: @DrChrisWatkin.

Samuel Webb is Teaching and Research Fellow (ATER) in the philosophy department of University of Paris IV (Sorbonne), where he completed a dissertation on Self-Knowledge and Practical Reflection in Sartre and recent analytic philosophy under the supervision of Claude Romano. He teaches courses on a variety of topics including personal identity, selfhood, belief, and philosophical translation. He has translated a number of French philosophical texts, including Rousseau's "Preface to *Narcissus*," in *Jean-Jacques Rousseau: Fundamental Political Writings* (Peterborough: Broadview, 2018).

Acknowledgments

This volume is one of the outcomes of the Research Group, *Atheism and Christianity: Moving Past Polemic*, which was very generously supported by Australian Catholic University through the Institute for Religion and Critical Enquiry from 2017 to 2019. We are ever thankful to our colleagues in that collaboration: Denys Turner (Yale/ACU), David Newheiser (ACU), Christiaan Jacobs-Vandegeer (ACU), Stephan van Erp (KU Leuven), Henning Tegtmeyer (KU Leuven), Charles Lockwood (ACU), Rachel Davies (ACU), and Jacob Benjamins (ACU/KU Leuven). We also acknowledge the enormous contribution of the invited international scholars who contributed so richly to the four ACU Rome Seminars held as part of the project: Nicholas Adams, Christine Alpers, Alda Balthrop-Lewis, Stefano Bancalari, Leora Batnitzky, Agata Bielik-Robson, William Cavanaugh, Sarah Coakley, Catherine Cornille, Ryan Coyne, Rick Elgendy, Fiona Ellis, Emmanuel Falque, Constance Furey, Phillip Goodchild, Eric Gregory, Christina M. Gschwandtner, Amy Hollywood, Tamsin Jones, Mark Jordan, Martin Kavka, Richard Kearney, Noreen Khawaja, Karen Kilby, Vincent Lloyd, Catherine Malabou, Jean-Luc Marion, Patrick Masterson, Vittorio Montemaggi, Jean-Luc Nancy, George Pattison, Andrew Prevot, Mary-Jane Rubenstein, Alec Ryrie, Devin Singh, Ted Smith, Anthony Steinbock, Kathryn Tanner, Susannah Ticciati, Linn Tonstad, Dennis Vanden Auweele, Rowan Williams, and Andre Willis, as well as our colleagues at the ACU Rome Campus, especially Claudio Betti, Marina Kavalirek, and Angela Marino, and Linda Tracey from the Institute for Religion and Critical Enquiry in Melbourne. We thank, too, those who contributed to our Australian events, including Lexi Eikelboom, Mark Kelly, Scott Kirkland, John McDowell, Jack Norman, Jon Roffe, Patrick Stokes, Geoff Thompson, Christopher Watkin, and Robyn Whitaker. Thanks especially to our editor at Bloomsbury, Jade Grogan, and to all those who have helped to bring this book into being. Finally, thanks must go to all those who suffer for our art, our families and friends.

1

Atheism, Faith, and Experience

Claude Romano and Robyn Horner

I. Atheism and the irreducible

The present volume has come about because of the conviction that it is timely to look anew at the question of atheism. Of course, there are already many fine books that have been written about atheism, but very often, they come down to an argument about whether or not one can reasonably believe in "God"—or in what one substitutes for God.[1] Such a polarization of views leads only to a stalemate, so that in the end there is nothing very interesting left to say. In late 2016, a group of scholars from Australia, Europe, and North America met in Rome to discuss the possibility that one can approach atheism otherwise, and very quickly it became evident that for many of us, it was not even clear what we meant when we used the term. There are many atheisms: some of these atheisms actually inhabit theism or are even seen to live out theism's ends. Between 2017 and 2019, three further meetings were hosted by Australian Catholic University at the campus in Rome to extend the work of that first group. This book arises in large part from the final seminar in 2019, where we pursued the question of the relationship atheism bears to experience. Why experience? Because in our view, as editors, while there are plenty of intellectual arguments to be made about atheism, atheism is not first a question of conceptual knowledge. People rarely argue themselves entirely to belief or unbelief in God; more commonly, they have already crossed a particular threshold before they begin to make such arguments—or at least, before they have reached their conclusion. We ventured to begin the conversation with the idea that atheism (or theism) is a way of finding oneself in the world, a characteristic of experience that is perhaps first affective rather than thetic. So, with this in mind, we asked our interlocutors to reflect on what the experience of atheism might look like.

This volume is characterized by conversations that have largely had their genesis in France, conversations that relate to the French reception and development of phenomenology. All the contributors to the book are readers of French philosophy

---

[1] Here we place the word "God" in inverted commas along the lines of the usage suggested by Kevin Hart, who writes: "the word and the concept 'God'... can never fail to divide and multiply once they enter dis-course." Kevin Hart, *The Trespass of the Sign*, 2nd. ed. (New York: Fordham University Press, 2000), 290.

and, more often than not, in phenomenology as it has developed in a particular trajectory from Husserl, whose thought was introduced to France in the early twentieth century and which, together with the work of Heidegger, has had a profound effect in that context and beyond. There is a certain way in which phenomenology shapes the present constellation of authors—even beyond their expressed concerns here—so that questions about the status, scope and limits of experience are frequently to the fore. In particular, while not all the contributors have an interest in the question of God, the question of the irreducible figures prominently in their work, and the irreducible is sometimes understood to mark experience prior to any division into concepts of theism and atheism. This is nowhere more the case than in the work of the two authors who have been chosen to "bookend" this collection: Jean-Luc Nancy and Jean-Luc Marion.

II. Atheism and alienation

It is well-known that atheism is a modern phenomenon, and that it is a phenomenon intrinsically related to our modernity. In the West, during a period that extends from early Christianity to the Renaissance, Patristic and Medieval apologetics had to engage in discussion only with other religions: Judaism, Paganism, Islam. The figure of the atheist makes its appearance in the course of the Renaissance period, with the renewal of Paganism and the resistance to the authority of the Church which accompanies it.[2] Giordano Bruno, Machiavelli, Aretino, and Vanini—and, soon after them, those who are called "the Libertines"—do not yet openly claim that God does not exist; instead, they reject the tutelage of the ecclesial institutions and oppose to them a free exercise of reason. It is only when Spinoza applies exegetical rules to the Scriptures which are comparable to those governing the reading of profane texts, and when he underscores the contradictions and inconsistencies of the Bible that betray, in his view, its human provenance, that an utterly new attitude toward monotheist revelation starts to take shape. And even then, Spinoza is far from considering himself an atheist: it is only in the view of his detractors that he personifies atheism for the seventeenth century.

The appearance of atheism is thus inseparable from the tide of secularization on which Western societies from the fifteenth century onwards have been carried. The word "secularization" is not only a political and institutional fact, an ever-sharpening separation between Church and State, but is often understood to reflect a privatization of religion or especially a decline of religious belief and institutional participation in our societies. It is a commonplace that this last view of secularization, which suggests that religion is simply no longer relevant or is dying out, has been largely set aside by

---

[2] Granted, we find "atheists" before that period. One example in the Greek world is the Pythagorean Hippon of Metapontion (or of Rhegion) who used to be called "Hippon the Atheist" because, according to John Philoponous, he claimed that the unique cause of all beings is water (*Commentary on Aristotle's Treatise of the Soul*, 88, 23). But it is hard to have a clear idea of what the word "atheist" was supposed to convey in that context. As we shall see, Oedipus himself is also called "atheist" in Sophocles' tragedy.

the sociologists, many of whom recognize the fact of pluralization.[3] Secularization—in the sense in which it accompanies the very possibility of atheism—should instead be understood according to the definition given by Charles Taylor, as the change "which takes us from a society in which it was virtually impossible not to believe in God, to one in which faith, even for the staunchest believer, is just one human possibility among others."[4] Secularization defines our present situation in so far as faith or belonging to a religious community only represents for us today *one option among others*, and certainly not a norm that should apply to everyone.

Nevertheless, this *prima facie* choice is complicated by the unfolding of a concomitant phenomenon that is sometimes known as detraditionalization, which refers to the manner in which the conditions for tradition-transmission in Western societies have changed.[5] This affects the ways in which individuals shape their identities, so that it seems not only that there are many possible options for religious belief but that the very conditions for religious believing are now different to what they might once have been. French sociologist Danièle Hervieu-Léger draws from the work of Maurice Halbwachs when she speaks of a radical forgetting that seems to have affected Western societies with respect to tradition, a forgetting that breaks lineages of belief.[6] Communities that were once bound together by strong frameworks of tradition have been fractured by the many elements which culminate in pluralization and globalization: ease of international communications, rapid transport and travel, mass migration, the explosion of media of all kinds, economic development, advances in education, increased individualization, and so on. In particular, the mass distribution of symbols weakens their particularity and capacity to speak. The recognition of the role of social memory in the continuity of religious and other traditions transposes the question of atheism into an entirely different key. In short, the secular age of the West seems to be accompanied by a haze of disorientation, in which it is sometimes hard to remember why the question matters in the first place.

The situation where adherence to a religious tradition becomes not only optional but also often strangely alienating deeply modifies the experience of the believer as much as that of the non-believer. For the believer, the possibility of atheism in the society to which he or she belongs should not, perhaps, be considered only as something

---

[3] See Peter L. Berger, "The Desecularization of the World: A Global Overview," in *The Desecularization of the World: Resurgent Religion and World Politics*, ed. Peter L. Berger (Washington, DC/Grand Rapids. MI: Ethics and Public Policy Center/Eerdmans, 1999); José Casanova, "The Secular, Secularizations, Secularisms," in *Rethinking Secularism*, ed. Craig J Calhoun, Mark Juergensmeyer, and Jonathan Van Antwerpen (New York: Oxford University Press, 2011); Peter L. Berger, *The Many Altars of Modernity: Toward a Paradigm for Religion in a Pluralist Age* (Berlin/Boston: De Gruyter, 2014).
[4] Charles Taylor, *A Secular Age* (Cambridge, MA/London: Belknap /Harvard University, 2007), 3.
[5] Paul Heelas, Scott Lash, and Paul Morris, *Detraditionalization: Critical Reflections on Authority and Identity* (Cambridge, MA: Blackwell Publishers, 1996); Lieven Boeve, "Religion after Detraditionalization: Christian Faith in a Post-Secular Europe," *Irish Theological Quarterly* 70, no. 2 (2005); Linda Woodhead, "The Rise of 'No Religion' in Britain: The Emergence of a New Cultural Majority," *Journal of the British Academy* 4 (2016).
[6] Maurice Halbwachs, *La mémoire collective*, 2 ed. (Paris: Presses Universitaires de France, 1968); Danièle Hervieu-Léger, *Religion as a Chain of Memory*, trans. Simon Lee (Cambridge: Polity Press, 2000).

regrettable. The possibility of atheism obliges that person to relate to faith in a different manner, possibly even with more depth and intensity, since it is no longer a commonly shared, obvious or uncontroversial attitude, but instead, a stance that is existentially lived-through and which potentially makes room for different forms of uncertainty. Such uncertainty includes doubt, of course, but it must also include challenges to particular forms of naivety.[7] This does not mean that believers never experienced uncertainty prior to the secular age: the experience of the "dark night of the soul" is a basic, inescapable experience reported by all the mystics. But even for the one who does not reach the peaks of mysticism, the possibility of atheism inevitably upends the very experience of faith or may even become indispensable to the living of that faith.

Moreover, as much as the theist, the atheist can perfectly acknowledge the dimension of mystery inherent to our lives, and so be open to dimensions of the religious phenomenon. Mystery does not only amount to the "problematic" of the meaning of all human life; it is, instead, something stronger which seizes us and in which we are always already engaged. Gabriel Marcel famously distinguished between a mystery and a problem: "It seems, indeed," he writes, "that between a problem and a mystery there is this essential difference: that a problem is something I encounter, that I find entirely displayed in front of me, and thus, that I can circumscribe and reduce—while a mystery is something in which I am myself engaged, which is therefore conceivable only as a domain in which the distinction of the 'in me' and the 'in front of me' loses its meaning and its initial value."[8] It is thus far from certain that the attitude of the atheist can only be defined as a stepping backward in the face of mystery or as a rejection of mystery, as it is also at play in faith, and one could even propose to broaden the meaning of the "religious" in order to understand it otherwise than as the belonging to a religious community defined by dogmas or beliefs. As Thomas Mann suggests: "We live and die in mystery, and one can eventually call 'religious' the awareness that one has of this fact."[9]

Neither of the two terms of the disjunction believer/atheist is, therefore, a simple one. Our living in societies including believers and atheists implies, first of all, the necessity of sharing different, but probably not incommensurable experiences. First, it should not be forgotten that the Christian was defined, at the beginning, as an atheist—with respect to the official religion of Rome until Constantine: Polytheism. One is often the atheist of someone else, of the one who does not share "the faith." Interreligious conflicts and even the resurgence of religious wars in our time remind us every day of this obvious fact.[10] Second, the word "atheism" can refer to very different experiences and dispositions. Hence, the importance of the notion of experience that we have placed at the heart of our investigations. If God cannot be defined, cannot be reduced to the measure of our thinking, but can be only *encountered* in a personal experience, in a paradoxical experience which pushes experience to its limits, the atheist is primarily the one who has not had such an experience, and not the one who denies the existence of

---

[7] See the final chapter of Paul Ricœur, *The Symbolism of Evil*, trans. Emerson Buchanan (Boston: Beacon, 1967).
[8] Gabriel Marcel, *Être et avoir* (Paris: éditions Montaigne, 1935), 169.
[9] *Lettres de Thomas Mann 1948–1955* (Paris, Gallimard, 1973), 424.
[10] Yet on the question of religious violence, see William T. Cavanaugh, *The Myth of Religious Violence: Secular Ideology and the Roots of Modern Conflict* (Oxford: Oxford University Press, 2009).

God. Now, no one can assert that such an experience can never be had. Nevertheless, the meaning of such an experience needs to be specified, and along with it, all the illusions to which such a so-called experience can give rise. Contemporary phenomenology, by attempting to broaden the concept of experience to allow it to include paradoxical experiences ("saturated phenomena," to borrow Marion's expression) cannot avoid the question of how to differentiate between a paradoxical experience that would only reflect our own desires or fantasies, and which is thus only illusory, and one that would *really* deviate from the conditions of our ordinary experience.

III. Literalist atheism

In its simplest form, atheism is often thought as the negation of belief in (a) divine being, and as we have already noted, this tends to limit any discussion to an exchange of irreconcilable truth claims. A dogmatic a-theism of this kind asserts the pure and simple non-existence of God as something that can be demonstrated: we observe this kind of atheism in the works of infamous atheists such as Richard Dawkins and Christopher Hitchens.[11] Now, such an atheism often borders on inconsistency. On the one hand, outside the realm of *a priori* sciences in which it is, indeed, possible to prove the non-existence of certain things (for instance, in Euclidian geometry, the non-existence or impossibility of a triangle the sum of whose angles would amount to more or less than 180 degrees), it is already very difficult to prove the non-existence of anything whatsoever in the world. If God is not only a concept, a mere object of thought, but a being who can perhaps be encountered, of whom it is perhaps possible to have an "experience," an *a priori* proof of God's non-existence does not even make sense. It makes probably even less sense than the traditional alleged "proofs" of the existence of God. The believer is here more rational than the non-believer, since the believer can at least allege an experience (perhaps illusory) as the basis of his or her belief, while the non-believer cannot for his or her disbelief: it does not follow from the fact that one does not experience something that this thing does not exist. Even more seriously, the atheist who wants to justify an assertion of the "non-existence of God" is committed inevitably to defining what the word "God" means. It is here, precisely, that the trouble begins. The atheist must rely at least on a *nominal* definition of what is intended by "God," and this definition often turns out to be arbitrary. Such is the argument of Jean-Luc Marion, who observes that the death of God asserted by Nietzsche is no more than the death of a particular idol that has come to stand for God.[12] In each case of such proofs, one must always ask whether it is the true God, the revealed God who is at stake in the question. As for negative theism or the assertive and militant type of atheism we have observed in exponents such as Dawkins, the question

---

[11] Richard Dawkins, *The God Delusion* (New York: Houghton Mifflin, 2006/2008); Christopher Hitchens, *God Is Not Great: How Religion Poisons Everything* (New York: Hachette, 2007).

[12] Jean-Luc Marion, *The Idol and Distance: Five Studies*, ed. John D. Caputo, trans. Thomas A. Carlson, Perspectives in Continental Philosophy (New York: Fordham University Press, 2001), 32; *God Without Being*, trans. Thomas A. Carlson (Chicago: University of Chicago Press, 1991), 29.

is always to determine whether such an atheism, grounded on an implicit, but often arbitrary definition of God, does not border on theological naivety. In a word, the God about whom it is possible to prove non-existence on the basis of a definition that is always dogmatic or chanced, can easily be suspected of not being the true God—granted, of course, that God exists.

If God were to exist, God would undoubtedly be the one who cannot be defined, that is, who defies our representational capacities, who cannot be measured by our conceptual resources. In order to claim that God does not exist, one necessarily has to claim to possess a concept of God, a definition of what God is, but this is precisely what is problematic from the outset. Even the "divine names" only reach God according to our own point of view. God can be characterized precisely—and in the Hebrew scriptures is shown to characterize Godself—as the one *who does not allow self-definition*. It is worth recalling that the primary meaning of the formula of Exodus 3, 14, *'ehyèh 'ashèr 'ehyèh*, which has been often understood as the first word of a "metaphysics of the Exodus," in no way amounts to a definition ("I am the one who is"), but is on the contrary *a refusal to be defined*: it means literally "I am who I am" (and so "you don't have to ask me this question"), or even more literally "I will be who I will be"—a reiteration of the promise which underlies the Alliance.[13] And so, to a request for nomination and definition, God answers with a reiteration of the oath: "I will keep my word, I will not betray my promise." Does this not make any dogmatic a-theism a contradictory undertaking? In this respect, the Marxist critique of Feuerbach's atheistic humanism is right on target: in some of its forms at least, atheism is nothing other than a reverse theology, a parody of a theology. William James already acknowledged such a possibility when he observed: "'He believes in No-God and he worships him' said a colleague of mine of a student who was manifesting a fine atheistic ardor; and the more fervent opponents of Christian doctrine have often enough shown a temper which, psychologically considered, is indistinguishable from religious zeal."[14]

IV. Atheism and the flight of the gods

However, a second form of atheism must be considered, according to which atheism is no longer a theoretical assertion about the non-existence of God, but a modality of our relation to the divine, be the latter purely chimeric: the experience of the loss of God, of the "flight of gods"—or God. Even Paganism was not unaware of this kind of experience. The tragic hero undergoes the experience of the withdrawal of the gods, of his abandonment by them. Oedipus defines himself as *atheos* in *Oedipus Rex* (verse 166), and this expression, of course, does not mean here "atheist" in the modern sense of the word. It means, instead, deserted by the god who has turned away from him, and

---

[13] See André Caquot, "Les énigmes d'un hémistiche biblique," in Paul Vignaux, éd., *Dieu et l'être. Exégèses d'Exode 3, 14 et de Coran 20, 11–24* (Paris: Institut des études augustiniennes, 1978), 18–26. See also Stéphane Mosès, *L'Éros et la Loi* (Paris: Éditions du Seuil, 1999) who insists on the double future and interprets it as an expression of the promise.

[14] William James, *The Varieties of Religious Experience*, in *Writings 1902–1910* (New York: The Library of America, 1987), 39.

so condemned him to a radical solitude that is testified to by his long perambulation in *Oedipus at Colonus*. "Atheist" does not mean in this context "the one who does not believe in the gods," in the first place because the very idea of a *belief* in the gods is problematic for Paganism. As Paul Veyne has stressed, the pagan religion never truly had "believers," even if it is true that it had "non-believers," that is, the early Christians.[15]

This other form of atheism, marked by the experience of the withdrawal of the gods (Hölderlin), and possibly even of a pure and simple death of the Christian God, is foreshadowed in Pascal's *Pensées* and fully developed for the first time by the young Hegel in *Faith and Knowledge*: Hegel identifies in this text "the feeling on which the religion of modern times rests—the feeling that 'God Himself is dead'"; it is of course taken over by Nietzsche in paragraph 125 of *The Gay Science*.[16] Such an atheism is utterly different from a negative theism or a dogmatic a-theism, and it addresses a challenge much more difficult for theology to meet. This time, the God who is dead is no longer a nominal definition, an idea of God. Instead, God has an intimate connection to "the Crucified," as Nietzsche calls him, and God's very disappearance gestures toward a *historical experience*, that of the "devaluation of all values" proper to the epoch of nihilism. Yet, on the other hand, as it has often been noted, the "death of God" of which Nietzsche speaks seems to have its place prepared in advance in theology and Christology: it is prefigured by the complaint of Psalm 22: "My God, my God, why have you forsaken me?," and the very words of Christ on the Cross (Matt. 27:46; Mark 15:34). Could such an atheism be understood as an element of the divine dramaturgy, liable to receive an eschatological meaning? Or else, is it the announcement of an end of Christianity and Monotheism as such? Whatever is the response to this question, that second atheism bears more intimate relationships to Christian theology than the first one. It raises especially the question of whether the God who "is dead" and whose death prescribes God's meaning in the age of "nihilism" is a mere metaphysical idol, as Jean-Luc Marion has claimed, or else is the Revealed God himself, according to Nietzsche's interpretation.

V. Before theism and atheism

Is it possible to describe an atheism that is not simply a denial of God, or does not co-implicate the loss of all value? Jean-Luc Nancy attempts to pursue this task, which means that he does not describe himself *simply* as an atheist.[17] In *Dis-Enclosure: The*

---

[15] Paul Veyne, *Le pain et le cirque: Sociologie historique d'un pluralisme politique* (Paris: Seuil, 1976) 589: "La divinité des souverains n'avait pas de croyants. En revanche, elle a eu ses incroyants, les chrétiens." ("The divinity of the sovereigns had no believers. On the other hand, it had its unbelievers, the Christians.")

[16] "Nature is such that she testifies everywhere, both within man and without him, to a lost God," Blaise Pascal, *Thoughts, Letters and Minor Works*, trans. by W. F. Trotter, The Harvard Classics 48 (Harvard UP: 1910), 148. G. W. Hegel, *Faith and Knowledge*, trans. Walter Cerf and H. S. Harris (New York, State University of New York Press, 1977), 190. Trans. modified.

[17] See the discussion of Nancy's uses of atheism, absentheism and atheology in Christopher Watkin, *Difficult Atheism: Post-Theological Thinking in Alain Badiou, Jean-Luc Nancy and Quentin Meillassoux* (Edinburgh: Edinburgh University Press, 2011) especially 53, 56, 113ff.

Deconstruction of Christianity volume 1, he argues that the force of Monotheism in Western thought builds toward its own overcoming. He declares that metaphysics is complicit with Christianity in that it "sets a founding, warranting presence beyond the world," and everything "is played out in the mutual referral of these two regimes of beings or presence."[18] The exhaustion of metaphysics is fulfilled in the nihilism of Nietzsche, yet at the same time, metaphysics "deconstructs itself constitutively" and reveals "the extreme limits of reason in an excess of and over reason itself."[19] Christianity as metaphysics thus harbors a resource within itself that is deeper than Christianity: in its Anselmian formulation, thought "thinks something in excess over itself. It penetrates the impenetrable, or rather is penetrated by it."[20]

Nancy thus maintains that both theism and atheism are positions defined by an appeal to a higher principle upon which reason is founded. However, he writes: "the signal weakness of any logic of the premise ... shows itself at the crucial point where theism and atheism prove to belong to each other ... The decisive point is this—it ought to be the task of the principle ... *to exceed qua principle principiation itself.*"[21] In this way, Nancy argues for the priority of a kind of experience or intentionality that he names "faith," but by this he refers neither to a relationship of trust with a transcendent being nor to a set of religious beliefs—as we might otherwise understand the term. This is described in his chapter in the present work, where we read: "No activity, no implementation, no praxis is possible without *an energy that allows one to devote oneself to a project without a program*, that is, not to the execution of a defined task but to the impulse and even to *the adventure or the experience of something that by definition is neither given nor presentable.*"[22] As a type of intentionality or consciousness, then, faith is "the act of reason" that bears witness to "the event" (to *the adventure or the experience of something that by definition is neither given nor presentable*) while having no-thing to show for it.

> Faith is not weak, hypothetical, or subjective knowledge. It is neither unverifiable nor received through submission, nor even through reason. It is not a belief in the ordinary sense of the term. On the contrary, it is the act of the reason that relates, itself, to that which, in it, passes it infinitely: faith stands precisely at the point of an altogether consequent atheism. This is to say that it stands at the point where atheism is dispossessed of belief in the premise or principle and in principiate, in general.... Reason does not suffice unto itself: for itself it is not a sufficient reason.[23]

For Nancy, "the name 'God,' or that of the 'holy'" always comes too late, but it is an "attempt to designate" where no designation can take place, "as that which exceeds thinking infinitely without in any way being principial to it."[24] Faith opens reason, then,

---

[18] Jean-Luc Nancy, *Dis-Enclosure: The Deconstruction of Christianity*, trans. Bettina Bergo, Gabriel Malenfant, and Michael B. Smith (New York: Fordham University Press, 2008), 6.
[19] Nancy, *Dis-Enclosure*, 7.
[20] Nancy, *Dis-Enclosure*, 11.
[21] Nancy, *Dis-Enclosure*, 22–3.
[22] See page 22 of the present work.
[23] Nancy, *Dis-Enclosure*, 25.
[24] Nancy, *Dis-Enclosure*, 25.

to its own insufficiency. However—and this is the crucial point for Nancy—while faith opens reason to its beyond, the event onto which faith opens is nothing *other* than reason.[25]

To the extent that Nancy relies on something deep within or deeper than Christianity to overcome Christianity, Jacques Derrida suggests that he is liable to the criticism that he is more Christian than the Christians. This would reinscribe Nancy within the very binary he seeks to evade.[26] However, Nancy's reference to the event whence faith opens reason to its beyond is an attempt to think the experience of what precedes the distinction between theism and atheism without becoming available as a principle for resolving their difference: this event is no-thing at all. Now, interestingly enough, Jean-Luc Marion seems to traverse the same terrain when he writes of "an opening of that which already no longer is . . ." It is here that Marion discerns the possibility of the event of the impossible: "If God ever has to appear to our eyes that have become blind to the twilight of the idols, clearly *it will be in this opening*, and no longer in the desertlike domain of the possible."[27]

What might such an experience look like? If it is unavailable except by means of a discursive reflection that always comes *too late*, how might it be known as such? For Nancy, the event prompting that discursive reflection comes as a *surprise* to thought.[28] For Marion, this event is known to feeling.[29] If we were to think this with a definitively Heideggerian inflection and not with a Schleiermacherian one, we might say that it is known to mood (*Stimmung*), which discloses our how of being in the world. Both atheist and theist would thus come to self-conscious reflection having always and already crossed a threshold. They would bring with themselves a mood that, according to Heidegger, is the co-condition of knowing. What would be at stake, then, in the difference between Marion and Nancy—our two bookends—is not so much that one believes in God and the other does not, but how each is fundamentally affected at that point of opening onto the world which is life, and how that is then understood and interpreted as experience.[30]

Let us say in concluding this brief sketch of a way of describing an atheism which is no longer an atheism but precedes the very distinction between atheism and theism—that it is echoed in the works of John Caputo and Richard Kearney, although in different ways. Caputo proposes that his notion of "religion without religion" "turns on a deeper resonance with the unconditional in our lives, which subtends the furious and futile

---

[25] "I propose here, simply, that nothing gives itself and that nothing shows itself—and that is what is." Jean-Luc Nancy, *The Creation of the World or Globalisation*, trans. François Raffoul and David Pettigrew (New York: SUNY, 2007), 123 note 24.

[26] Jacques Derrida, *On Touching: Jean-Luc Nancy*, trans. Christine Irizarry (Stanford: Stanford University Press, 2005), 220.

[27] Jean-Luc Marion, *Negative Certainties*, trans. Stephen E. Lewis (Chicago: University of Chicago Press, 2015), 62. Emphasis added.

[28] Jean-Luc Nancy, "The Surprise of the Event," in *Hegel after Derrida*, ed. Stuart Barnett (London/New York: Routledge, 1998), 91.

[29] Jean-Luc Marion, *In Excess: Studies of Saturated Phenomena*, trans. Robyn Horner and Vincent Berraud (New York: Fordham University Press, 2002) 162.

[30] For an extended argument along these lines, see Robyn Horner, *Experience of God: A Phenomenology of Revelation* (forthcoming).

debate between theism and atheism."³¹ In contrast, Kearney emphasizes that his anatheism comes both before any division between atheism and theism as well as after them.³² Moreover, since his anatheism rests on a wager, he does not exclude (as Caputo does) that "God" might have passed or will pass again.

VI. A very brief introduction to the works in this book

The atheistic desert

According to Jean-Christophe Bailly, "atheism has not found a way to irrigate its own desert." But what would it mean for atheism to perform such a task? What kind of energy could vivify the desert created by the absence of God? By investigating Marx's theory of spirit, Jean-Luc Nancy questions the paradoxical proximity of atheism to Christianity. What defines Marx's view of Christianity is the lack of real love, and by contrast, Marx's atheism is characterized first of all by a trust (a faith?) in the reality of a genuine love taking place between concrete individuals in concrete socio-economic conditions, a trust in what Marx sometimes calls "spirit." Marx's atheism is not, therefore, the substitution of a material god for a spiritual god; instead, it is the deepening of a resolute faith whose character as a "faith" stands out through the fundamental trust that Marx puts in the possibility of a reality of spirit. With that example—which is not unparalleled—it is possible more generally to suggest that there is no atheistic existence that does not imply a faith of some order. This faith is even stronger in the atheism of intellectuals of our time (philosophers, artists, scientists) because of the fact that it is not related to any god. Yet –Nancy asks—is this enough to vivify the desert of atheism?

The atheism of desire

If atheism and theism are ways of being in the world rather than ways of believing, no one brings this out more poignantly in the present volume than Jeffrey Bloechl, who describes the atheism of those who, wanting to believe, nevertheless find themselves unable to do so. Bloechl introduces us to the character of Jack Boughton, the main protagonist in Marilynne Robinson's novel *Home*. Everything in the story suggests that Jack lives and moves wholly outside the grace of God, though neither because we can be sure that grace is in no way extended to him nor because he is simply unwilling to see it. Jack has only his adhesion to the world and the things of the world, and they answer more readily to his cares than does the God whose love he nonetheless wishes to have – across a gulf of alienation as old and deep as his very life. The character of Jack reveals that existence is such that we are not predetermined to faith in God's love, but only called to it from a condition that admits the real possibility of living instead as if the world is all there is.

---

[31] John D. Caputo, *The Folly of God: A Theology of the Unconditional* (Salem, OR: Polebridge Press, 2015), 2.

[32] Richard Kearney and Jens Zimmerman, eds., *Reimagining the Sacred: Richard Kearney Debates God* (New York: Columbia University Press, 2016) 7.

Anarchic atheism

In her consideration of critiques of the metaphysical "archic paradigm"—that is, of the ontological sovereignty of the *arche* and what derives from it—Catherine Malabou credits French Politician Pierre-Joseph Proudhon with being the author of a semantic "revolution" in the use of the term "anarchy." Before Proudhon, anarchy refers to disorder, or chaos. Proudhon gives anarchy a new, positive meaning: politically, it is not a rejection of power as such, but a rejection of the domination or abuse of power. Malabou argues that this idea underlies theological and philosophical attempts at a deconstruction of the archic paradigm, and she illustrates this using the work of three thinkers. Christian anarchists, like Jacques Ellul, try to subtract God—so to speak—from all idea of domination and so to liberate Christianity from the domination of the Church. In contrast, Levinas advocates a dismantling of the archic paradigm in ethics under the form of "anarchic responsibility," because he suspects Heidegger's "Being" of being unable to resist the archic paradigm of Western metaphysics. In contrast again, Reiner Schürmann shows in relation to Heidegger that "anarchy" is the name of the destiny of thinking after the deconstruction of metaphysics. In these ways, is anarchy an atheism? Are the various deconstructions—undertaken by Ellul, Levinas, and Schürmann—deconstructions of God? Alternatively, Malabou asks: do they pave the way for a new way of approaching religion, in such a way that "God" is here a name for the deconstructive force of the archic paradigm, the self-dismantling move of the *arche*?

The "death of God" and "the death of God"

In his 1953 study of Stéphane Mallarmé, Jean-Paul Sartre writes about the author of "Un coup de dés": "More and better than Nietzsche he experienced the death of God." Quentin Meillassoux actually maintains an opposing thesis: contrary to what has been advanced, Mallarmé's famous letter on the Nothing (April 28, 1866)—from which all his later research proceeds—cannot be understood as the discovery of such a *topos*. The experience of the death of God had, indeed, already nourished his writing before that date, and led him to an impasse. The profound originality of Mallarmé's crisis of 1866 is, instead, that it is an experience of nothingness that constitutes a break with this theme of his youth. By introducing a new writing centered on this discovery, Mallarmé will avoid both a return to religious transcendence and the renewal of the death of God as a poetically exhausted commonplace.

Ana-theism

One of the lasting contributions of Richard Kearney to philosophy of religion will be his coining of the term to which we have already referred, "ana-theism." Anatheism is a "returning to God after God": a critical retrieval of sacred things that have passed but still bear radical potentialities that may be reanimated in the future. As such, anatheism proposes a future for the forgotten or still unfulfilled calls of divine history: it is an "after-faith," which is more than any "after-thought" or "after-affect." After-faith is eschatological: something ultimate in the end that was already there from the beginning. Yet anatheism is not a dialectical third term which supersedes theism and atheism in some Hegelian synthesis or final resolution. It contains a moment of atheism within itself, as it does a moment of theism, or to be more precise: anatheism pre-contains both, for it operates from a space and time before the dichotomy of atheism and theism (as well as after). The double "a" of anatheism holds out the possibility, but not the necessity, of a second affirmation once the "death of God" has done its work. Resisting the logic of theodicy, anatheism is always a wager—a risk that can go either way. It is a matter of discernment and decision on our part, responding to the Call of the instant. As such, anatheism reactivates suspended or unsuspected possibilities often experienced in the a-theism of non-knowing; the "a-" marking an act of abstention and withdrawal rather than passive privation. Such a-theism is less a matter of epistemological argument against God than a pre-reflective lived experience of lostness and solitude—a mood of *Angst* or abandon, an existential "dark night of the soul" which most people experience at some point in their lives.

Atheism as apocalypse

A discourse on "the end times" has renewed relevance during a period of catastrophic climate change. For Emmanuel Falque, the end times is not only a religious concept, but also finds an atheistic meaning in the scientific discourse of climatology. How can a Christian concept of the apocalypse as revelation interact with an atheistic discourse on the end, today? There is an amphibology in the concepts of "revelation" and "apocalypse"; thinking revelation as "unveiling" in Greek thought and the "removing of the veil" in Judaism, it is possible to argue that these traditions are united and transformed in a Christian understanding. The Christian apocalypse, as the revelation of Jesus Christ, integrates the various meanings of revelation and apocalypse in order to suggest that God dwells with humanity in even the most cataclysmic events. The possibility of such a transformation is central to thinking about the future of humanity in the midst of a climate crisis.

Atheism as loving critique

Anthony Steinbock observes that participation in being is a belief posture that can be characterized phenomenologically as naïve participation. This naïve belief posture includes a belief in the God of religion. Evidently, there is also another possibility—the possibility of a critical approach to religion which entails holding this belief attitude in abeyance: a phenomenological atheism that would thus call into question the being of God. This is a very common stance in contemporary philosophy.[33] Yet, he argues, atheism can also evolve from love, and could be described as a different kind of critique, a discernment of the heart. Steinbock maintains that we should speak about the "religious" in critical terms in order to keep the discourse attuned to religious experience.

---

[33] Hent de Vries, *Religion and Violence: Philosophical Perspectives from Kant to Derrida* (Baltimore: Johns Hopkins University Press, 2002), xii.

Atheism and Indifference

Philippe Cabestan asks about the significance of philosophical responses to the proclamation of the "death of God." On the one hand, this event provokes a positive humanism, which reads it as the triumph of modern sciences over obscurantism. Cabestan argues that this approach is simplistic: amongst other things, it ignores the historicity of the events which concern the Christian God. On the other hand, in the works of Heidegger and Sartre, the death of God assumes a very different character. For Sartre, the death of God relates largely to his personal atheism. His indifference to the event ultimately leads to his assumption of a Marxist materialism that is ironically linked once more to a narrative of progress. For Heidegger, the death of God is intrinsically tied to the end of metaphysics. From this perspective, Heidegger maintains that Nietzsche's death of God is only an inadequate interpretation of nihilism: to Nietzsche's limited sense of nihilism, Heidegger opposes the nihilism of being. Cabestan argues this demonstrates Heidegger's failure to deal with modernity and the real questions that are raised by the event of the death of God.

Atheism and intersubjective experience

Tamsin Jones considers the question of how excessive experiences signify intersubjectively through the lens of debates within the disciplines of religious studies and trauma theory. Within religious studies—which most recently has been occupied with a return to the material—social constructivist positions argue that all forms of religious experience are humanly constructed. Historians, however, argue against foreclosing the limits of legitimate objects of study according to an enforced naturalism or positivism within the study of religion. Thinkers such as Robert Orsi develop this position materially: it is a radical empiricism because it attends to what appears on bodies, in communities, in ritual and performance. Jones demonstrates how an analysis of undergoing and interpreting a traumatic experience can challenge this divide between social constructivist and radical empiricist positions. Through an analogy with the excess of traumatic experience, religious experience can be understood in both a persistently realist mode and, at the same time, only made meaningful through an interpretation that is socially constructed.

Atheism in metaphysics and phenomenology

Many contemporary philosophers of religion abandon metaphysical speculation and take up the challenge of attending to the traces of God's phenomenality through the discipline of phenomenology. Most famously, Jean-Luc Marion claims that phenomenology "relieves" theology of metaphysics. Patrick Masterson argues that a realist metaphysics has as important a role to play as phenomenology in the philosophical elucidation of religion. They offer complementary rather than incompatible approaches; each being both appropriate and incomplete. Phenomenologically, God is affirmed as existing in salvific correlation with religious experiences of contingency, finitude and hope. In metaphysical realism, by way of contrast, the relationship between humanity and God is affirmed as an asymmetric one of radical causal dependence upon an ontologically independent and utterly transcendent Infinite Being. The asymmetry involved in realist metaphysics between independently existing being and our intuition of it resembles what is presupposed by the various ways in which God can be envisaged phenomenologically as correlative to the religious exigencies of our conscious subjectivity.

Atheism and revelation

Christina M. Gschwandtner asks: does the line between theist and atheist experience run through *what* phenomena one experiences or *how* one experiences them? Do atheists and theists have different experiences, or do they, instead, respond to or interpret the same phenomena differently? Can experience distinguish between or provide a basis for a theist rather than an atheist or non-theist position? What makes them different, and does either have a more convincing, more coherent, more phenomenological position? Jean-Luc Marion, she argues, attempts to provide such phenomenological distinctions in his work. While the positions he suggests are all recognizable, by his own admission, it ultimately proves impossible to give an account of an experience of revelation, because the (atheistic) blindness that refuses to see is indistinguishable, on phenomenological terms, from the (theistic) blindness that is bedazzled by the overwhelmingly, paradoxically saturated phenomenon. Marion makes various attempts to distinguish the first kind of blindness from the second—that is, what might be called various "atheist" or non-theist experiences versus a more genuinely "theist" one, although this is not language Marion himself employs. Gschwandtner complicates his account of the first kind of blindness and challenges Marion's assurance that the latter kind is evidence of having experienced a phenomenon of revelation.

Jean-Luc Marion

In his essay, "Doubling Metaphysics," Jean-Luc Marion underlines the indeterminacy of the concept of "philosophy of religion" which has entered a crisis today insofar as it derives from the establishment of metaphysics, starting from Duns Scotus, and more clearly still with Suarez, that is to say, from the movement by which, by making the *metaphysica* a *scientia transcendentalis*, one subordinates God to the question of *ens in quantum ens*. In subordinating God to the transcendental device, we conceive God as the supreme being (*ens supremum*) whose function is to found all beings (as *principium*, *causa*, and even ultimately *causa sui*). God is thereby subject to the requirements of human representation and thought, and subordinate to the *ens cogitabile* in general. So, the main consequence of the establishment of ontotheology is an idolatrous determination of God.

The need for a post-metaphysical theology therefore passes through the deconstruction of the metaphysical device, beginning with its founding opposition between the possible and the impossible: to God, nothing is impossible, which also puts the principle of sufficient reason out of play. Hence, the possibility that takes shape for the thought of God, not to "go beyond" metaphysics, but rather to "double its cape," which requires ratifying the gap established by Pascal between theology and philosophy through his doctrine of the three orders—the third order, that of the "divine truths," being characterized by the fact that here "one only enters truth by charity": we must therefore love the truth to know it. A Christian thought can only be built starting from *agapē*, that is to say, in formulating an autonomous and strong doctrine of love—or better, by letting itself be built up and edified by *agapē* as such. Such thinking does not need the foundation of the *metaphysica* in any of its versions, but, in it, love must prevail over any other metaphysical rationality and "submit everything to the one who submits all to the Father."[34]

VII. Postlude

It will be apparent from this brief survey of our interlocutors that there are many shades to debates about atheism, most especially in relation to experience. What is clear, however, is that a view that restricts the concept of atheism to an argument about belief in God will often miss the point. In the context of Western societies, particularly, where such belief and its attendant dogmatics can appear simply to make no sense, there must be other ways to engage with questions of ultimate meaning. It is our hope that in the richness of the responses in this volume, such ways may be explored by our readers.

Australian poet, Bruce Dawe (1930–2020), was once asked by a priest to write about his "experience of God." In the poem which forms Dawe's reply, he observes that this is "like being asked to write about/ what it's like to be good at maths or the world's best/ ocarina-player." Dawe cannot respond, because such an experience—as he claims in his response—has simply passed him by. For some people, he writes, "when the one special thing comes along/ they're out of town for the day and the vision of the godhead/goes to the bloke next door."[35] The impossible, it seems, resists experience, but experience also resists the impossible. It is this resistance that we explore in these pages.

---

[34] See page 198 of the present text.
[35] Bruce Dawe, *Sometimes Gladness: Collected Poems*, 1954–1987, 3rd ed. (Melbourne: Longman Cheshire, 1988), 237.

Part One

The Experience of Atheism

2

Atheistic Experience

Jean-Luc Nancy

There is only one means for me to approach atheistic existence. It is to question my experience. One sentence in particular has, since my first reading it, singularly informed this experience. It was penned by Jean-Christophe Bailly, an atheist like myself (like so many of those we call "intellectuals") but more tenacious, exempt from any religious past (which is not the case for me) and quite allergic to any evocation of the theological or the spiritual, whatever its content, even taken as problematic.

The sentence appears in his book *Adieu*, published in 1993.[1] Its title takes leave of God and of the gods. How it does that, I will perhaps come back to. In any case, the sentence I'm referring to, which comes early on, gives a major motive or impetus for this atheist book. He writes: ***Atheism has not found a way to irrigate its own desert.***

I. The spirit of a spiritless world

I believe that this sentence is the first, to my knowledge, to echo in a severe way Nietzsche's still joyous expectation: ***how many new gods!***

Bailly is saying that there have not been any new gods and that we have not given birth to new energies capable of vivifying what he admits is a desert, even if he in no way regrets the absence of the one named God. It is a desert because along with the one and capital-G God, the multiple gods dotted with proper names (Zeus, Shiva, Horus) have also deserted.

This sentence sends me directly back to the question: the one who knows and feels himself to be in the desert, he knows and feels what an irrigation would be. He does not only have the historical memory of it. Nor does he only have a utopian vision of it. This sentence, itself at least, is already irrigated. It is already a trickle of water at the bottom of a dry gully.

This sentence repeats Marx's stigmatizing religion as ***the spirit of a spiritless world***. Indeed, Marx thus attests that he knows at least something about "spirit." It could even be argued that Marx knew more about it than we do. When he speaks of "individual

---

[1] Jean-Christophe Bailly, *Adieu: Essai sur la mort des dieux* (La Tour-d'Aigues: Editions de l'Aube, 1993).

property" which comes to erase collective property with private property, he has in view—in an imprecise way, of course—each individual's appropriation of the value of what he produces and which is, above all, social existence itself.

Granted, this view is limited by the very idea of an "appropriation" as well as by that of "production" which it presupposes. This double motif signals, in spite of Marx's intentions (in this, Marx conforms precisely to the *spirit* of his times), a displacement of "value" in itself from "being" or "life" to "having" or "having the power to"—if I may help myself to this necessarily clumsy shorthand. Nevertheless, in speaking of "spirit" Marx knows full well what vocabulary he is mobilizing, even if he does not know very clearly what he is trying to theorize.

II. Ownness and property

Of what he is thus obscurely searching for, it can be said at least that "property" is displaced from meaning the possession of an object to meaning "being properly oneself" or "being one's own self" ["*être proprement soi*"]. Let us re-read his sentence in its entirety. "Religion is the sigh of the oppressed creature, the soul of a heartless world, the spirit of spiritless conditions."[2] One cannot miss the subtle way in which Marx employs a religious lexicon: the sigh of the creature resembles the exhale of opium smoke but it is no less the groan under real oppression. In the same way, the heartless soul and the spiritless spirit are fake, illusory, but their names indicate the character of what they should be in truth. In kind, opium must be understood both as vain smoke and as real relief (Marx himself experienced its medical use). The illusory "spirit" of religion therefore bears the name of a genuine spirit, one which must actually respond to human suffering.

How and in what capacity does it bear the same name? One thing that seems understandable enough is that the heart and the spirit should properly be what they are—thereby properly be the heart and the spirit of a man who is no longer reduced to sighing and could properly be what he is: no longer a creature but a human being who produces his own existence. The "spirit" to which Marx can entrust the truth of the illusory spirit of religion is defined by what distinguishes created being from being that creates itself.

Such an expression is not to be found in Marx's writings and I am only using it for its provocative suggestiveness. Self-creation is not meant not refer to a mysterious doubling of the individual but simply the fact that there is no real human except in the individual (the rest—genus, species, universality—is only an abstraction) and that this reality therefore consists in this irreducible own-being [*être-propre*] within the collectivity itself. This own-being is also an own-acting and this acting is wholly distinguished from the appropriation of a good (be it privately or collectively). Own-ness [*Le propre*] here stands for that which cannot be substituted, in contradistinction to property, which by its very essence is substitutable (exchangeable).

---

[2] Karl Marx, *A Contribution to the Critique of Hegel's Philosophy of Right*, trans. Joseph O'Malley and Annette Jolin (Cambridge: Cambridge University Press, 1844; 1977), 131.

III. The faith of Marx

Without extending the analysis of this motif in Marx, I limit my claim here to this: the *spirit* that the world of (private or collective) ownership of goods lacks is *own-ness*, which is not a good but a self-relation, which also means, necessarily: as a relation of self to other selves. This can be shown in Marx, as one could also show how profoundly this is influenced by Hegel, the caveat being Marx's emphasis on the real, on the concrete and practical actuality of relations, as opposed to their representation.

In the same vein, we can show how Hegel himself carried to a certain level of intensity a theory of spirit characteristic of Christianity, and singularly of the mystery of the Trinity. In saying this, by the way, I do not mean to speak in terms of "secularization": on the contrary the provenances of Christianity itself are to be reserved for further research.

However, we must conclude that Marx describes religion as a lack or a distortion of its own-most truth, that is to say, in a word, as a lack of what was called love. It is not overstating the case to say, and more than one Marxian text allows us to confirm, that *real* love—it too, of course—belongs to the real relation of real individuals. This suffices to situate the atheism of Marx as constituted by a more than essential trust—should we say a faith?—in what I would refer to as the spirit of the real or the reality of the spirit. I say "more than essential" because it is indeed real, actual and palpably at work at the heart of his texts.

This claim has nothing to do with secularization, nor with some unmasked religiosity (in the manner of the often evoked "messianism" of Marx, unless, in this regard, one were to take a closer look at Derrida). I have only taken this Marxian detour in order to provide a basis for this claim: Marx's atheism is held, not by substituting a material god for a spiritual god, but by a deep and resolute faith whose character as a "faith" stands out through the fundamental trust that Marx puts in the possibility of a reality of spirit. This trust alone, more decisive in Marx than any kind of knowledge or analysis—but which animates all his work—accounts for (if it can thus be expressed) the exemplary energy that would shine forth from his works.

IV. Atheistic faith

On the basis of this example, which is certainly privileged but far from unique, I would like to suggest that there is no atheistic existence that does not imply a faith of this order. To do this, I return to my experience: if Jean-Christophe Bailly's sentence struck me, it is because in it an atheist is making an observation not so much critical as regretful of a general failure of atheism to give rise to an existence proper to itself, a communicable existence, endowed with a vitality comparable to that which cannot be denied in the history of so many religions. I could, of course, do an analysis of Bailly's own *oeuvre* analogous to the one I just sketched of Marx's. It, too, would be based on certain words—in his work, among others those of "meaning" ["*sens*"] and "opening" ["*ouvert*"]. But the point is not to multiply examples. I intend instead to take as a starting point that which this sentence—along with those of Marx, Nietzsche and many other thinkers and artists I could evoke—awakened in me for myself.

I simply asked myself how it happened that for so long (in 1993 I had already spent thirty years not only as an atheist but as a philosopher well-assured that there was no religious philosophy) I had not felt the aridity of the country in which I found myself. Around me, nothing had given rise to an impression of this kind. Janicaud's book, *Le tournant théologique de la phémonénologie française*, would only appear four years later and would then leave me rather indifferent.[3] Even if I had for some time an interest in what I would later call a "deconstruction of Christianity" I knew only too well how detached I was from any belonging to and any feeling connected to religion or to belief, both long dissipated.

But as at the same time preoccupation began to grow surrounding what we would soon call "the return of religion" (and which Harvey Cox had already suspected as far back as 1968) I found myself forced to provide myself with an explanation. This only happened slowly, intermittently, bit by bit. And yet the answer seemed to me simple and luminous once it presented itself: it was obvious that, with a few exceptions, the collective group of philosophers, writers, artists, scientists and more broadly the so-called "intellectuals" was irrigated by a faith all the stronger and more faithful—one could say—in virtue of the fact that it was not related to any god.

Whether it involves creating forms, working on concepts, expressing feelings or revealing the real, no activity, no implementation, no *praxis* is possible without an energy that allows one to devote oneself to a project without a program, that is, not to the execution of a defined task but to the impulse and even to the adventure or the experience of something that by definition is neither given nor presentable. If faith is distinguished from belief as impulse is distinguished from expectation, then this is indeed a faith—and all faith refuses assurances, even while finding its own in a form of trust which puts itself on the line without guarantee, beyond any backing or attestation.

V. The refusal of assurance

One could say that this disposition of trust is the one in which both Greek philosophy and the Jewish Covenant established themselves almost at the same time and in conjoining contexts. In Plato there is a whole theory of the courage of thought or of philosophy as risk-taking. It could be shown that all great philosophy knows and implements something of this audacity. And the trust in the Covenant does not rest on guarantees but on the very act of trusting: a testimony to which subsists in all the forms of faithfulness and trust-dependent-value [*fiduciarité*] (even the most self-interested).

What characterizes the atheism of intellectuals (in the broad sense still) is the capacity to refuse the certainty of assurance. An artist is never someone for whom the

---

[3] Dominique Janicaud, *Le tournant théologique de la phénoménologie française* (Combas: Éditions de l'Éclat, 1991); Dominique Janicaud et al., *Phenomenology and the "Theological Turn": The French Debate*, ed. John D. Caputo, trans. Bernard G. Prusak, Perspectives in Continental Philosophy (New York: Fordham University Press, 2001).

rules of the beautiful are given and as such implementable. A philosopher is not someone for whom knowledge or wisdom is given: that is the very meaning of the word "philosophy."

Of course, it is the same for any action that cannot be reduced to mere execution. Having children, cultivating a field, marrying someone, governing a people, and standing in solidarity are all practices of faith. It could even be claimed, in a Kantian spirit, that in religion it is not possible to distinguish—at least in many cases—what in the practices of the faithful belongs to the assurances of belief and what to the trust of faith.

It is no less true that assurances are necessary each time it is not possible to put them aside: that is, whenever the valorization of the un-given and the taste for the "beautiful risk" (according to Socrates' famous expression in the face of death) no longer function. For this to work, cultural, social and personal conditions are necessary which no doubt are shared, in every collectivity, by those who can risk atheism and those who cannot—without this distinction conferring on one or the other an advantage, much less an ethical privilege.

No doubt, in every society, those who possess the sacred and its secrets are always in one way or another aware of the intangible character of these secrets, or even of their non-existence. A pope does not necessarily believe in God, even if it is certain that most often he trusts in a mission he sees for the Church or for himself. But that is still quite different from giving oneself over to the intangible, or the unknown, or even to the nonsensical or nothingness as such.

VI. Opening to the infinite

So, we must recall the lasts words of Marx's text: the opium of the people. The metaphor of opium to indicate a religious or ideological numbness is not new (it can be traced back at least to Sade and seems to have passed to Marx by way of Heine) and it has no doubt often implied a disposition to let oneself be lulled to sleep, as in the medical use the patient willingly welcomes the analgesic. Yet here, this disposition is specified as that of the "people."

The usage of this term in Marx is not always very clear-cut. It is often tied to the nation—obviously not the case here. It is the metaphor that sheds light on the meaning: opium is not a sedative available to all. Without even speaking of the "artificial paradises" cultivated long before being named (and which it cannot be ruled out that Marx has in mind), therapeutic opium is not at everyone's disposal in a society where medicine in general is not. The metaphor has a two-fold significance: religion offers an illusory appeasement and it is especially received by the people. The very possibility of the metaphor implies the social distance of the one who employs it.

A question therefore presents itself: since Marx is an atheist, what is it that for him brings consolation to his suffering condition? What is the non-illusory opium? The answer is clear: science. No need to linger on how exactly Marx understands this word. In the broadest sense of "knowledge" one can no doubt find less the justifications than the deep motivations for atheism: one can think one knows a material constitution of the world or think that one must give oneself over to a "non-knowledge" or to a "gay-science"; the very exercise of this thought (in whatever practice it takes form) is in itself an assurance.

It is not the assurance of a presumptuous pride (as atheists we were once accused of) and it is not that of an indifference too wrapped up in the world (as La Bruyère judges the atheism of the "great" [*les grands*]). Neither is it, at least not for a long time, the conviction of giving a rational basis to the world and to existence. But it is properly the assurance of being carried by a movement that experiences itself more or less clearly as capable of—to put it in a word—the infinite. Or, staying close to Jean-Christophe Bailly, of what he more gracefully calls "the opening."

VII. Atheism and the a-theological

In many ways, this assurance uncoupled from certainty, from proof, and of course from all overarching fiction has continually been confirmed and even become more refined all throughout a modernity that began no doubt always a bit earlier than we tend to think. Well before Hegel, Eckhart asked God to free us from God and well before Eckhart, Plato or Moses refused any figure of what we must, according to Montaigne, "imagine unimaginable."

All these great names have fashioned our thoughts. But these thoughts have not irrigated the existence of the sighing creatures. One may well wonder if they have not, instead, opened an ever deepening rift between what we continue to call vaguely "the people" and those whom we no longer know what to name because they should be in charge of the "spirit" even as we feel more acutely than ever how much that is not a profession or a defined knowledge.

On the contrary, the people of the "intellectuals" is dislocating itself at the same time as the "people" as such rejects them more and more. There are experts, there are researchers, be it in art, in ethics or in philosophy, and there are—many—popularizers, consciousness-raisers, lookouts, there are "scientists" who examine the psycho-social behaviors and discourse of the others. That is quite a crowd—in principle, mostly atheist. But it also resembles the atheistic spirit of a world devoid of all spirit. On the one hand, around this intellectual people swarms another people ever more desiring sometimes of religion, sometimes of diverse beliefs named nation, identity, nature, tradition, sovereignty, power, growth, efficiency …

On the other hand, there are those who in the intellectual world are most interested in showing that atheism is a false problem—at least in the monotheistic and or Buddhist countries. If the meaning of monotheism (and perhaps the ultimate meaning of all great religion) is to be found in the erasing or in the retreat of the god figure itself, and under these conditions it is not religion, those people are even farther removed from all those for whom the name "religion" (or "faith," "belief," all these terms becoming synonymous) refers to the register of an assurance guaranteed by more or less divine inheritance (the latter functioning thenceforth as the absolute presupposition of the assurance itself).

Since what we call Western monotheism is in solidarity both with the philosophy and with the techno-scientific rationality that governs the existence of humanity as a whole, it can be said that today an ever larger gap is widening between the conditions of existence that we could technically call atheistic and the conditions of thought which, with Bataille, we could name "atheological." Increasingly, neither side has anything to say the other, while each seems to be incorporated into the general structure of the present time. Has atheism, instead of irrigating itself, irradiated itself, and has its desert become nothing but a scorch mark?

November 2018
Translated from the original French by Samuel Webb

3

Desire and Inertia

Jeffrey Bloechl

I. Four forms of atheism

When we propose to speak of atheism, we fall immediately into equivocation if we overlook the fact that it is always a matter of a specific context, which is to say a specific *theos* or indeed, remembering the Greek context in which the word seems to have been coined, *theoi*.[1] In its intended usage, the alpha privative *a*-theism has precisely this range: one negates a particular sense of divinity, and in this way opens up possibilities that this sense of divinity would otherwise suppress. As for positive senses of divinity, we should distinguish between something that is properly without predicates, and something—god or gods—to which predicates can be properly applied. In affirming the existence of "something" that is properly without predicates, one can only say, finally, that it *is* (whereupon there arises the difficult question of whether the existence that is asserted is not itself a predicate). Any more than this would come down to conceding that certain predicates do in fact apply properly to the divine, as distinct from certain others that do not, in which case the notional theism of a divinity without predicates would in fact be qualified by the manner in which divinity makes itself truly known. Conversely, the refusal of any predication risks promoting a sense of the divine that it is no way truly known and indeed, strictly speaking is in no way knowable. Such a theism passes as close as possible to atheism. And one easily anticipates asking of its proponents quite how much it would truly matter, at least for our practical comportment, whether we begin from the idea that God is without predicates or rather from the idea that there is no God at all.

To recognize instead certain predicates of the divine, to take the position that I have just invoked, is to adopt what I propose to accept as "qualified theism." It is to relate oneself to the divine from within the horizon of human understanding, even if one also insists that the divine is capable of making itself known there without submitting to its limits. The history of these qualified theisms—or if one prefers, the set of their distinct

---

[1] Instances appear by the fifth century BCE, when Greek thought reached critical consciousness about the historical and anthropological dimensions of their conceptions of the gods. But it was uncertain whether the various positions taken by Protagoras, Democritus, or Xenophanes were strictly atheistic or only guilty of impiety (*asebia*). Cf. Walter Burkert, *Greek Religion* (Cambridge, MA: Harvard University Press, 1985), 311–18.

forms—makes up the context in which to consider the atheisms that have appeared in our tradition. This is not to say that in each case we will find that an atheism has emerged from an active rejection of some prior or contiguous theism, not if by "active" we mean a knowing and deliberate turn away from something else. To be sure, in some instances this has evidently been the case. What is sometimes called the "atheist humanism" of twentieth-century Europe is to an appreciable degree born of a searching dissatisfaction with some implications of nineteenth and twentieth century Christian theism, whether or not either the theism itself or the implications were well understood. One thinks, perhaps inevitably, of Henri de Lubac's claim that the philosophies of Feuerbach, Marx and Nietzsche each propose to liberate new possibilities for being human by overturning the idea that we are created in the image of God, which is thought to be alienating and suppressive.[2]

Close to this is the atheism that abandons or is deprived of the idea of God according to a profound experience of suffering that, one often feels, cannot be reconciled with any notion of supreme love or justice. The suffering is of course undeniable, and that God wills it or only permits is unbearable.

Now, there is also an atheism that does not answer to these descriptions, since it belongs to a way of life that is no longer coordinated either positively or negatively to the question of religion. It has become unmistakable in our own time: a considerable number of people live not only without any faith in God, but also without any sign of resentment, nostalgia, or longing in its place. To the contrary, their lives are often plainly happy, productive, and attentive to much of what is valuable in the world. And to be precise, they do not claim that one can or cannot know whether God or gods exist but are simply not interested in that effort. It is difficult to think that this originates in active refusal of faith in God. There is, instead, only the tacit closure that is constituted by indifference to the entire question.

Somewhat apart from the atheism of refusal, the atheism of loss, and the atheism of closure is the atheism of those who want to believe but, without knowing why, find themselves unable. One sees immediately that whereas the other atheisms live and think at some distance from faith in God, this last one remains strangely close to it. But these differences are more richly distributed at the level of affect: the atheism of refusal is animated by zeal for what is thought to be positive liberation, the atheism of loss often issues in bitterness or regret, the atheism of closure is generally dispassionate about the entire matter, and the non-belief of those who would like to believe but are unable is restless and agitated. Their condition is striking not least because, as we learn from the testimony of Augustine, it does not clearly respond to a deficient or incomplete understanding of the faith in question. There are those among us who understand the principles and practices in great depth, yet only long actually to live from them. Nor can it be reduced to a problem of desire, since plainly enough desire for God is often there in abundance.

This is already enough to shake our confidence in some familiar thoughts. One thinks first of the pronouncement by some theologians that faith is given by God to

---

[2] Henri de Lubac, *The Drama of Atheist Humanism* (San Francisco: Ignatius Press, 1994), Part I.

some of us but not to others. Can one comfortably uphold it, given the testimony of those who wish to believe but cannot? After all, this would be the case according to the will of a God who is also said to be perfect love. How (and why) would the graces of perfect love not extend to all of the beloved? The question provokes an entire theodicy, and from theodicy one seldom receives an improved understanding of what is difficult to bear, so much as assurances that it is necessary.

The evident alternative is to look more deeply into our own finitude, for impulses or dimensions that might interrupt the relation with God, contrary to one's own awareness and desire, in the hope that we—that is, we who struggle to believe—may recognize and overcome them. Of course, we might suppose that this will be a matter of addressing ourselves to the human propensity for self-deception and the base insistence on self for which it provides cover. This, at any rate, has been the teaching of moral theology and depth psychology, each in its own way, and the weight of evidence makes it impossible for us to ignore it. It may seem that this is where the investigation must go, if one refuses to accept that the divine will lies at the root of these phenomena. Yet one may nonetheless hesitate, and indeed hesitate even earlier than this—already at the prospect of having to settle the matter at the level of culpability, that is, between divine and human agency. We have only to ask whether it is true that when we have determined that a person believes or does not believe in God we have therefore said everything there is to say about her, to remember that in any case we are *beings in the world*. And this suggests a somewhat different approach to the matter at hand. This would also be my point of departure for engaging suggestions that one can get beneath or around the alleged difference between belief and non-belief, for example by calling into question the history of the concepts in play or else appealing to a more general anthropology of which each would be a variant. The practical motive for avoiding emphasis on differences is event enough, and appreciable, yet there is no avoiding a phenomenological account of different ways of being, and of what moves them and sustains them—even if phenomenology is not everything.

Here, then, is a word from phenomenology, and in its train a simple hypothesis. While it is correct to say that I have a world and indeed things in a world that are oriented by the cares from which I engage them, it is incorrect to suggest that the world is only this. The world is always more than what I am able to make of it, and in that sense always lies beyond and ahead of each particular moment in which this occurs. Conversely, the fact that the world transcends me without therefore being unintelligible suggests that it is implicated in whatever I may make of it. It lends itself to my cares without being coextensive with them, or better, *it is adequate to my attention*. Now, unless God and world are one and the same, this means that on the matter of interpreting a person's belief or non-belief, there is also its relation to its world to consider. And unless we are to think that a human life can be without world, it also means, further, that the world may claim our attention in a manner that cannot be due either to the specific will of God for this or that person, or to some fault or defect in the person herself. In short, between God and person there is a *hiatus*. This hiatus is the world, and it is a primary condition of our existence. Perhaps we do not see it in this way among the lives of those who refuse the possibility of religious belief or are indifferent to it, since they do not recognize any tension between the proximity of the world and the possibility of God. But those who believe in God certainly do encounter it, and in practice struggle to overcome it when, as often happens, sincere efforts to place themselves fully in God's presence come to nothing. In the lives of those who desire faith but do not have it, the same phenomenon is no longer only a recurrent interruption but something much closer to a defining condition.

This form of atheism, I submit, is more puzzling and therefore more interesting than are the others. We have already seen enough of it to recognize the need of an ontology of belief and non-belief capable of attending to phenomena that cannot be parsed between divine and human agency. But before addressing that need (and I will say almost nothing at all about this here), there is still some work to be done toward better understanding the thing itself—the frustrated atheism of those who wish to believe—in relation to the specific theism that is known but not believed. Needless to say, there can be no universal account of the thing, since in every case it is a matter not only of a specific theism but also a specific human being. And this is only to repeat what everyone already knows: in every case of non-belief, and indeed every case of belief, there is finally a complexity that would elude even the most determined conversation. Our next best recourse is to literature, which, under the condition of necessary artifice, affords us access to the inner movements of the soul. I take up the character of Jack Boughton, in Marilynne Robinson's novel *Home*.[3]

II. The atheism of desire

Jack Boughton is the estranged son of Reverend Robert Boughton, a Presbyterian minister in small-town Iowa during the 1950s. The father is aging and near death. The son left home some decades ago, after a childhood and early adulthood marked by emotional turbulence and moral transgressions. As an adult, while away, he has been in prison and has a common-law relationship with an African American woman whose father does not accept him. Jack's mother, the Reverend Boughton's wife, died some years ago, and Jack did not return home for the funeral. He has three brothers and three sisters, of whom only Glory, the youngest, figures importantly in the story. She is home to care for Reverend Boughton in his final weeks. Jack has come home to see him one last time. Despite all of the trouble that Jack has brought to the family, his father waits especially for him, and upon his arrival it is to him that his father gives most of his concern and attention.

Robinson's story is evidently a retelling of the parable of the prodigal son (Luke 15:11–32), but in this case there is an unhappy ending. Although Reverend Boughton and eventually Glory, who has to overcome considerable jealousy and resentment, both give Jack their unqualified love and forgiveness, he finds himself unable to accept them, and in the final pages of the story returns to what one may assume is his former life of estrangement. But the story is about considerably more than the difficulty of accepting the unconditional love of one's parents and siblings. According to Jack's father, his

---

[3] Marilynne Robinson, *Home* (New York: Farrar, Straus and Giroux, 2008).

problems run deeper than, and probably antedate the actions that gradually distanced him from his family. "I just never knew another child who didn't feel at home in the house where he was born," he remarks at one point.⁴ Stealing, vandalism, and sexual improprieties did not produce the alienation, but were forms of struggle within it. Things are not significantly different in Jack's adult life, and in all of his time at home his restlessness never quite subsides.

It is also clear that Jack's difficulty is as much with God as with the father, Reverend Boughton, who taught him, in word and deed, everything one might wish to know about divine love and forgiveness. Readers of Robinson's previous novel, *Gilead*, which is essentially a first telling of many of the same events that occur in *Home*, already know that Jack has a keen theological mind and a pronounced interest in the topic of predestination. When he takes it up with Reverend Ames, a friend of his father's, the discussion does not go well because Ames doubts his sincerity. In *Home*, we find that Ames was mistaken, and also that over the years the topic has been debated often between the two ministers. Jack knows full well the meaning of his words, and is deeply invested in their stake, when he asks Ames: "Do you think some people are intentionally and irretrievably consigned to perdition?"⁵ Let us be clear about what "perdition" can mean for him here. He worries not only from the weight of guilt about his transgressions, but also from a deeper sense that he has always been outside the reach of divine love, and that this must always be the case. Ames' thought only underlines the nature of Jack's difficulty. He reminds himself that *sozo*, the Greek root of the English word "saved," can also mean "healed" or "restored," and suggests that we can be *salved* (aided, comforted) by Christianity even if we do not feel confident of being *saved*.⁶ But this salving that would be found outside faith, which is to say without a sure experience of grace, must be sought by the exercise of one's own freedom. And this, the reader certainly knows, Jack cannot do. If there are signs of God's help, if God is present and perhaps approaches in subtle ways, Jack has never been able to see this. As this begins to dawn on him, he feels confirmed in a growing sense that, all things considered, it is best for him once again to leave home.

What, then, is Jack Boughton's true condition? Everything in the story suggests that he lives and moves wholly outside the grace of the loving God, though neither because we can be sure that grace is in no way extended to him nor because he is simply unwilling to see it. And this, it would seem, has always been the case for him. This is how Glory sees Jack when, near the end of *Home*, she associates him with the biblical description of the Messiah as "a man of sorrows and acquainted with grief, and as one from whom men hide their face."⁷ Jack has only his adhesion to the world and the things of the world, and they answer more readily to his cares than does the God whose love he nonetheless wishes to have—across a gulf of alienation as old and deep as his very life.

---

⁴ Robinson, *Home*, 115.
⁵ Marilynne Robinson, *Gilead* (New York: Farrar, Straus and Giroux, 2004), 176. The reference is to 2 Thess. 2:3. I will return to this.
⁶ Robinson, *Gilead*, 283.
⁷ Robinson, *Home*, 318, invoking Isa. 53:3.

Jack's self-understanding, I repeat, runs deep, as does his theological insight. He is on a remarkable track when in his discussion with Ames he asks about "perdition" (*apóleias*, destruction). The word harkens unmistakably to 2 Thess. 2:3, in which the author (it is probably not Paul himself) delivers to us the image of a man who "opposes and exalts himself against every so-called god or object of worship, so that he takes himself to be seated in the temple of God, proclaiming himself to be God." Perhaps it is Jack's moral conscience that leads him to a passage that imputes responsibility for lawlessness to the man himself, but if he were to have looked more deeply into all of the chapter he would have been led, as the tradition has been led, to concentrate instead on the question of the origin of the lawlessness itself. Moreover, the lawlessness in question is not active trespass of the prevailing order, but rather detachment, distance, or alienation from it: not *paraptoma*, but *anomia*. If, as one is entitled to think, the law in question is thus the principle of goodness and grace, then the *anomias* invoked in 2 Thessalonians 3 plainly resembles the experience of Jack Boughton. Fundamentally, he is at some distance from God, and in his struggle with that condition he trespasses against God's expressed will. A few verses later (2:7), it is said that "the mystery of lawlessness [*mysterion tes anomias*] is already at work," whereupon there unfolds an apocalyptic vision of the end times. Let us leave aside the apocalypse, apart from reminding ourselves that the letter is written at a time when it was thought that the *Parousia* was immanent, and that this left the community exposed to the danger of mistaking false signs for the real coming of salvation. The son of perdition would be the one who proposes his own vision of salvation, commanded by his own interests and reliant on his own freedom. Whether or not this refers to a specific figure, as is often supposed, it also describes the condition of one for whom the world is all that there is. It hardly needs to be said that human beings can find themselves to be precisely thus. This may be some of what is meant when it is said that lawlessness is already underway. Our existence is such that we are not predetermined to faith in God's love, but only called to it from a condition that admits the real possibility of instead living as if the world is all that there is.

Theology has never truly doubted this. And if we want to understand better why it is that someone like Jack Boughton, a man of intelligence and longing, cannot answer that call, phenomenology has prepared us to consider the complex nature of our adhesion to the world. At the root of Boughton's affliction is the torment of constraint. Desire for salvation, even if it is mitigated by a conviction that it is impossible, is born from a sense that the world is not enough. Jack Boughton has this sense and knows that the Christian faith promises more—indeed, he knows a good deal about what that would mean. Constrained by everything that makes the world appear evident and urgent, he nonetheless returns home as if to find another way in life. Nothing in the story suggests that he can conceive of this as anything more than sheer liberation. At bottom, what he asks of his father, Reverend Boughton, and what he plainly wants from his Father, the Lord, is only the freedom to live and move without limits. On this point, Robinson's story agrees with Jean-Luc Marion's interpretation of the story of the prodigal son. According to Marion, what the son asks of his father is not merely property and money (*ousia*, substance), but freedom to be entirely and only himself in the world. His return to his father implies disillusion with the way of the world, and a new willingness to bow to something higher.[8] But this is not yet the freedom from constraint to the world that comes only, according to the religious paradox, through surrendering one's freedom to something still higher again. The persistence of this desire for freedom marks a woundedness that is not self-inflicted, but also not inflicted by anyone else—and which, in some cases, seemingly cannot be healed.

Christian thought has recognized this phenomenon as evil—since it implies distance from salvation and is cause for suffering—and has on occasion proposed to ground it among the primordial conditions of our existence. Hans urs von Balthasar situates it in the drama of relations among human and divine persons, and proposes that its possibility is ingredient to the creation of a freedom that is necessarily finite.[9] In Gabriel Marcel's philosophy of hope, also sometimes worked out in the register of plot and characters, it emerges from what he calls our ontological brokenness.[10] Thinking in terms closer to my own, Simone Weil describes an unresolvable tension between a desire to give oneself fully to God and the "inertia" of forces binding one essentially to a world governed by necessity—an elevating desire, then, and the weight of attachments that work against it.[11] What these various efforts strongly imply is that the peculiar atheism of someone like Jack Boughton—of anyone who wishes to believe but cannot, and due to no fault of his or her own—is a possibility contained within Christian theism itself. And yet what they seek lies beyond our reach. The intellectual consequence is striking. The *mysterium iniquitatis* invoked already in 2 Thessalonians necessarily lies beyond our understanding because it is always already in place, even before any attempt to come to terms with it. Perhaps this sheds new light on the nature of theology, as it returns time and again to the problem of evil, though it knows just how deeply it lies, and as if unable to let the matter rest.[12] Theology is endless, because the world will never be free of evil and yet hope is undying.[13]

---

[8] See Jean-Luc Marion, *God Without Being*, trans. Thomas A. Carlson (Chicago: University of Chicago Press, 1982), 95ff.
[9] Hans Urs von Balthasar, *Theodramatik*, 2 vols., vol. 2 (Einsedeln: Johannes Verlag, 1976), 425ff.
[10] See, for example, Gabriel Marcel, "Sketch of a Phenomenology and a Metaphysics of Hope," in *Homo Viator* (New York: Harper and Row, 1962); "The Broken World," in *Gabriel Marcel's Perspectives on the Broken World* (Milwaukee, WI: Marquette University Press, 1998) and so on.
[11] Simone Weil, "The Love of God and Affliction," in *Waiting for God* (New York: Harper Colophon, 1973), 74–6. Although in some of his writings Dostoyevsky seems to take a similar view, finding in the "inertia" of natural forces a draw away from the sublime freedom experienced in Christian faith, he invests the former with a Newtonian mechanics that he fears will distract us from the potential of redemptive love.
[12] My thought only reformulates Ricœur's remark that theology can never definitively overcome tragedy, since it is "powerless to account for the position of evil in the world." Ricœur, *The Symbolism of Evil*, 326 note 7.
[13] The present work has profited greatly from the insights of my friends in Arlington, Vermont, who prefer to remain anonymous.

4

No Gods, No Masters—Anarchism and Religious Experience

Catherine Malabou

I. The fact of being left alone

"No gods, no Masters" is undoubtedly the most famous anarchist motto. Originally coined by Auguste Blanqui as a name for the journal he created in 1880, it then became the radical expression of the core tenet of anarchism: the rejection, not of power as a whole—as one too often thinks—but of domination, that is, of excess or abuse of power. Since the end of the nineteenth century, in different ways and at different moments, anarchism has fought domination in all its forms: political, philosophical, and religious. Such a fight is the attempt at dismantling what one might call the "archic paradigm" that has governed the whole Western political and spiritual tradition. In politics, the archic paradigm coincides with the nexus that bids the question of politics and the political to the logic of government exercised within the domain of state sovereignty; in philosophy, the archic paradigm refers to the ontological sovereignty of the archè understood as both inception and domination. The religious meaning of anarchism, on which I will of course focus here, is much more ambiguous. Anarchism presents itself, as we know, as an atheism. Emma Goldman characterizes anarchism as the "Philosophy of Atheism."[1] Nevertheless, as I intend to demonstrate, anarchism has also been and still is paradoxically considered a modality of religious experience itself, and this by taking Proudhon's general definition of anarchism as a point of departure, not by rejecting it, or by creating a different definition of anarchism. It is as if the detour by means of the atheist meaning of anarchism was, in a certain sense, necessary in order to access a new, an-archic, vision of God.

Let me first briefly examine Proudhon's definition. Proudhon is said to be the inventor of the "positive" sense of anarchy, contemporaneous with the invention of the terms "*anarchism*" and "*anarchist*" that entered the *Dictionnaire de l'Academie de langue française* in 1877. Before Proudhon, anarchy meant chaos; disorder; absence of a chief, direction, or meaning. In Herodotus' *History*, IX, 23, anarchy is characterized as the

---

[1] Emma Goldmann, "The Philosophy of Atheism," first published in February 1916 in the *Mother Earth* journal.

"state of a people deprived of government." In Sophocles' *Antigone*, it is synonymous with "lack of authority" (v. 672). In the *Iliad*, it describes the state of an army after its general has passed away. In Aristotle's *Politics* 1302B 29, *Anarchia* finds itself associated with *anomia*, and hubris.

In *What is Property?*, Proudhon undertakes a semantic revolution of the term, in the literal sense. He turns it against itself, so that anarchy can from then on mean "the highest expression of order." The highest perfection of society, Proudhon writes, is to be found in "the unity of order and anarchy."[2] He declares (and this was the very first occurrence of this expression) "I am an anarchist."[3] The absence of a chief, of an *arkhē*, the fact of being left alone—instead of creating chaos—ceases to appear as something negative, and starts to qualify the emergence of another experience of order. It is in this semantic revolution, presented as a radical, atheistic U-turn, that religious anarchism paradoxically finds its source.

I will briefly present three different forms of this phenomenon: first, the important tradition of Christian anarchism; second, the way opened by Levinasian ethics by the notion of "anarchic responsibility" (*Otherwise than Being or Beyond Essence*), understood as transcendence and as a path toward God, and toward what Levinas calls "the State beyond the State" (in *New Talmudic Readings*), or "The State of Cesar and the State of David" (in *Beyond the Verse*); and third, Reiner Schürmann's reading of Heidegger through the concept of "ontological anarchism," a reading that is not, strictly speaking, religious, but that contains important elements on the destiny of a principle when dislodged from its role as a principle.

II. Christian anarchism

The important tradition of Christian anarchism includes thinkers and writers like Leon Tolstoi, Ivan Illitch, and Felix Ort, and in France, among French Catholics, the young Paul Claudel, or later the philosopher Jacques Ellul, on whom I will focus. Anarchism in this context consists in thinking God independently from the traditional vision of God as a dominating power: thinking God as liberated from God so to speak, from God apprehended as a master. As Claudel beautifully writes: "*choisir Dieu est le seul moyen radical de n'avoir aucun maître*" (choosing God is the only radical possibility of having no master).[4] For Ellul and many other Christian anarchists, subtracting God, so to speak, from all idea of domination implies to liberate God from the mediation of the Church. This is a very first level of analysis. The Church, not God, is the origin of the archic paradigm that has been superimposed on God. The idea of a dominating God is, then, the result of an excess of human power. An anarchistic approach to God

---

[2] Pierre-Joseph Proudhon, *What is Property? An Inquiry into the Principle of Right and of Government*, trans. Benjamin R. Tucker, vol. 1, *The works of P. J. Proudhon* (Princeton, NJ: Princeton University Press, 1876), 286.
[3] Proudhon, *What is Property?* 272.
[4] Cited in Michel Autrand, "Les saisons noires du jeune Claudel (1882–1895)," *Revue d'histoire littéraire de la France* 99, no. 3 (1999): 400.

subsequently implies a direct access to God through biblical hermeneutics, an idea that we will also find in Levinas.

In his interesting short book, *Anarchy and Christianity*, Jacques Ellul is well aware of the paradoxical character of his position. "It is taken for granted that anarchists are hostile to all religions (and Christianity is classified as such)," he writes. "It is also taken for granted that devout Christians abhor anarchy as a source of disorder and a negation of established authority." He adds: "It is these simplistic and uncontested beliefs that I propose to challenge."[5] Further:

> My next task is to show by a "naive" reading of the Bible that far from offering us a sure basis for the state and the divine authorities, a better understanding will, I believe, point us toward anarchy; not, of course, in the common sense of disorder, but in the sense of an-arche: no authority, no domination. We commonly talk of sheer anarchy when we see disorder. This is because we in the West are convinced that order can be established in society only by a strong central power and by force (police, army, propaganda).

We see here the reference to Proudhon's redefinition of anarchy, to which Ellul is explicitly referring throughout the book. What Ellul calls authority, and what he challenges, is the alliance between State and the Church that has endured, according to him, since Emperor Constantine's reign and up to our times. This alliance has never been dismantled, even where an official separation between them has been enacted. "The Roman Catholic Church is less compliant, but we must not forget that under Hitler, if it did not directly aid the regime, it did support it, even in Germany. The pope even made a concordat with Hitler. The point is that no matter what the form of government, at the higher level and in its directives the church is always on the side of the state."[6] We can, of course, reverse the proposition: the States always find themselves on the side of the Church.

What about God's power? This question addresses the theological aspect of the archic paradigm:

> Now it is true that for centuries theology has insisted that God is the absolute Master, the Lord of lords, the Almighty, before whom we are nothing. Hence it is right enough that those who reject masters will reject God too. We must also take note of the fact that even in the 20th century Christians still call God the King of creation and still call Jesus Lord even though there are few kings and lords left in the modern world. But I for my part dispute this concept of God.... I realize, finally, that many biblical passages call God King or Lord. But this admitted, I contend that the Bible in reality gives us a very different image of God.... For beyond power, there is the being of God ...[7]

---

[5] Jacques Ellul, *Anarchy and Christianity*, trans. Geoffrey W. Bromiley (Grand Rapids: Eerdmans, 1988), 1.
[6] Ellul, *Anarchy and Christianity*, 29–30.
[7] Ellul, *Anarchy and Christianity*, 32–3.

God would then ontologically dismantle any supposed political domination and appear as an an-archic opening toward non-teleocratic economy: "But we are now returning to the simple and essentially biblical truth that God does not serve any outside purpose."[8]

III. Anarchic responsibility

I turn, now, to Levinas and his dismantling of the archic ethical paradigm. The concept of anarchic responsibility appears very early in his work, in texts like *Humanism of the Other*, which includes a chapter called "Humanism and An-archy."[9] However, it is in *Otherwise Than Being or Beyond Essence* that anarchy finds itself most strongly elaborated. We know that for Levinas, being [*l'être*]—in the traditional as well as in the Heideggerian sense—cannot be said to resist the archic paradigm. On the contrary, it is at one with it. In Levinas, domination pertains to the power of totality, and totality in its turn pertains to the sovereignty of the subject. In Western tradition, subjectivity, be it understood as substance or as the ego on the one hand, and *arkhē*, on the other, have always been intimately linked. God himself has always been considered a subject, even the supreme form of subjectivity. Of course, there is a strong link between anarchy and what, according to Levinas, lies "Beyond Essence": a space that does not obey any principle, which economy does not derive from a pre-existing being, the utterly other, alien to any command, any beginning. "Indatable substitution," Levinas says.[10] Anarchy starts with the Other, from the Other, which means that it does not start. The "I," in that sense, is always already held hostage by the Other. Levinas speaks of an "an-archy more ancient than any beginning and even freedom."[11]

It is clear that "Levinas refuses a purely political vision of anarchy."[12] Levinas is explicit on that point: "It would be contradictory to set [anarchy] up as a principle (in the sense that anarchists understand it). Anarchy cannot be sovereign, like an *arkhē*."[13] Nevertheless, he does not entirely dismiss the political value of anarchism, and his attacks on State power are numerous. At this point we find religious anarchism. "Anarchy can only disturb the State [political turmoil]—but in a radical way—making possible moments of negation without any affirmation. The State then cannot set itself up as a whole."[14] Ethical anarchism is metapolitical, it carves out a dimension of transcendence in the immanence of the political, and such a transcendence is nothing

---

[8] Ellul, *Anarchy and Christianity*, 36.
[9] Emmanuel Levinas, *Humanism of the Other*, trans. Nidra Poller (Chicago: University of Illinois Press, 2005).
[10] Emmanuel Levinas, *Otherwise than Being or Beyond Essence*, trans. Alphonso Lingis (The Hague: Martinus Nijhoff, 1981), 29.
[11] Levinas, *Otherwise*, 167.
[12] Cf. Miguel Abensour, *Democracy Against the State: Marx and the Machiavellian Moment*, trans. Max Blechman and Martin Breaugh (Malden, MA: Polity, 2011), 123–4.
[13] Levinas, *Otherwise*, 194n3. Quoted in Abensour, *Democracy Against the State*, 122.
[14] Levinas, *Otherwise*, 194n3. "Anarchy cannot be sovereign, like an *arkhē*. It can only disturb the State—but in a radical way, making possible moments of negation without any affirmation. The State then cannot set itself up as a Whole."

but God's "significance." In *Adieu*, Derrida rightly comments: "Beyond-in: transcendence in immanence, beyond the political but in the political. Inclusion opened on to the transcendence that it bears, incorporation of a door that bears and opens onto the beyond of the walls and partly framing it. At the risk of causing the identity of the place as well as the stability of the concept to explode."[15]

According to Miguel Abensour, transcendence in Levinas is the anarchic plot that brings trouble into politics in order to prevent the State of justice from locking itself up in a closed totality.[16] It is the enigmatic movement of the State toward its outside. What outside? The answer is contained in the title of Levinas' work, "Beyond the State in the State."[17] Anarchy, as transcendence, is the opening of a passage from the State of Caesar to the State of David, that is a path toward God. A God here also who is not a master, even in a different sense than in Ellul. Anarchy clears the way to sanctity understood as the end of domination, as a non-coercive political organization, that of the "messianic State."

If, once again, Levinas certainly did not define himself an anarchist, we see here also that his concept of anarchy is indebted to that of traditional political anarchy. The critique of State Power, the significance of the absence of principle, the link between anarchy and otherness, would, of course, not have been conceivable without the semantic revolution I mentioned earlier.

IV. Ontological anarchism

The word "teleocracy" brings me to Schürmann's famous book *Heidegger on Being and Acting: From Principles to Anarchy*.[18] Teleocracy is a term coined by Schürmann precisely in this work. Following Heidegger, Schürmann shows that the archic paradigm operating in metaphysics consists in the existing solidarity between *arkhē* and *telos*: "*Telos*," as he suggests, is not only "the complementary notion of *arkhē*," it is synonymous with *arkhē*.[19] In Metaphysics XI, 8, 1050 a 7sq, Aristotle declares: "Everything that comes to be moves toward an *arkhē*, that is, a *telos*: in fact, that for the stake of which a thing is, is its *arkhē*, and becoming is for the sake of its *telos*."[20] The *arkhē*, the principle, Schürmann remarks, "commands" everything, and teleocracy then designates, once again, the explicit unity between inception and domination.[21] Metaphysically conceived, the origin has always appeared as a beginning, as a principle determining a hierarchical order. For Aristotle, politics borrows from ontology its governing structure. Individual actions and ends are determined by collective ones, the ones of the city, just like

---

[15] Jacques Derrida, *Adieu To Emmanuel Levinas*, trans. Michael Naas and Pascale-Anne Brault, Meridian: Crossing Aesthetics (Stanford, CA: Stanford University Press, 1999), 76.
[16] Abensour, *Democracy Against the State*, 75.
[17] Emmanuel Levinas, *New Talmudic Readings*, trans. Richard Cohen (Pittsburgh: Duquesne University Press, 1999).
[18] Reiner Schürmann, *Heidegger: On Being and Acting, From Principles to Anarchy* (Bloomington: Indiana University Press, 1987).
[19] Schürmann, *Heidegger*, 107.
[20] Aristotle, *Metaphysics* XI, 8, 1050 a 7sq. Cited in Schürmann, *Heidegger*, 103.
[21] Ibid.

accidents are determined by the substance. Substance is then thought of as the ultimate chief, political as well as ontological, that confers unity, *pros hen*, to the army of predicates. Teleocracy secures order from arbitrariness and chaos. Anything "*adynaton*" (impotent) is excluded from the realm of being.

The sub-title *From Principles to Anarchy* indicates a trajectory, a passage from traditional metaphysics to what Heidegger calls "the other thinking." Anarchy is the name of the destiny of thinking after the deconstruction of metaphysics, that is, of the archic paradigm as the core structure of philosophy. The Heideggerian *Abbau*, precisely translated by Schürmann as "deconstruction," tends to let "the an-archic, anti-teleocratic element" freely appear, and liberate its force of dislocation and fragmentation.[22] "To deconstruct action is to uproot it from domination by the idea of finality, the teleocracy where it has been held since Aristotle" and to dislodge it "from the attributive schema."[23] The an-archic thinking is visible in Heidegger through the motives of the "without why," "without a goal," or "without reason."

There would, of course, be much more to say on these points, but I return to my immediate topic. One may object to my development that there is no mention of religion, or religious experience, or even of God, in Schürmann's book—outside his critique of the God of onto-theology. Nevertheless, his trajectory as a student in both philosophy and theology, his Dominican priesthood and his renouncement of it, constitute a complex archive that allows one to postulate that an-archic thinking, in Schürmann, and for Schürmann, is certainly not alien to religious experience. This aspect of Schürmann's thinking is perhaps more visible in the article he wrote on negative theology, "*L'hénologie comme dépassement de la métaphysique*" ("Henology as transgression of metaphysics").[24] Schürmann shows how the One, in Plotinus, exceeds the traditional ontotheological concept of God—teleo-theo-cracy, if I may say so. The One, he says, has to be thought not as a principle but as an event (*un "événement"*) a unifying event (*un "événement d'unification"*).[25] Such an a-principiality is a "non-foundational but evential economy" ("*une économie non fondationnelle mais événementielle*"), that nothing prevents us from interpreting as a divine one. This is the way Stanislas Breton understands it in his book, *Du Principe* (in which he refers to Schürmann's article).[26]

As remote as it seems from traditional anarchism, this metaphysical reflection on the principle, I have to say, once again, would at the same time not have been possible without it. Schürmann is very dismissive of Proudhon: "Needless to say, here it will not be a question of anarchy in the sense of Proudhon, Bakunin, and their disciples. What these masters sought was to displace the origin, to substitute the 'rational' power,

---

[22] Schürmann, *Heidegger*, 16.
[23] Schürmann, *Heidegger*, 10. Justifying the paradox of the title "Principle of Anarchy," Schürmann declares that it "locates the Heideggerian enterprise, it indicates the place where it is situated: still implanted in the problematic of ... 'what is being?' but already ... dislocating it from the attributive [teleocratic] schema" (6).
[24] Reiner Schürmann, "L'hénologie comme dépassement de la métaphysique," *Les études philosophiques*, no. 3 (1982).
[25] Schürmann, "L'hénologie," 349.
[26] Stanislas Breton, *Du principe* (Paris: Cerf, 2011), 294.

principium, for the power of authority, *princeps*—as metaphysical an operation as has ever been."[27] However, as I suggest, *From Principles to Anarchy* is more indebted to Proudhon than Schürmann recognizes.

V. Religious anarchism

I would like to insist very precisely on what is not anarchistic in the traditional sense in the three thinkers. It is clear, in all three contexts, that God is not the result of the deconstruction of the archic paradigm. God is the deconstructive force of the archic paradigm, the self-dismantling move of the *arkhē*. Religious, ethical, and ontological anarchism are understood in the three contexts, even if very differently each time, not as the outcome of an external deconstructive gesture, but as a dynamism immanent to Godself, to tradition itself, to the principle itself. An identical mechanism—and I use this word purposefully—is at work in the three thinkers, a mechanism that is clearly identified as a mechanism of auto- or self-regulation. In Ellul, God is said to limit God's own power: "[God] is a self-limiting power, not by arbitrariness and fantasy, but because to act otherwise would contradict God's very being."[28] Levinas shows that a hermeneutical self-regulated principle lies at the very heart of the Torah—is the Torah itself. He insists on the meaning of the word "time" and shows that Torah is like a watch that tells a double temporality: profane and sacred, so that every event happening in the world, even the events to come, can be inserted in the sacred calendar.[29] Schürmann names his conclusion "Of Economic Self-Regulation and its Foci": "Without a form of systemic self-regulation," he declares, "it would seem difficult to speak of identity and difference in history, that is, to think change."[30] Further:

> Deconstruction directly concerns the self-regulation of epochal economies. It is the method for uprooting the very event of *phainesthai*, of manifestation, from past manifest configurations of phenomena. It is the method by which the phenomenologist gathers presencing as the synchronic event-or advent-from the cultural fields of presence and their diachronic shifts."[31]

It is on that point that religious and ontological anarchism part ways from political anarchism more broadly. For political anarchists, there is nothing like a political self-regulation. The mechanism is missing that constitutes the social as autonomously governed or managed. This means that political anarchy has to be conquered, fought for, and is always precarious, fragile, contingent. Can the semantic revolution of

---

[27] Schürmann, *Heidegger*, 6.
[28] Ellul, *Anarchy and Christianity*, 33, trans. modified.
[29] Emmanuel Levinas, *In the Time of the Nations*, trans. Michael B. Smith (Bloomington/London: Indiana University Press/Athlone Press, 1994), 7.
[30] Schürmann, *Heidegger*, 282. On the same page, Schürmann speaks of anarchy versus pure and simple disorder.
[31] Schürmann, *Heidegger*, 283–4.

anarchism, the turning of anarchy against itself, happen without conflicts, without struggles, without change? Self-regulation would appear to anarchists as just another means of domination, a robotic production of new masters. Does self-regulation, by definition, prevent all experience? Such would be the paradox of religious anarchism, that its revolutionary force might proceed from a powerful automatism—that is, from a terrifying, mechanistic version of domination.

5

Nothingness against the Death of God— Mallarmé's Poetics after 1866

Quentin Meillassoux

I. The poetic renouncement of the divine

"More profoundly than Nietzsche, he experienced the death of God."[1]

With this declaration on Mallarmé, in a 1953 article which displays his admiration for the author of "Un Coup de dés," Sartre supposes that the poet, like Nietzsche, endorsed and faced the death of God throughout his work. Something like a "difference of degree" is thereby established between the Dionysian philosopher and the poet of Nothingness [*le Néant*], which allows Sartre to present the thought of the latter as deeper and more radical.[2] But is it actually in those terms that these thinkers should be distinguished? Sartre's judgment does suppose that Mallarmé was in fact a poet of the death of God. As it happens, that opinion is still quite common today, including among many commentators—but for what reason, exactly? In the first place, everything depends on the interpretation of the "Tournon crisis," attested by the so-called "Letter on Nothingness," or the Void [*le Néant*], sent by Mallarmé to his friend Henri Cazalis on April 28, 1866.

To grasp the nature of this crisis, we must go back to the period of Mallarmé's published poems, to those written between 1862 and 1865. Up until then, his poetry had been dominated by an exacerbated Baudelaireanism, as a classic study by Bertrand Marchal emphasizes.[3] Indeed, during that period we find numerous splenetic themes: Satanism ("Le Sonneur," 1862), the sordid poverty of the poet ("Le Guignon," 1862), sterility in the face of a cruel Ideal ("Les Fenêtres," 1863), disillusioned histrionicism

---

[1] Jean-Paul Sartre, *Mallarmé, or the Poet of Nothingness*, trans. Ernest Sturm (Philadelphia: University of Pennsylvania Press, 1991/1953), 146.
[2] [Sartre's *le néant* is normally translated as "nothingness," hence the English title of Sartre's essay on Mallarmé, *The Poet of Nothingness*. Mallarmé's use of the term, however, is sometimes rendered by "the Void," as in the translation of the famous letter referred to below. I have translated *Néant* by Nothingness, except in some cited translations—Trans.]
[3] Cf. Bertrand Marchal, *La religion de Mallarmé* (Paris: José Corti, 1988), 41–67.

("Le Pitre châtié," 1864 for the first version), degradation in prostitution ("À une putain," 1864), or invitation to journey ("Brise marine," 1865). From 1865 on, the influence of the Parnassian movement (Gautier, Leconte de Lisle) no doubt becomes more important: it colours with its avowed "impassivity" the disdainful and metallic virginity of Hérodiade, whose "Scene" was written in that year. But the main evolution at work is elsewhere. For, starting in 1864, it is above all Edgar Allen Poe and his ideal of premeditated composition (discovered in "The Philosophy of Composition"), as well as the desire to invent a poetry of effect ("paint, not the object, but the effect it produces") which progressively takes center stage, in particular in the composition of "L'Azur" or the "Scène."[4]

Still, it remains the case that until the "Overture" of "Hérodiade"—the text from 1866 left unfinished, through the drafting of which Mallarmé experienced the "counter-revelation" of Nothingness [*le Néant, le Rien*]—Baudelaire's influence, although in competition with that of Poe, never disappears. The poetics of *Spleen* did allow the young poet, according to Marchal, to supplement a largely neglected God by an aesthetic ideal, posed as inaccessible, certainly, but as such assured to be a source of obsession. It is this substitution of a cruel Ideal for a fading God—a way to avoid until then endorsing atheism too directly—that Mallarmé would definitively reject in his letter from April 28, 1866, stating resolutely henceforth the absence of any beyond to which one could aspire.

Let us cite the essential and well-known passage of that "Letter on Nothingness":

Unfortunately, in the course of quarrying out the lines [of the "Overture" of "Hérodiade"] to this extent, I've come across two abysses that leave me in despair. One is the Void [*le Néant*], which I reached without any knowledge of Buddhism, and I am still too distraught to be able to believe even in my poetry and get back to work, which this crushing awareness has made me abandon.

Yes, I know, we are merely empty forms of matter—but we are indeed sublime for having invented God and our soul. So sublime, my friend, that I want to gaze upon matter, fully conscious that it exists, and yet launching itself madly into Dream, despite its knowledge that Dream has no existence, extolling the Soul and all the divine impressions which have collected within us from the beginning of time and proclaiming, in the face of the Void [*le Rien*] which is truth, these glorious lies! That is the plan of my Lyrical volume, and that might also be its title: *The Glory of the Lie* or *The Glorious Lie*. I shall sing it as one in despair!

If I live long enough! For the other void that I found is that of my chest.[5]

---

[4] See the two letters to Cazalis of 7(?) January 1864 and October 30, 1864, in Rosemary Lloyd, ed. *Selected letters of Stéphane Mallarmé* (Chicago: University of Chicago Press, 1988), 59–61. «Genèse d'un poème» is the 1853 translation by Charles Baudelaire of "The Philosophy of Composition"— see Edgar Allan Poe, *Complete Essays, Literary Criticism, Cryptography, Autography, Translations & Letters* (Cleveland, OH: Musaicum Books, 2017/1846). In a doubtlessly fictive manner, Poe narrates there the ptinciples which have governed the writing of *The Raven*, which he describes in the form of a necessary series of deductions having a mathematical appearance.

[5] Lloyd, *Selected letters of Stéphane Mallarmé*, 60.

According to the standard interpretation, then, Mallarmé, from that period until the end of his life, would face the experience of the death of God.[6] But is that really what this passage teaches us?

That there is in this letter what might—for lack of a better term for the moment—be called a declaration of "atheism," or "materialism" ("Yes, I know, we are merely empty forms of matter") is clear enough. But it seems paradoxical to say that Mallarmé's avowed materialism means that he is discovering, at that date, something that could properly be called the "Death of God." Simply because, for one thing, the statement that by far most resembles "God is dead" in all his published poetry, is to be found before 1866 and not after, that is, in "L'Azur," completed in 1864 and published in 1866, with a few modifications, in the *Parnasse contemporain*. In the first line of the sixth stanza, that poem, sent in January 1864 to Cazalis, does, indeed, contain the declaration: "The Sky is dead."[7] Now, not only did Mallarmé write this sentence more than two years before the letter on Nothingness, but he bluntly deprecates its meaning in the commentary that gives of it to Cazalis in that same letter. As he explains, it is merely the "grotesque exclamation one expects from a schoolboy who's been set free."[8] In other words, it all seems as if the theme of the death of the Sky—synonym for the Baudelairean Azure, itself a substitute for God—was already at that point, before the letter on Nothingness—an old thing, belonging to an already outgrown adolescence, for which Mallarmé feels compelled to apologize to his correspondent. How are we to understand this attitude?

"L'Azur" seems to carry to its conclusion a logic of exacerbating Icarian poetry, exacerbation which was already at work in "Les plaintes d'Icare."[9] Indeed, in that poem, Baudelaire is no longer content to compare the failure of the poet to the fall of the son of Daedalus, as others had before him. Instead, he describes a "splenetic" version of the Icarian drama, in which the poet fails even in this fall, no longer managing to conserve for it any grandeur or renown since; unlike his "model," he does not succeed in giving his name to the ocean, to the abyss which serves as his tomb. The poet no longer even manages to be maudlin, and stumbles in perennial misfortune ("Le Guignon"). Thus falling from the fall initiates a seemingly repeatable process in which each failure can itself fail, and so on exponentially. "L'Azur" presents a kind of final step of such a movement, where the poet manages this time to fail even in his attempt to become a philistine. Riveted, indeed, to the arid and sterile soil of his "suffering," he seeks to plug the sky to flee the irony of an Azure that definitively escapes his art: fogs, rags of mist, Lethean *ennui*, and the soot of sad chimneys are conjured up, until the apparent death of the sky. But the Azure passes through this veil by the song of a bell, indifferent to

---

[6] This is what Bertrand Marchal maintains, who regularly uses the expression in *La religion de Mallarmé*, pp. 58, 64, 99. Patrick Theuriault does the same in a recent study: "Entre postulat de raison et postulation du désir: l'athéisme de Mallarmé," in Patrick Thériault and Jean-Jacques Hamm, eds. *Composer avec la mort de Dieu. Littérature et athéisme au XIXè siècle* (Québec: Presses de l'Université Laval, 2014).
[7] With, in 1864, a capital letter for "Sky" which disappears in the version of 1866.
[8] Lloyd, *Selected letters of Stéphane Mallarmé*, 60.
[9] The poem appears for the first time in 1862 and is inserted in the third (posthumous) edition of *Les Fleurs du Mal* in 1868.

what made it invisible—and continues to haunt the one who dreamed of joining the happy herd of humans without genius. The poet is thus summoned to return to the torture of writing, but the loyalty to his office now only seems to be the consequence of his inability to fail in everything—even mediocrity. His vocation is now nothing more than the residue of a failed failure.

What is Mallarmé actually up to in this poem? He seems to be playing one poetics of impotence against another, and attempting to destroy, as if through a desperate escape, the solar figure of Icarian poetry with that of the night of dead gods, of exiles and fled gods. Icarian impotence is due to the inability of the poet to approach a sky which is too ardent for him; the impotence of the poet facing the night of dead gods is due to the disappearing of the celestial Ideal. It is not, in the latter case, the ascent toward the Azure that is lacking, it is the Azure itself. Impotence is no longer the consequence of the poet's inadequacy in reaching his ideal, but the result of the extinction of the absolute for his entire age. It is no longer the climb that fails, but the summit which comes up short. For the artist, there would therefore seem to be a form of consolation in forgetting the limitations of his art by hoping for the disappearance of the Ideal itself. The death of the gods provisionally relieves the perpetually intensified Icarian fall. That is the whole dynamic tension of the poem. But when the Azure makes itself heard again by its unsullied celestial music, this attempt to transform his own failure into an anonymous nightfall dissipates and the poet is brought back, in the last line, to the specter of what he believed himself to have slain.

For I am haunted. The Sky! The Sky! The Sky! The Sky!

But why this reference to the "grotesque exclamation one expects from a schoolboy," about the dead Sky? Most obviously because for Mallarmé at the time, the death of the sky refers to a poetry that considerably predates the Baudelairean *Spleen*—by more than half a century, in fact. And no doubt also because it corresponds, in our poet's eyes, to one of his long-since abandoned poetic influences, at least at the scale of his rapidly evolving literary youth: that is to say, Alfred de Musset. Indeed, thanks to a study by L.J. Austin, we know that Musset, with Lamartine and Hugo, was a major influence on the collection of poems entitled *Entre 4 murs*, that Mallarmé wrote between in 1859 and 1860 while still in high school.[10] The last poem of the collection ("Pan") contains in particular two lines which are obvious reminiscences of Musset's "Rolla," sufficient proof, if any were necessary, that the young Mallarmé read it closely.[11] Now, this poem opens on one of the most famous declamations of the death of the gods in French poetry. It is a long lament by the rake, Jacques Rolla, who belongs to a generation that is incapable of believing, after a century of incredulity dominated by the "hideous smile" of Voltaire. The desolation of one whose faith is exhausted in a world deserted by the ideals of the fathers, and not the frustration of a literary man incapable of raising himself toward what he continues to ardently desire for his pain,

---

[10] Lloyd James Austin, "Les 'Années d'apprentissage' de Mallarmé," in *Essais sur Mallarmé* (Manchester: Manchester University Press, 1995).
[11] *Essais sur Mallarmé*, pp. 4 and 17n13.

Rolla is therefore only a literary love of the first hours for Mallarmé, set aside as early as 1860 by his passionate discovery of *Les Fleurs du mal*. Thus to return, as the poet of "L'Azur" does, from Baudelaire to Musset, to attempt to free himself from the Icarian Spleen by lamenting the dead Sky, would no doubt, for the intransigent Mallarmé of 1864, be understood as both a desperate and a pathetic return of immaturity.

Let us add the following as well, which reinforces the impression of distance. About "L'Azur", Mallarmé wrote in his letter from 1864 that there was not "a single word which hasn't cost [him] several hours of research" and that he had composed it, as we have said, attempting to follow the principles of composition of Edgar Allen Poe, ruling out any intervention of chance or gratuitous inspiration.[12] In fact, the profound struggle of the poem happens between a principle of composition mobilized by the author of the poem, coldly aware of the calculus of its effects and already sensing the possible fecundity of this mode of writing, and the splenetic Azure which imposes a disease of impotence on the voice within the poem, sterilizing it. But the principle of composition is also thematized within "L'Azur" itself, since in it we see the poet voluntarily mobilize, to mask the ironic sky, fogs, *ennui*, Lethean water, and murderous night, like so many theatrical effects, openly artificial. Hence, the death of the Sky is itself already thought of, and reflected on as a simple procedure, a poetic artifice and not as a destiny to which the whole age would be submitted. A demystification is at work which shows that Mallarmé already no longer really believes in the staging of the dead God.

All this makes it rather implausible to think that, two years later, Mallarmé would have had a crushing revelation of a Nothingness, identified with something as already well-known as the poetics of the death of God. Instead, it seems to us that the letter on Nothingness from which Mallarmé's whole later aesthetic does proceed, is fascinating not because it marks the quite belated discovery of what, in the meantime, had largely become a cliché, but because it breaks with the poetics of the dead God just as much as with the poetics of *Spleen*. In 1866, Mallarmé experiences a poetic renouncement of the divine which is not a form of its death—and that is what his originality consists in. But in what does it consist, this experience lived at the heart of the nineteenth century? What is this thing whose name is *Néant*? That is what we must now attempt to elucidate.

II. Atheism as a stigma of the age

To grasp the full importance of Mallarmé's gesture, we must begin by bringing more precisely into view what it allows us to move beyond. Let us start with Musset. It is well-known that he belonged to that "1810 generation" who, with Gautier and Nerval, developed in France the theme of the exhaustion of belief, in the wake of the translation from the German of *Le Songe de Jean-Paul* by Madame de Staël.[13] This is a generational effect, since the first feature of the death of God is characterized by its being lived as an

---

[12] Lloyd, *Selected letters of Stéphane Mallarmé*, 26.
[13] On this generation, cf. Paul Bénichou, *Romantismes français II. L'école du désenchantement. Sainte-Beuve, Nodier, Musset, Nerval, Gautier* (Paris: Gallimard, 2004).

inheritance—a historical inheritance: that of collective unbelief, of sworn faith having left the earth, since the Enlightenment and the Revolution.[14]

At the beginning of the nineteenth century, unbelief is no longer a battle or a cause, but a legacy: it no longer takes the form of the militant, determined, offensive reason of the deistic or materialist philosophers. It is no longer the choice of a struggle led against dominant and oppressive superstition, with the help of the weapons of empiricism and the new science. Instead, unbelief is what is given at birth, to all the children of the new century—those who came "too late in a world that is too old," according to Rolla's lament. As Sartre puts it (this time correctly), speaking of the Parnassian generation: "they had been turned into atheists, they had undergone de-Christianization before they reached the age where they could decide for themselves."[15] Consequently, atheism is no longer a mark of the strong mind who freely endorses it, but of the mind natively too weak, too exhausted to be able to believe, or at least not able to believe as innocently as in glorious ages past, imagined to be fervent. Atheism is no longer an individual decision, but the stigma of the present time.

The statement "God is dead" is, therefore, essentially of a historical time period, and directly contains a devaluation of the theoretical statement "God does not exist," for the latter is the result of philosophical inquiry, instead. Consequently, this devaluation occurs not in favor of the opposite metaphysical statement (itself conceived of in terms of proof): God exists—but in favor of a historical experience condemning theory in general, since that is the source of its present unhappiness. At the same time, when it leads to forced atheism, this experience is a vital experience—that of the weakening of the ability to believe, to adhere to any higher values. When it comes to putting into words this loss that reveals itself to be deeper than any rationalization, the poets are in their role, even more than the philosophers.

Furthermore, this death is not only a question of the age, but it is lived as a particular distress, and, above all, an elective one. For it confers a form of spiritual aristocracy on those individuals, by definition rare, who are capable of feeling it. The elect recognizes herself by the suffering she feels from a legacy of which she cannot rid herself. The counter-model is no longer the priest and superstition, but the philistine and his satisfaction—the latter being the representative of the age as happy with his inheritance. A recurrent, negative figure in the French nineteenth century, he can already be found in 1798 in Novalis' "Pollen."[16] The death of God is thus an atheism of the time, but not necessarily of the poet and his fictional characters. Novalis is not an atheist, of course—but from 1800 he deploys, in his *Hymns to the Night*, the figure of a stellar night fallen on the present of the peoples, in which the remoteness and exile of the divine celestial

---

[14] It is, indeed, from this historical situation that the meaning of the "death of God" is to be theorized—and not by relying on the presence of that expression in an author's writings. It is little used by the poets of the time, Nerval being one of the few—in his retranslation of the "Songe"—to write "God is dead" as an epigraph to his "Christ aux Oliviers (Christ on the Mount of Olives", 1844). On this point, cf. Claude Pichois, *L'image de Jean-Paul Richter dans les lettres françaises* (Paris: José Corti. 1963), part II, chapter VII: "Le 'Songe' dans la littérature romantique."

[15] Sartre, *Mallarmé Poet of Nothingness*, 18.

[16] Margaret Mahony Stoljar, ed. *Novalis: Philosophical Writings* (Albany, NY: State University of New York Press, 1997), 37.

bodies becomes visible, cast aside from a nature henceforth delivered to the cold, calculating reign of narrow Measure and pure Number.[17] And the image of this night of exile, which shows us the immensity which separates us henceforth from the gods, crosses the half century up to Leconte de Lisle's "Dies Ira."[18]

But night is not necessarily darkness, that is, deep and black night: it offers the vision of retreating stars, therefore a remainder of luminosity by which the residue of a possible salvation remains visible, albeit barely. If the Gods seem dead, they are perhaps in exile, ready to make a return. We can therefore perceive some quite diverse attitudes within the theme of the death of God—from the wait for the return of a golden age of European Catholicity (Novalis), to the deploratory irreligiosity of the rake (Musset).[19] If the death of God nonetheless possesses a unity, that unity seems to come from a determinate affective dynamic, a recognizable "passional schema." For the one who is in distress has a right to expect something from the ordeal of the departed gods, from the suffering itself that is endured in thinking of their disappearance: either their return as they were before, or the arrival of another form of salvation or divinity which confirms the definitive abolition of the old gods, better to welcome what could constitute a substitute.

The Night of the gods therefore continues to nourish *expectation*, even as it remains night. The night is thus, for Hölderlin, both "time of distress" and "source of wonder" ("Bread and Wine").[20] Its length, its depth, its indifference to humanity seems to be the guarantee of what it continues to offer, for it is by getting through, or better, by aggravating one's own despair that the expectation comes to join the promise of a salvation—since the peril is posed at the "spring" of its reversal:

But where the danger is, also
Grows the saving power[21]

But the various substitute salvations—which the poet wants to hope for insofar as he confirms and intensifies his despair—seem in turn to contain the mark of the process of loss from whence they come. Thus, Nervalian salvation, which seems to be accomplished in the safeguarding through memory of past religions, or in the precious reminiscence of the youth of the poet, also confirms the irreversibility of a past that will never return, "a perspective not exempt from bitterness and secret despair," as Bénichou writes about "Delfica."[22] And the love which—in Musset—allows Octave, in

---

[17] "Nature stood alone and *lifeless. An iron chain held it in arid count and strict measure.*" Novalis, Hymn V, in Novalis, *Hymns to the Night*, trans. Dick Higgins (Kingston, NY: McPherson & Company, 1988), 26.
[18] "Dies Ira" (1852) in Charles Leconte de Lisle, *Poèmes antiques 1818-1894* (Charleston, SC: Nabu Press, 2011).
[19] Novalis, "Christianity or Europe: A Fragment," in *The Early Political Writings of the German Romantics*, ed. Frederick C. Beiser, Cambridge Texts in the History of Political Thought (Cambridge: Cambridge University Press, 1996).
[20] "Bread and Wine" (1801), in *Friedrich Hölderlin: Selected Poems And Fragments*, trans. Michael Hamburger (London: Penguin, 1998).
[21] "Patmos" (1803), ibid.
[22] "L'école du désenchantement," 1804.

"La confession d'un enfant du siècle," to attain profane redemption in a lost generation, only exists through the betrayal of the woman he loves.[23] Even Novalis tints his prophetic announcement of the future times with a "desire" or an "impatience" for death (*Sehnsucht nach dem Tode*), expressed in the sixth and last of the *Hymns to the Night*—individual promise which cuts off historical expectations. Hence the impression, in these various remissions of disaster, of a nagging, perpetual repetition of the death and the suffering they are supposed to exorcise. The salvation keeps renewing the strength of the affliction that it promised to overcome. And so it is easy to understand why the poet of "L'Azur" does not long find relief in a dead Sky: for as splenetic poetry keeps exacerbating the failure of the creator, the poetry of the death of God keeps reproducing, in the one who attempts to escape it, the catastrophe that he is attempting to flee. How better to fuse the destructive recurrence of these two disasters than by the obsessive and unnerving final litany:

The Sky! The Sky! The Sky! The Sky!

Although he reinvents it with an unprecedented power, Nietzsche still belongs, at the end of the century, to this configuration. It is through "nihilism" that the philosopher ultimately comes to theorize the death of God. Now, nihilism is understood by Nietzsche as a historical process whereby the "highest values are devalued," which affects much more than our conscious opinions, because it involves a vital depreciation of a morality that has been embodied for millennia.[24] Again, what is at stake here is to theorize the eclipse of the gods in the form of a history independent of conscious choices and which manifests itself as an exhaustion—in part physiological—of belief. That is why we find again in Nietzsche the idea that the death of God is deeper than the theoretical declaration of God's inexistence: it is ancestral ways of living, largely unconscious in the preferences by which they guide our behavior, which are at stake in this death—not the theses of a school of thought. The loss of the gods—which becomes that of meaning in general—is moreover maintained as a superior form of distress for those who are capable of feeling it. Aphorism 125 of the *Gay Science*, which presents the vignette of the madman and his lantern in broad daylight, contrasts to his solitary perdition in the face of the death of God a prosaic and mocking crowd, indifferent to the somber grandeur of the event. That is a crowd that is made up of what Nietzsche could have dubbed, from one book to another, the "philistines of culture," the "freethinkers," or the "last men."

---

[23] And that love, even before the betrayal, only exists for Octave through the consented suffering of voluntarily wearing the spiked plate of a medieval "discipline whip" on his chest, which bloodies the body of the overcome lover, continually reminding him of the intensity of his passion. Cf. Alfred de Musset, *Confession of a Child of the Century*, trans. David Coward (London: Penguin Classics, 2014/1836).

[24] "Nihilism: the goal is lacking; an answer to the 'Why' is lacking. What does nihilism mean?—That the highest values are devalued." Friedrich Nietzsche, in Rüdiger Bittner, ed. *Nietzsche: Writings from the Late Notebooks* (Cambridge: Cambridge University Press, 2003), 146. [No complete translation of the critical edition of Nietzsche's works yet exists in English, though a relevant section can be found in *Nietzsche: Writings from the Late Notebooks*, cited immediately above. Subsequent references to Nietzsche's notebooks are to the German *Werke*—Trans.]

Of course, on two fronts, the philosopher takes a remarkable step forward in thinking about our figure. First, he unifies into one movement the lineages stemming from the atheism of the Enlightenment and those coming from the death of God. In the nineteenth century, the first major heirs of French materialism—in particular of Baron d'Holbach and his System of Nature—participated in the so-called "chemical" or "vulgar" materialism which developed in Germany in the 1840s, of which the physician Ludwig Büchner, the naturalist Carl Vogt, or the Dutch physiologist Jacob Molleschot are the main representatives.[25] Now, there exists a direct line between this German materialism and nihilism. In *Fathers and Sons*, indeed, Bazarov, the original figure of the Russian nihilist, reveals himself to be a reader of *Force and Matter*, the most highly touted work of Ludwig Büchner.

Nietzsche did not wait for his discovery of Dostoevsky, in 1887, to take an interest in Russian nihilism. He had read Turgenev's novel as early as 1873, and knew of Chernyshevsky's *What is to be done?* by the presentation that Brunetière gave of it, in 1884, in *Le Roman naturaliste*.[26] But the discovery of the author of *Demons* is probably decisive in his understanding of the destructive capacities of the most radical revolutionaries.[27] His gesture consists, then, in reunifying the two radically opposed branches of atheism: the one, offensive and rationalist, which goes from the Enlightenment to the Russian nihilists, and the other, deploratory and largely poetic, initiated by early Romanticism. While the century had taken them for two evidently opposed forms of relation to the divine, Nietzsche makes them two degrees of impotence in the face of values: a "passive nihilism" which refers to the exhaustion of any form of belief, and an "active nihilism" which still possesses the power to destroy existing values, but without having the strength to create new ones. For a frontal conflict, Nietzsche substitutes a hierarchization of psycho-physiological weaknesses.

The second step forward consists in making the values in danger of extinction the very cause of the process of their own exhaustion: "why is the rise of Nihilism henceforth necessary? Because it is our values themselves that draw their final conclusion in it."[28] The elegy of the departed gods gives way to a genealogy of the ascetic ideals which, since the "revolt of the slaves"—the Judaism of the second Temple, Christianity, various forms of idealism—turn life against itself, nourish its hatred of the sensible, eat away at it by *ressentiment*, to the point where they make this life ill, incapable of belief in general, of adhering to any meaning. The history of the loss of values appears, consequently, no longer as a thought-defying political catastrophe (the

---

[25] On this movement, too little-known considering its importance, cf. Leo Freuler, *La crise de la philosophie au XIXème siècle* (Paris: Vrin, 1997), chapter III: "Le matérialisme naturaliste ou vulgaire et la Naturwissenschaftliche Welenshauung," pp. 55–86.

[26] Cf. Michèle Cohen-Halimi, "Partition I. Cloots, Jacobi, Netchaïv, Nietzsche," in Jean-Pierre Faye and Michèle Cohen-Halimi, *L'histoire caché de nihilisme: Jacobi, Dostoïevski, Heidegger, Nietzsche* (Paris: La Fabrique, 2009) 117.

[27] We know that Nietzsche recopied, starting in the winter of 1887, multiple dialogues between Stavroguine-Verkhovenski, or Kirilov-Verkhovenski. See Friedrich Nietzsche, NB 11 [fragments 331–52], Nov. 1887-Mar. 1888, in *Werke: Kritische Gesamtausgabe*, ed. G. Colli and M. Montinari (Berlin/New York: W. de Gruyter, 1967), section VIII.

[28] Nietzsche, NB 11 [411], in *Werke*, section VIII. Translation taken from J. Doomen, "Consistent Nihilism," *The Journal of Mind and Behaviour* 33.1/2 (2012) 112.

French Revolution), or an enigma of destiny, instilled by the departure of the gods, but as an implacably necessary and immanent becoming.

Yet, in doing so, Nietzsche actually extends, more than he contradicts, the Hölderlinian adage about the greatest danger being a condition for the growth of the saving power. Because the necessity at work in the history of nihilism is, once again, its aggravation, that makes it possible to glimpse its Dionysian overcoming: it is necessary to go through the reactive values to bring out their meaning and surpass them as they open the way to their self-abolition.[29] Until exhaustion leads to the "perfect nihilism," that Nietzsche himself espouses, that is, the "accomplished nihilism" of the Eternal Return.[30] Only the most extreme intensification of the epoch's powers of death promises to yield the reversal of *ressentiment* into affirmation.

This last doctrine brings us back to the "deathly salvation," the dynamic of which we have already encountered, but in a form where the repetition of suffering, in what is supposed to save one from the doom one was seeking to flee, is now thematized, lucidly, in its openly appalling aspect. Indeed, the Return, although placed under the sign of the Dionysian evaluation of life, is in fact the bringer of death. First, as a "negative" choice that must lead to the annihilation of an immense number of wills judged to be sick, which Nietzsche, among other formulations, calls "the remorseless destruction of all degenerate and parasitic elements."[31] But also as a "positive" choice, since those who could pass the most difficult test—Nietzsche or potential "free spirits" that are his contemporaries must endorse, as their only future, the indefinite repetition of historical nihilism at the worst moment of its evolution—the one which accompanied their existence, they who are of that time. It is a nihilism that they are eternally condemned to relive—each time until their end, itself always beginning again. For the Return is not an immortality but the same life constantly destined for the same death. Nietzsche did not construct any other salvation than his perpetual rebirth within the negation of life, at the height of its triumph.

We are not seeking to shed light on the reason why here, but it is as if conceiving of the end of Christianity according to a statement that is still Christian—"God is dead"—led inevitably to believing in various possible resurrections of such a God, which would succeed God's current crucifixion on the altar of the time. The resurrections can, of course, take different forms, as we have seen: the salvation may become love, reminiscence, a golden age, Dionysian life, and so on. But these rebirths are in turn affected by the structure of the loss from which they remain derived and appear to lead only to a return of the divine still encumbered by its initial death. One does not escape from the death of God other than in the direction of a deathly God. The life of this process stems from the life of this metamorphosed death, reflected back from one end to the other. Consequently, it seems impossible to get out of the death of God if one accepts that it has taken place. Because, in that case, you are caught in a cycle where the divine and the lethal become continuously

---

[29] "[W]e must first live nihilism in order to find out what in fact was the value of these 'values.'" Ibid.
[30] Ibid; Nietzsche, NB 9 [1], in *Werke*.
[31] "Why I Write such Good Books," "The Birth of Tragedy," in Friedrich Nietzsche, *Ecce Homo*, trans. R. J. Hollingdale (London: Penguin Classics, 1992/1888), §4, p. 51.

bound up with each another, imbuing one another with their power of prestige and misfortune.

What is left then is *not to enter into it*: that is, not to accept the premises of such a belief in the deceased god, so as not to be caught in the snares of its harmful circularity. But is that possible without falling back into the dogmatic belief in past religions, the satisfaction of the philistine, or the active destruction of the nihilist? In particular, can one—while confirming the expiration of Christianity—refuse both the narrow atheism of the Enlightenment and the bitter atheism of Romanticism? This is what Mallarmé, like no other, begins to attempt in April 1866.

III. The hole in the fullness of things

In his letter to Cazalis, Mallarmé recounts his loss of faith in the form of a back and forth movement: we are, to be sure, mere "empty forms of matter," and yet "indeed sublime for having invented God and our soul." Hence it is an equivocal experience that makes him escape as much from the serenity of the narrow-minded materialist as from the melancholy of the bereaved poet. This discovery, indeed, discourages him from practicing his art ("I am still too distraught to be able to believe even in my poetry") but also inspires in him the idea of a poetry devoted to "The glory of the Lie." Now, this idea of "glory" supposes a reinterpretation of the present of poetry which contradicts the notion that the contemporary offered nothing but a form of loss. For in grasping itself finally *as* a lie, poetry verily re-appropriates the whole scope of its instrument, but in such a way that the latter appears, by turns, as sublime or empty.

If no God guarantees the value of the poet's ecstasy, the poet, indeed, discovers the retrospective glory of having been not inspired by the divine, but composer of it. In return, however, such a God is revealed, by that very fact, to be a mere illusion. And thus, for the poet, at the very moment when he grasps the full demiurgic power of his art, what could have been given to him as a kind of masterpiece melts into thin air. He writes all the way to God, but that God, consequently, only roams on his page. Since everything comes from the poet, nothing flows from him anymore. Hence Mallarmé's paradoxical conclusion: that he will sing glory "as one in despair."

There exists, however, beyond this still affective back-and-forth, a deeper level of oscillation, which the 1866 letter only announces, but which will occupy Mallarmé's mature poetry extensively. Indeed, Mallarmé specifies, and emphasizes, that his new conviction is a kind of knowledge—but that of poet, not a man of science or a philosopher, for it comes exclusively from his work on the "Overture" of *Hérodiade*. "Unfortunately, in the course of quarrying out the lines to this extent, I've come across two abysses that leave me in despair.... Yes, I know, we are merely empty forms of matter." The point here is not to undertake an analysis of the unfinished text that is the "Overture"—an uncommonly difficult task. But this much needs to be said about it: never before had Mallarmé eroded the object, the situation, or the event so well that someone—even a person familiar with his preceding poems—should find him or herself at such a loss to determine simply what is at issue. And, conversely, never had Mallarmé declared himself so enthusiastic about the splendor thus produced—being hardly disposed, during that period, to sing the praises of his texts. In the same letter from April 28, 1866, he announces: "I've written the musical overture, which is still almost completely in draft stage, but I can say in all modesty that it will create an unparalleled effect and that in comparison with these lines, the dramatic scene you know is like a mere vulgar scrawl compared with a canvas by Leonardo da Vinci."[32]

Here, we have a sketch of a different relationship to what Mallarmé will later call "Fiction" and whose point is no longer lying but suggestion. "To name an object is to remove three-fourths of the enjoyment of a poem ... to suggest it, that is the ideal."[33] In a lie, either the fiction is not given as such, masking itself in favor of the object (God is), and thus eliciting desire; or the fiction is explicitly given as being what it is (God is only an illusion), cancels the object, and disappoints desire. In suggestion, on the other hand, the fiction is given as such and manages nonetheless to elicit desire ("the Dream"): to erase the real in favor of the linguistic screen of the poem, which makes the referent and even the meaning opaque, producing an "unparalleled effect" not by the object, but by its avowed absence. This constitutes the knot of the paradox Mallarmé experiences in the "Overture": *subtracting* from the consistency of being can—if the poetic operation is successful—*add* to the intensity of desire. And let it not be supposed that everything is reducible to the musicality of the verse: by his most obscure poems, Mallarmé does not produce an instrumental music without any meaning. He produces a difficult meaning that, by the well-ordered annihilation of the thing barely said, elicits our investigation and our elevation toward that which thereby makes a hole in the fullness of things.

Cazalis responded to Mallarmé's letter that his ideas on nothingness were absurd, for, he writes, "*ex nihilo nihil*, therefore thinking cannot come out of matter, or nothingness would create life."[34] For Cazalis, we could not be "empty matter" since the latter cannot engender thought: that would be to believe in creation *ex nihilo*, an irrational notion par excellence. But such is, indeed, the poetic value of Fiction, whose nothing elicits poetic aspiration as a vacuum produces a call for air. Of this causal mechanism—nothingness intensifies desire—there is neither science nor metaphysics, since it involves, for all (at least classical) rationality, pragmatic absurdity. But the poet *knows*, through a poet's knowledge, that his instrument is potentially loaded with such an efficacy, insofar as he manages to master his art.

One understands consequently how Nothingness [*le Néant*] could bring a new source of legitimacy to the writer without God. The "glory"—which Mallarmé will later name "consecration" (*sacre*)—evokes the possibility that poetry matters, and that nothing matters more than poetry, even though no transcendence grounds its legitimacy.[35] Not only is the art of verse not a futile occupation, a word game without any bearing, but it touches on what is most fundamental in the human condition.

---

[32] Lloyd, *Selected letters of Stéphane Mallarmé*, 59–60.
[33] "Sur l'évolution littéraire», interview with Jules Huret" (1891), *Œuvres complètes*, Bibliothèque de la Pléiade Collection, vol. II, ed. Bertrand Marchal (Paris, Gallimard, 2003) 700.
[34] Stéphane Mallarmé, *Correspondance avec Henri Cazalis*, 1862–97, recueillie, classée et annotée avec la collaboration de Lawrence A. Joseph (Paris, Nizet, 1977).
[35] "Poetry, consecration ..."; "L'action restreinte," *Divagations* (1897), *Œuvres complètes*, 217; "Limited Action," trans. Mary Ann Caws, in Mary Ann Caws, ed. *Stéphané Mallarmé: Selected Poetry and Prose* (New York: New Directions Books, 1982), 109.

Indeed, nothingness is not the abandonment of the Divine, for Mallarmé, but rather its redefinition. Not in the style of a negative theology, of course, for nothingness gives us access to "Divinity, that is nothing but Self."[36] Divinity is nothing more than the capacity of "the Self" [*le Soi*] of the poetic subject to access what is not of this world—that is, the nothing [*le rien*], because nothing is outside the world: "There must be something obscure deep inside everyone. I do firmly believe in something abstruse, by which I mean closed and hidden, which dwells in common folk."[37] There is indeed, therefore, still a "beyond," that fiction burdened with non-being, of which the poet does not have to compose an ontology—like the philosopher heir to Plato's *Sophist*—but to understand how it manages to elevate us far from the ordinary things of this world. As has been said, Nothingness is approached from the angle of desire.

> We know, we captives of an absolute formula, that of course, there only is what is. But to thrust the bait aside forthwith, under a pretence, would reveal our inconsequence, denying the pleasure we would like to take; for that beyond is the agent, and what I would call the motor of our pleasure, if I did not disdain to perpetrate in public the impious dismantling of fiction and consequently of the literary mechanism—to display the principle piece or nothing at all.[38]

If Mallarméan poetry is reflexive, that is because its aim is to say this nothing and its power of consecration. A Mallarméan poem is often the description of the crown of nothingness with which it adorns itself, which it possesses only through the course of its own writing. But how exactly does such a ceremony play out? This, in truth, is where Mallarmé's great originality resides. Indeed, he never renounced, at least in the expression of his most profound poetry, the possibility that his art might be in vain: for Nothingness can never be attested in Mallarmé's work, like a thing, a law or an event could be established in their reality by objective thought. This paradoxical notion oscillates between "nothing" [*rien*] and "nothingness" [*le rien*], between being actually nothing—pure illusion, paltry fiction—and being a nothing whose efficacy guarantees poetic splendor. How could the poet have access to certainty concerning the value of his art, given that no reality, neither in this world—made banally of what is, nor in the other—assuredly reduced to illusion—grounds its essential character?

To pronounce the poetic consecration within a poem is to state the eternal hypothesis that there was perhaps a consecration within such a poem. This is what Mallarmé manifestly begins to do in "L'après-midi d'un Faune" (1876), first expression of his new poetic art: an idyll in which a satyr, upon waking, wonders if his encounter with a duo of nymphs was a dream or a reality. The poem is thus entirely devoted to the uneasiness of the poet about whether his rhyme (symbolized by the conjoined naiads) has actually taken place, and whether poetry has been the result of his art or not;

---

[36] "Catholicisme," *Divagations, Œuvres complètes*, 238: "Divinité, qui n'est jamais que Soi." "Catholicism," trans. Jill Anderson et al. in *Mallarmé in Prose* (New York: New Directions books, 2001), 120, trans. modified.
[37] "Le mystère dans les lettres" (1896) *Œuvres complètes*, 229–30; "Mystery in Literature," ibid., 46.
[38] "Music and Letters," trans. Anderson et al., ibid., 36.

whether there was a genuine rhyme or a mere consonance devoid of value. And the art of writing thus becomes analogous to the way in which the Faun ceaselessly proposes new hypotheses about the erotic and undecidable event—a revival of poetry's desire for itself concerning its value, never certain and always investigated anew. Such is the art of suggestion and its three operators of consecration: subtraction, reflection, indecision, always fundamentally with the sentence from "Un coup de dés" in its sights: "Nothing will have taken place but the place except perhaps a constellation."

Why then, is Mallarmé so often thought of as a poet of the death of God? For serious reasons, quite certainly. His poetry is dotted with twilights, nights without a dawn, tombs, shipwrecks, various disasters—Icarian bird, distraught swan. So many symbols of poetic failure in which it is traditional to read a radicalization of the literary despair that emerged at the beginning of the century. And yet our reading is wholly different. If Mallarmé does take up these themes, it would be disappointing to think that he endorses them, even to take them to an extreme, since, as we have said, they were already well-trodden at the time. We believe what Mallarmé is up to is more singular: while it is true that he often proposes, on a first reading, a form of perdition, in fact, through the subtle motif of his allusions, he allows his reader to discover the exact opposite of what at first seems to constitute the theme of his poem. Under the essential failure, we discover the possibility of a paradoxical triumph. It is in this sense that Mallarmé provides us with a counter-diagnostic of his century in the form of a hypothesis whose essence is to never be able to be decided: "Is God dead, or does Nothingness triumph at last?" It is by this suspended possibility that the *pathos* of the flight of the gods is neutralized, as well as its structure of expectancy, which runs ultimately all the way to Heidegger ("Only a god can save us"). For Mallarmé's poetry is not a poetry of patient waiting, or of imminence—it is a poetry of recency. Something exceptional and infinitely discreet has perhaps just occurred, and not loudly proclaimed distress. Instead of projecting ourselves toward a disappointing salvation to come, let us turn back to the past event to interpret, ever further, its enigmatic fertility.

IV. The destitution of the night of exile

Our point will appear less arbitrary if we give an example of the type of reading which follows from it, applied to the sonnet *Le vierge, le vivace, le bel aujourd'hui* (*Sonnet of the Swan*), first published in 1885:

> The virginal, enduring, beautiful today
> will a drunken beat of its wing break us
> this hard, forgotten lake haunted under frost
> by the transparent glacier of unfled flights!
>
> A swan of old remembers it is he
> magnificent but who without hope frees himself
> for never having sung a place to live
> when the boredom of sterile winter was resplendent.

His whole neck will shake off this white death-throe
inflicted by space on the bird denying it,
but not the horror of soil where the feathers are caught.

Phantom assigned to this place by pure brilliance,
he holds still in the cold dream of contempt
Put on in useless exile by the Swan.

Putting aside various difficulties in the details, the general gist of the sonnet seems, at first, fairly clear. A swan, stuck in the ice of a lake, comes back to itself and remembers its former magnificence; it shakes off the frost that covers it, but unable to free itself from the ground, holds still in a final movement of contempt. Up until Émilie Noulet, commentators tended to associate Mallarmé's swan with that of Baudelaire ("Le cygne") or Banville ("Les Torts du cygne"): its contempt was thought to be addressed to a cold and hostile environment, incapable of appreciating its genius. Émilie Noulet argued—and many have followed her in this—that the sonnet in fact describes, as in "L'Azur," the contempt of the swan-poet for its own sterility.[39] It is contempt for his inability to sing the celestial Ideal ("a place to live"), for his "useless [infertile] exile," on a ground that he abhors. But in both these interpretations we find, in any case, the idea that the poet is abandoned on a desolate earth, a prosaic and desert-like here-below, from which he cannot manage to escape to join the Sky of his inspiration. Yet it is possible to show that the theme developed in this little masterpiece of ambiguity is actually precisely the opposite. And not only is it not necessary to "force" the text in order to show this, but we will see that it is actually the traditional interpretation which finds itself obliged to do violence to what is written in the poem.

Let us take the stanzas one by one, proposing our counter-reading each time:

The virginal, enduring, beautiful today
(*Le vierge, le vivace, et le bel aujourd'hui*)
will a drunken beat of its wing break us
(*Va-t-il nous déchirer avec un coup d'aile ivre*)
this hard, forgotten lake haunted under frost
(*Ce lac dur oublié que hante sous le givre*)
by the transparent glacier of unfled flights!
(*Le transparent glacier des vols qui n'ont pas fui*)

The "us," rather than being expletive, refers to the readers contemporary to Mallarmé, faced with a book—a poetry that has never been read. Under the whiteness of the flyleaf—under its "frost"—is situated the still whitened mass of a "hard lake" (the book itself). This lake is "forgotten," for the poets have not sung the book, they have sung in the book of the Sky that was supposed to be the sole value, located beyond the grimoire. The reader takes a letter-opener. This is the thin blade of the present, of the "beautiful

---

[39] Émilie Noulet, *L'œuvre poétique de Stéphane Mallarmé* (Paris: Librarie E. Droz, 1940), 263–5.

today" which separates him or her from the imminent reading of the first page—this thin blade being "virginal" and metallic, according to a symbolic of coldness that Mallarmé has already employed, we note, to evoke "Hérodiade." In a lively (*vivace*) gesture, the reader cuts the page. Will the Book, perhaps forgotten until now in favor of the referent of its signs, be discovered *for itself* for the first time? Once the page is "broken" (*déchirée*), it turns, curling slightly, like a drunken wing: "drunken wing beat" (*coup d'aile ivre*)—book beat. And under the whiteness of the flyleaf the reader discovers: "the transparent glacier of unfled flights!"

The book is, therefore, a glacier that lets text be seen in the transparency of its whiteness, and it is constituted by the successive wing beats of each page turned, of their "flights" which, nevertheless, have never fled, since every page's flight is destined from the start to fall back against the book—against the original glacier.

The second stanza presents what we can discover at the level of the signs of a poem taken in a time where the poet's Icarian insufficiency and the retreat of the gods mix together:

A swan of old remembers it is he
(*Un cygne d'autrefois se souvient que c'est lui*)
magnificent but who without hope frees himself
(*Magnifique mais qui sans espoir se déliver*)
for never having sung a place to live
(*Pour n'avoir jamais chanté la legion où vivre*)
When the boredom of sterile winter was resplendent
(*Quand du stérile hiver a resplendi l'ennui*)

Our reader, once the book is open, discovers the text of a poetry, represented here by the signs (*cygne/signe*)—by its regime of signs.[40] This sign is vivified by the first reading that it has ever received (recall that the book had never been cut until now). It then comes back to itself, remembers its magnificence—and through its meaning aims for its referent, the Sky, the Ideal, the stellar Night of the departed gods. But it is "without hope" that it attempts to tear itself from the matter of the book—that it "frees itself."[41] For it has not sung "the place to live." This "place" (*région*) is ordinarily interpreted as being the Azure that the poet, by his impotence, finds himself unable to sing. But in that case, it would be necessary to say instead that the swan did sing the Sky—what has it done more since the beginning of the century?—but that it has sung it badly. Yet Mallarmé says literally that the swan has not sung, and not that it has sung badly—and if we take this choice of words seriously, we are led to understand something else entirely. The swan frees itself without hope because it has never sung the book and therefore the Earth—since the absolute Book, for Mallarmé, ought to be an "Orphic

---

[40] [The author is referring to the homophony between the words for "swan" and "sign" in French, that is, *cygne* and *signe*, respectively—Trans.]
[41] [The author is proposing to read the line "*qui sans espoir se délivre*" as a play on words, where *se délivre* means both "frees himself" (in the ordinary sense of "deliverance") and, literally, "de-books himself" (*se dé-livre*)—Trans.]

explanation of the Earth."[42] And it is precisely because he has not sung the true place to live—the ground where he has always found himself—that the here-below sickens him, and the same poet has sterilized—in the desert of his pains, as L'Azur put it—the ground of his existence. The poet never sang the site, the original place, of his existence. He had always-already exiled himself toward faraway gods that masked the intimate meaning of his office: to write signs on a page and insert the thread of nothingness into the materiality of things.

> His whole neck will shake off this white death-throe
> (*Tout son col secouera cette blanche agonie*)
> inflicted by space on the bird denying it
> (*Par l'espace infligée à l'oiseau qui le nie*)
> but not the horror of soil where the feathers are caught
> (*Mais non l'horreur du sol où le plumage est pris*)

The poet is caught in the "horror of soil" [*l'horreur du sol*]. Let us pay attention to the phrasing: the swan is not said to be prisoner of a soil that is horrible in itself, but he is captive to the subjective horror that he feels for it. This feeling is the source of his imprisonment in the glaciation of what he does not sing, because he does not sing it. He is horrified by the immanence of the book given over to its own power—because he was incapable of discovering the means to poetize the nothing from whence his whole art comes. His desire is deathly because it aims for the elsewhere and not the here.

The last tercet is particularly emblematic of the general reversal that we can discover in it:

> Phantom assigned to this place by pure brilliance
> (*Fantôme qu'à ce lieu son pur éclat assigne*)
> he holds still in the cold dream of contempt
> (*Il s'immobilise au songe froid de mépris*)
> Put on in useless exile by the Swan.
> (*Que vêt l'exil inutile du Cygne*)

The first line of the last tercet is particularly difficult to explain in the usual perspective on the sterility of the swan: the swan is said to be a phantom "assigned to this place by pure brilliance." No doubt "pure brilliance" is in continuity with the "Magnificent" from the second stanza: but how are we to understand, if the swan's vocation is to take off for the Sky, that the perfection of its brilliance assigns it instead to the place where it is, that is, the frozen ground? How are we to understand the swan being suddenly assigned to its lake, not because of its supposed impotence, but on the contrary because of what constitutes its distinctive splendor? And if the swan is a "phantom" because it is merely a "shadow of itself," because its hour is passed and it is sinking into failure and death, where does this brilliance come from that makes this site the one where it is meant to

---

[42] "Lettre à Verlaine" (1885), Lloyd, *Selected letters of Stéphane Mallarmé*.

be? Gardner Davies who, in his classic interpretation, follows Noulet's interpretation of the sterility of the swan, honestly admits to not seeing how to account for this line. On the other hand, the line becomes luminous if we understand that the poet will only draw his true brilliance from finally deciding to sing the place where he has always been—the earth, the Book. Ghostly as long as he has not made that decision, he is on the verge of becoming embodied at last.

The swan, therefore, "holds still" [*s'immobilise*]. That is not to say that it dies, for to hold still is yet a movement—it is not to be immobile, but to become immobile. The swan folds its wing and reorients its flight—it accepts at last that the flight of the page's wing is destined to fall back into the book and to hold still to allow the page to be read. And the book, open on itself at last, immobile, represents by its shape (let the reader examine the shape of the volume he or she is reading) the idea of such a grounded flight of a bird with open wings—finally an earthly flight, and not heavenly one, poetry returned to its proper place. The swan can therefore hold still in the dream henceforth "cold with contempt" that it feels for the exile that has become useless of his celestial double—Cygnus, the constellation of the "Swan" (as the initial capital attests) and of its gods who have fled. Gods that it has at last ceased to desire, with that deathly desire that hindered its glory. There is, indeed, a destitution of the night of exile, night that from Novalis to Leconte de Lisle represents the departure of the gods and their perpetual distancing as far as possible from Earth. We must stop attempting to join them—in order finally to re-appropriate our living space—the Earth, the Page, Nothingness.

That is not to say, if we accept this reading, that the triumph has become as certain as the disaster was beforehand. For the Nothingness is undecidable, just as is the right interpretation amongst the two, directly opposed, that are given to us. Instead, once again, we are presented with an oscillation between victory and defeat. Thus, I have insisted on the material elements of reading—letter-opener, page, shape of the open volume—as symbols of the "place to live." But, in the strict sense, Nothingness, the power of fiction over desire, is no more present in the apparently celebrated matter of the Book and its reading—matter which like all things, is content simply to be—than in the deploring of poetic impotence. One is inevitably disappointed if one thinks that everything is actually resolved in what we have before our eyes: *that is all poetry was, then—book, fold, page, ink*? The meaning of the poem was all contained in this astute little riddle? The promise transforms in turn into a collapse—for nothingness [*le rien*] is not held in either of the two certainties, but rather in the making fragile through writing of each option in play—death of God, life of the book—in favor of its rival. That is what allows the meaning, and with it the desire, to circulate according to the faunesque questioning of a possible encounter with the consecrating power of poetry. Forever, beyond the endless elegy of the lost skies, some black diamond may be able to take place.

No longer death of God but pulse of Nothingness.

Translated from the original French by Samuel Webb

6

There Is No Experience of Pure Atheism—Michel Serres and the Schema of Unbelief

Christopher Watkin

Can we call our secular civilisation atheist? It is a question I often ask myself.[1]

I am an atheist three quarters of the time.[2]

There is no experience of pure atheism. This is in part because atheism itself, like Oscar Wilde's truth, is rarely pure and never simple. It is also because the very idea of an experience of atheism is itself problematic. Let us begin with this latter problem: the question of experience. What is an "experience of atheism"? Does the genitive indicate an experiential structure or mode ("Everything I experience, I experience atheistically"), or an experiential content ("I experience some object or phenomenon as an atheistic object or phenomenon")? Or is it perhaps an amalgam of both? Who decides what it means to experience something atheistically and, for that matter, what it means to experience something theistically? What is more—and this is perhaps the thorniest question of all—how would we recognize if we were having an experience of atheism, such that we could be confident in labeling it as such? What would be its characteristic affects, impressions or representations, and would they be unique to atheistic experience or shared with other ways of being in the world? In other words: what would it be like to experience experiencing atheism?

This set of questions would be easier to answer if there were one consistent set of ideas designated by the term "atheism." But there is not, as I have argued at length elsewhere.[3] There are at least three dominant types of atheistic thought today, two of which will be the focus of this chapter. They are attended by radically different experiential modes, though none of these modes can be called an "experience of atheism" *simpliciter*. They all have their complexities, but those complexities are very different in each case.

The late French philosopher Michel Serres (1930–2019) has a particularly nuanced sense of the relationship between ostensibly theistic and purportedly atheistic forms of

---

[1] Michel Serres and Michel Polacco, *Petites Chroniques du dimanche soir: Entretiens avec Michel Polacco* (Paris: Éditions le Pommier, 2006), 155.
[2] Michel Serres, *The Troubadour of Knowledge*, trans. Sheila Faria Glaser and William Paulson (Ann Arbor, MI: The University of Michigan Press, 1997), 151. Translation modified.
[3] See Christopher Watkin, *Difficult Atheism: Post-Theological Thinking in Alain Badiou, Jean-Luc Nancy and Quentin Meillassoux* (Edinburgh: Edinburgh University Press, 2011).

thought and experience, and he offers a subtle account of how we might think about the relationships between any such seemingly contradictory accounts of the rhythms and patters of experience. It is through a Serresian lens that I propose to examine the experience of atheism in this chapter, first considering the "umbilical" atheism he rejects, and then the "translational" atheism he embraces. Before we can embark on that investigation, however, it behoves us to reflect on the intricacies of Serres' own profession of faith … and of atheism.

I. Is Serres an atheist?

The complexity of Serres' account of atheism is mirrored in how he speaks about his own (lack of) faith. In *La Guerre mondiale* he testifies to a conversion to mysticism precipitated by the acute lack of food at his wartime childhood lycée, born of a need to "still believe a little in another world than this banal plain littered with scattered limbs."[4] It is an experience that parallels his atheist father's turn to Christian faith two decades earlier in the "hell" of the Verdun battlefield.[5]

Asked directly in a 2005 interview whether he is a Christian, Serres replies:

> Ah, that's another question that calls for a little reserve, given that it relates to God. I am from a Christian tradition, I have always been interested in the history of religions, but I will withhold my answer about what I am myself.[6]

This response is not as evasive as it may sound. It raises the question of whether being "from a Christian tradition" suffices in order to have an "experience of Christianity," in order to see the world with the characteristic sensitivities, values, and blind spots of that particular religious tradition. If it does indeed suffice, then avowed atheists can just as easily have an "experience of Christianity" as the most devout of believers.

It is in *The Troubadour of Knowledge* that we find Serres' most developed account of his own conviction and experience:

> I do not know if I believe in God. I know that often I cannot believe in God: I am an atheist three-quarters of the time. Yet, through intermittent flashes, I know that the divine is there, present, in my neighbourhood, and that it reigns through the universe.[7]

It is instructive to probe a little deeper into what Serres means by the "divine" that "reigns" here. He has in mind not an individual deity but a shape or a pattern of experience:

---

[4] Michel Serres, *La Guerre mondiale* (Paris: Éditions le Pommier, 2008), 12.
[5] Serres, *La Guerre mondiale*, 9.
[6] Michel Serres, Sylvain Michelet and Patrice van Eersel, "Mutations: L'imprévisible reste la règle." *Nouvelles Clés* 46 (2005). http://www.cles.com/debats-entretiens/article/l-imprevisible-reste-la-regle.
[7] Serres, *The Troubadour of Knowledge*, 151. Translation modified.

Here, reign does not refer in any way to a king, but to that means of construction that a tiler indicates when he says that a hexagonal and red floor tile reigns in, is spread throughout, all the rooms of the same house. Everywhere in the universe, the divine is the fabric, the others say the law, I prefer to describe its matter or flesh, of which I am certain, not now, but sometimes, rarely, in an ecstatic manner.[8]

The divine, then, is the shape of things; it is their rhythm, the way everything in the universe is figured. Not a garment but the fabric from which all garments are made: the warp and woof of reality. It is the "flesh" of the universe, not its brute matter but the constellations and patterns into which that matter resolves itself.

This divine does not take the form of any determinate deity. The language of "fabric" and "flesh" here helps us to situate Serres' experience in terms of the distinction between what he elsewhere calls structure and model, or schema and content.[9] Serres' experience of the divine is not as an object of experience, a what, but as the structure of experience, its how.

It is not surprising, then, that Serres embraces a pantheism for which the divine is coextensive with everything, and that everything is an experience of the divine:

> I believe, I believe above all, I believe fundamentally that the world is God, that nature is God, white waterfall and laughing seas, that the changing sky is God Himself: I have navigated in God, flown in the midst of God, received his true light on my back at dawn in the ice corridors high up on the mountains; I have even sometimes written, under his breath, naively tracing my humble path across the divine page, and because of this vocation, I have never ceased to live through him, with him and in him.[10]

It is perhaps strange, then, given this ubiquity of the divine, that Serres also, and equally emphatically, describes himself as without the gods, *a-theos*. His use of the term is ambiguous. As well as referring to unbelief, the motif of the *a-theos* can refer to the state of being abandoned by the gods, which is how Sophocles describes Oedipus in *Oedipus the King* and again in *Oedipus at Kolonos*. In *The Troubadour of Knowledge* we see Serres embracing both unbelief-atheism and abandonment-atheism:

> And when the long eclipse follows the brief, intuitive flash, I am certain that God is not: it's an outdated and unnecessary hypothesis. Maybe, then, he abandons me,

---

[8] Serres, *The Troubadour of Knowledge*, 151.
[9] Serres defines a "model" as "a meaningful content that can fill an empty form. And, given that contents vary, there can be several models for the same form." (Michel Serres, *Le Système de Leibniz et ses modèles mathématiques* (Paris: Presses Universitaires de France, 1968) 309–10). A "structure" (or, sometimes, a "form"), by contrast, is defined as "a set [*ensemble*] of undefined meaning, [...] grouping elements of any number (the content of the elements being unspecified) and relations, finite in number, the nature of which is undefined, but the function of which is defined in relation to the elements" (Serres, *Le Système de Leibniz*, 4). For an extended discussion of model and structure in Serres, see Christopher Watkin, *Michel Serres: Figures of Thought* (Edinburgh: Edinburgh University Press, 2020), 40–7.
[10] Serres, *The Troubadour of Knowledge*, 152. Translation modified.

doubtless he damns me, in abandoning my intelligence to this misery. Did God abandon all of us ever since that recent day when we abandoned him?[11]

The respective experiences of these two atheisms of unbelief and abandonment are, of course, not mutually exclusive: even if God does not exist one can still feel abandoned by him, feel the presence of his absence, if only as a result of being "from a Christian tradition" in which intellectual and social life is built on the foundation of this now conspicuously absent deity. The experience of abandonment does not presuppose the reality of the subject of abandonment.

Serres proceeds to add a cruel twist to his pantheism however, one which draws him vanishingly close to Sophocles' wretched Monarch:

> I am sure, absolutely certain beyond all hope, that there exists a hole, a bizarre flaw in this massive and dense pantheism, a strange exception, source of all pain, that I and I alone, in this divine concert shot through with noise, am not God; this fault line of nothingness is alone not God; a new, very pointed, meaning of the old word "atheist." Here, no God. Here, only, God is absent. My portion of destiny is this place of atheism. Everything is God except the one who writes him, who lets fall His pen amid tears.[12]

So for Serres, the experience of atheism is decidedly complex: (1) The fabric of the universe is experienced as divine; (2) he is certain that God is not; and yet (3) he is equally certain that he, alone, is not God, the rent in pantheism's garment.

This account of Serres' own unbelief is far from stable and simple. As such, it fits well with his account of atheism more broadly. In the rest of this chapter, I will argue that this lack of stability and simplicity is no diffidence or deficiency of self-awareness on Serres' part, but an experientially faithful account of the intertwining of belief and unbelief and their respective experiences and expressions.

II. Umbilical atheism

For Serres there is no atheism *tout court*. His account of unbelief can be divided into two distinct and irreconcilable modes. The first of these, what we will call "umbilical atheism," is itself subdivided into two interrelated tendencies: an atheistic monotheism and an atheistic polytheism.

Atheistic monotheism

Serres is emphatic that the attempt simply to negate theism provides no exit from theism: "An idea opposed to another idea is always the same idea, albeit affected by the negative sign. The more you oppose one another, the more you remain in the same

---

[11] Serres, *The Troubadour of Knowledge*, 151.
[12] Serres, *The Troubadour of Knowledge*, 152. Translation modified.

framework of thought."¹³ As well as remaining within the tractor beam of theism in this way, Serres also dismisses any atheism that frames itself as the straightforward negation of theism for the same reason that he rejects dogmatic theism itself: its claim to control and condition all other discourses. As early as his 1968 thesis on Leibniz he rejects what he calls "umbilical" thinking or any "queen science" or "queen discipline" that claims to ground and give the irreducible truth of all other discourses. In anatomy, the umbilicus is the navel, the fixed, central point through which the fetus is fed. In geometry, it is a (now obsolete) term describing a focus, or the point on a surface through which all lines of curvature pass. More broadly, both in French and English "umbilical" carries the sense of "occupying a central point or position" (OED). A discourse or way of thinking is umbilical if it claims to offer a pure, privileged access to plain, unvarnished truth, which all other discourses distort or falsify to one degree or another. Atheism is umbilical when it claims to be able to exclude all vestiges of faith and create a pure domain of unbelief uncontaminated by vestigial religiosity.

However, Serres characterizes this type of dogmatic atheism as inextricably dependent on the theology is denies. Three examples will suffice to sketch this argument: space, time, and the universal. In terms of space, Serres considers the unique, homogeneous Cartesian extension of modernity to be a relic of Newton's *sensorium dei* and to be an attempt to create a sacred temple of flat space unencumbered by the inconvenient obstacles, undulations and striations of the secular wasteland now banished beyond its borders.¹⁴ As for time, the modern paradigm of a progressive movement from benighted superstition to enlightened atheism is a relic first of the Hebrew prophets who "invented history, in the singular sense we give this word in the West," and of the Christian philosophy of history of Pascal and Bossuet (and before them, we might add, of Augustine) that has merely replaced religion with science as the driving force of progress.¹⁵ The labels may have been swapped, but "[i]nstead of believing in history because one believes in God, or rather in Jesus Christ, we believe in history by extrapolating from what goes on in the sciences.... The structure [*schéma*] hasn't changed."¹⁶ Both space and time in modernity have qualities of emptiness and absoluteness "whose resemblance to eternity strikes anyone who knows how to see knowledge as secularised religion," and the idea of history as an irreversible progression is "only another name for the one Judaeo-Christian God": an atheistic monotheism.¹⁷

The universal is similarly reliant on Christian foundations. Christianity opens the door to universalism through its rejection of the limits of genealogy and embrace of filiation through adoption.¹⁸ More abstractly, the idea of a cosmos, a universal order

---

[13] Michel Serres and Bruno Latour, *Conversations on Culture, Science and Time*, trans. Roxanne Lapidus (Ann Arbor, MI: University of Michigan Press, 1995), 81.
[14] Michel Serres, *Le Passage du nord-ouest: Hermès V* (Paris: Éditions de Minuit, 1980), 74.
[15] Michel Serres, *The Incandescent*, trans. Randolph Burks (London: Bloomsbury, 2018), 101. See also Michel Serres, "Paris 1800" in Michel Serres, ed., *A History of Scientific Thought: Elements of a History of Science* (Oxford: Blackwell, 1995), 422-54, 446.
[16] Serres, "Paris 1800," 442.
[17] Michel Serres, *Éloge de la philosophie en langue française* (Paris: Fayard, 1995), 126. Serres, "Paris 1800," 443.
[18] Michel Serres, *Hominescence* (Paris: Éditions le Pommier, 2001), 201.

and law, is a theological idea with the result that "the most theologian-like of the men of the world is the contemporary scholar when he puts his trust in that old universal order," even though "most often such a man calls himself an atheist."[19]

The irony of such a dogmatic mode of atheism is that while it may, intellectually, be the contrary of belief, experientially it is its perfect imitation because it apes the schemata, the forms, the warp and woof of a theistic (specifically, a Protestant) mode of being in the world, with its view of a flat, qualitatively uniform space, its universalism, and its linear, progressive view of time. The experience of this sort of atheism is a decidedly theological one, in the sense that the structure of experience informed by theological traditions is maintained, with only minor alterations to the labels on different parts of the structure.[20] The layout of the furniture is unchanged, but the upholstery is renewed.

In a further irony, the very notion of the secular is a religious idea: it is the Christ of the gospels who endorses a separation between heavenly and earthly dominion with his "Render to Caesar what is Caesar's, and to God what is God's" (Matt. 22:21; Mk. 12:17; Lk. 20:25); in the Middle Ages the "secular clergy" referred to any ordained ministers outside of monastic orders; and it is Thomas who insists on the distinction between civil law and canon law.[21] Umbilical atheism builds itself a house only to find that, brick for brick, it has followed a religious blueprint.

Atheistic polytheism

Atheistic monotheism is not the only mode of umbilical unbelief that Serres discusses. The second variety of atheism replaces God not with a single, universal, scientific placeholder, but with a variety of deities in what we might call a poly-a-theism: a pantheon of secular gods reminiscent of Max Weber's famous diagnosis of the condition of disenchantment:

> We live as the ancients did when their world was not yet disenchanted of its gods and demons, only we live in a different sense. As Hellenic man at times sacrificed to Aphrodite and at other times to Apollo, and, above all, as everybody sacrificed to the gods of his city, so do we still nowadays, only the bearing of man has been disenchanted and denuded of its mystical but inwardly genuine plasticity. [...] Many old gods ascend from their graves; they are disenchanted and hence take the form of impersonal forces. They strive to gain power over our lives and again they resume their eternal struggle with one another.[22]

---

[19] Michel Serres, *Genesis*, trans. Geneviève James and James Nielson (Ann Arbor, MI: University of Michigan Press, 1995), 107. The gender-specific language is Serres', and I have left it as he wrote it.
[20] This is what, in a different context, I called "imitative atheism." See my *Difficult Atheism*.
[21] Michel Serres and Michel Polacco, *Petites chroniques du dimanche soir 6: Entretiens avec Michel Polacco* (Paris: Éditions le Pommier, 2014) 102. See also Michel Serres and Michel Polacco, *Petites chroniques du dimanche soir 4: Entretiens avec Michel Polacco* (Paris: Éditions le Pommier, 2011), 72–3.
[22] Max Weber, "Science as Vocation," in *From Max Weber*, ed. and trans. H. Gerth and C.W. Mills (New York: Oxford University Press, 1946), 148–9.

Echoing this claim, in *The Incandescent* Serres asserts that:

> The previous centuries had put the single god of monotheism to death. Did they understood that, in doing so, they were reinstating the old pantheon of Olympic gods? For fifty years, drugged with ambrosia, we have been feasting the way these latter did, or so they say.[23]

What has expired is not theism, but monotheism, and it has been replaced not by a pristine atheism but by a return to the polytheism that preceded it. Even more bluntly in a 2005 episode of his long-running radio program *Le Sens de l'info* ("The Sense of the News"), Serres affirms that "[o]ur civilisation, proud as we are of it having become atheist, secular, even anticlerical, appears to me to be submerged today under a huge wave of polytheism and idolatry."[24]

The nature of this atheistic polytheism is most fully explored by Serres in his engagement with Georges Dumézil's discussion, in *Archaic Roman Religion* and elsewhere, of the "Archaic Triad" of Jupiter, Mars, and Quirinus.[25] For Serres' Dumézil, the Western rejection of religion is not a turning away from the divine *tout court* but rather a substitution of one god for a plurality of deities. The modern West has rejected Jupiter, the god of priests and of religion, along with the concomitant claim that the religious is the umbilical mode of experience and the discourse to which all other ways of living in the world ultimately owe their origin and can be reduced. Bluntly, what has been rejected is that "everything is religious."

It is worth noting that this claim is theistic both in its content and in its structure or schema. The "everything is" is just as religious as the "religious," because it relies on the universalism that, as we have seen, bears theological fingerprints. Serres calls this umbilical religiosity "the all-religious" (*le tout-religieux*), and he counts it as a very good thing that we have turned away from it:

> You know that living in the Middle East exposes you right away ... or rather converts you to the secular ideal [*à l'idéal laïc*] from the moment the all-religious exposes these countries to endless fighting that has carried on for four millennia[26]

However, this local laicism is not to be confused with a general atheism. In fact, the demise of the all-religious facilitates the rise of Dumézil's two other deities, Mars and Quirinus, each with their own fundamentalism to set alongside the religious variety: the all-military and the all-economic respectively. If the ancient and medieval world was all-religious, then the early modern was all-military and, since the end of the Second World War and the rise of the European Union and the United Nations, the

---

[23] Serres, *The Incandescent*, 170–1. See also Serres, *Éloge de la philosophie en langue française*, 77–8.
[24] Serres and Polacco, *Petites chroniques du dimanche soir 1*, 156. See also Michel Serres, *Andromaque, veuve noire* (Paris: L'Herne, 2012), 50.
[25] See Georges Dumézil, *Archaic Roman Religion*, trans. Philip Krapp (Baltimore, MD: Johns Hopkins University Press, 1996).
[26] Serres and Polacco, *Petites chroniques du dimanche soir 6*, 103.

scales have tipped in favor of the all-economic.[27] Our own society is just as religious as ancient cultures, with the difference that its god is not Jupiter but Quirinus:

> Everything is economic, just as everything was religious or military in the past: daily life, work, timetables, gestures, human relationships. Everything is economic, and the financial Popes, the priests of Quirinus, force us to live as economic monks, as economic clergy.[28]

In his description of our present state of economic fundamentalism, Serres shows that the structures and forms of religious experience remain intact, but are now filled with different, purportedly secular content.

The primary structure that remains unchanged is that of domination, the absoluteness of the "all-" itself. There remains one zero-degree or fundamental mode of experiencing and engaging with the world that conditions all others, at the bar of which all others have to answer, into which they are converted. This single, fundamental mode of experiencing and engaging with the world extends across the whole of experience, making certain features of the world and of human relationships visible while veiling others, making some values or desires dominant while muting others, and making some actions meaningful while evacuating meaning from others. What remains constant here is the ideology of the universal: the economic that, as Marx so vividly puts it, dissolves all fast-frozen relations[29] and makes a market of everything from love and life to identity and security.

In the course of a discussion of Zola's novel *l'Argent* (*Money*), Serres enlarges the range of religious language he uses to talk about the economic:[30]

> "Gold, silver, currency, notes, precious stones and ingots were the gods of the pagan pantheon";
>
> "polytheism turns into monotheism ... Money is God, it is the Christ";
>
> "The ships and the Mediterranean ocean liners, the Turkish railways, carriers to Holy places."[31]

What this adoption of religious language shows is that "God," "Christ," and "Holy Place" are structures that can be filled with various different contents. They happen to carry religious labels because it is religious content that has predominated for most of the West's collective history, but the "Christ" can just as easily be economic or martial as religious.

The same substitutability obtains for other modern social practices as well: our wars are elaborate sacrificial rituals, and the television through which we learn of them is a fetish, voicing priestly proclamations of violence and death: "Do you not see therein

---

[27] Serres and Polacco, *Petites chroniques du dimanche soir* 6, 103.
[28] Serres and Polacco, *Petites chroniques du dimanche soir* 6, 103.
[29] Karl Marx and Friedrich Engels, *The Communist Manifesto*, in *Marx-Engels Collected Works*, vol. 6 (London: Lawrence and Wishart, 1976), 486–7.
[30] Michel Serres, *Feux et signaux de brume: Zola* (Paris: Grasset, 1975), 296.
[31] Serres, *Feux et signaux de brume*, 296.

an archaic religion founded on human sacrifice? It is a constant, perpetual state of sacrifice."[32] We fancy ourselves as a society that has had done with the religious millstone of guilt, but if that is the case, "[h]ow is it that our atheistic and secular [*laïques*] societies, drugged up as they are on spectacle, do not stop inviting us to look for someone to kill?", all in an insatiable drive to "[f]ind the guilty party."[33] These similarities are for Serres anything but superficial or trifling: "These spectacles repeat, with a stunning precision, the rites of archaic religions all the more easily because modern religions are declining and increasingly losing their audience for condemning these sacrifices."[34] The ceremony of religion is repackaged in the society of the spectacle, and the spectacle we are presented with—in the news, in films, in TV series—is the dead body, such that "we unknowingly live in the polytheism of the bloody manufacturers of glory."[35] In the words of a passage from the end of Bergson's *The Two Sources of Morality and Religion* that Serres is fond of quoting, human beings and human societies are "machines for creating gods," some of which are divine. As Judeo-Christian monotheism withdraws, ancient polytheisms flow in to take its place. To be sure, the religious "changes sides" but it does not go away, and "[w]e remain archaic in three-quarters of our actions and the quasi-totality of our thought," for "under the atheist exterior we silently practice a secular religion [*religion laïque*]."[36]

This modern polytheism results in a peculiar situation in which religious believers, as those with a point of reference outside Dumézil's modern pantheon, find themselves cast in the role of contemporary atheists. Why?

> because they believe neither in the gods of politics and the spectacle, nor in the reigning gods of money and economics, technology and science, nor in this power and glory to which we ruthlessly sacrifice more than a hundred lives every week. They are known to say that if God exists, he is not here.[37]

Serres echoes here the words of Justin Martyr written around CE 150:

> Hence are we called atheists. And we confess that we are atheists, so far as gods of this sort are concerned, but not with respect to the most true God, the Father of righteousness and temperance and the other virtues, who is free from all impurity.[38]

---

[32] Michel Serres, Martin Legros and Sven Ortoli, *Pantopie: de Hermès à Petite Poucette* (Paris: Éditions le Pommier, 2014) 294–5. See also Serres, *The Incandescent,* 253–4.
[33] Michel Serres, *Biogea*, trans. Randolph Burks (Minneapolis, MN: Univocal, 2012), 19.
[34] Serres, *The Incandescent,* 16.
[35] Michel Serres, "Le balancier, la pierre philosophale," in *Cahier de l'Herne Michel Serres*, ed. François L'Yvonnet and Christiane Frémont (Paris: Éditions de l'Herne, 2010), 101–11, 108.
[36] Serres, *The Incandescent*, 39. Michel Serres, *Statues: The Second Book of Foundations*, trans. Randolph Burks (London: Bloomsbury, 2014), 122. Serres, *Hominescence*, 335–6.
[37] Michel Serres, *Angels: A Modern Myth*, trans. Francis Cowper (Paris: Flammarion, 1995), 193.
[38] Justin Martyr, "The First Apology of Justin," available at http://www.ccel.org/ccel/schaff/anf01.viii.ii.vi.html.

The atheists are those who, in any age, do not believe in the dominant gods of the culture. How can one be an unbeliever today, Serres muses? Answer: read the news theologically![39]

There has been no experience of atheism

The inexorable conclusion to be drawn from Serres' discussions of atheistic monotheism and atheistic polytheism is that modern society has not in fact had an experience of atheism at all. It has instead transferred its worship from religious to martial, and from martial to financial deities, recycling the content of its theism while its fundamental structure remains untouched. The experience of theism is structural, not tied to any particular content, and it can be lived just as easily through Mars and Quirinus as it can through Jupiter.

It might be objected to Serres' arguments that he is confusing religion (a set of practices) with theism (a set of beliefs). Society may well be religious in its ceremony or its fascination with guilt and sacrifice, but that does not mean it invests these practices with theistic content. However, to say that theism can only refer to belief in a transcendent God—and cannot denote a general disposition that can have as its focus war or money as well as a divine being—is to divorce the structure of experience from the content of experience, assuming that "the experience of atheism" or "of theism" can only ever indicate the content of experience, and never its mode. Such a stance would be unpardonably naïve about the extent to which our mode of experiencing the world—what we notice, what matters to us, how we feel about the world—is a product of religious or secular ideology. If it is possible to experience theistically or atheistically, rather than simply to experience a thing that is deemed to be theistic or atheistic, then theism cannot be limited to assent to specific doctrinal propositions, and it is legitimate to call the worship of Quirinus not only religious but also theistic.

This raises a further question however: to what extent are the structures that sometimes carry labels such as "sacrifice," "Christ," "Holy place," or "sacred" themselves irreducibly theistic, regardless of their content? If money is one's Christ, as it is in the case of Aristide Saccard, the protagonist of Zola's *Money*, is the experience of that Christ a theistic one? Expressed more abstractly: if something that is not "God" occupies in our experience the place originally carved out for, and traditionally occupied by, God, then can our experience of that thing be properly qualified as an atheistic experience? Not, I would suggest, if we are careful to pay attention to the schema as well as to the content of experience.

Let us return to Serres' warning quoted above: "An idea opposed to another idea is always the same idea, albeit affected by the negative sign. The more you oppose one another, the more you remain in the same framework of thought."[40] Why is that? A passage on Alexander the Great in *Detachment* helps us to see Serres' logic more clearly:

---

[39] Serres, *Angels*, 193.
[40] Serres and Latour, *Conversations on Culture, Science and Time*, 81.

I would have to oppose myself to the king. But if I oppose him, strong or weak against strong, rich or poor against rich, lowborn or bigwig against fetish, I will camp in Alexander's space, in the battlefield; I will confirm, within their law, the relations of value and the heights of idolatry. Alexander will then rule over me just as well, the relation of order imposing its law upon me. Alexander rules over all, including those who oppose him. He is such a powerful king that he has no contradictors. To contradict the king is to belong to the king, to oppose power forces one to enter into the logic of power, to contest wealth imposes an actuarial arithmetic, to destroy idols causes one to enter into the sacred. If I win this struggle, I lose for having accepted the relation of order, and if lose, I lose.[41]

So why is opposition synonymous with identity? Because ideas—and a fortiori ideologies—are not reducible to a content devoid of all structure or form. They instantiate patterns and relationships, categories and shapes that can be occupied by other ideas. To oppose Alexander's power is to affirm a rival power; to raise an army against him is to play his martial game. And, yes, "to destroy idols causes one to enter into the sacred": if I topple the idol I have succeeded only in erecting a substitute idol, and if I fail then the idol remains.[42]

So, is this the choice we face today in relation to theism: either it topples and a new atheistic god takes its place, or it remains and atheism fails? For Serres' own translational atheism there is a third, more attractive option.

III. Translational atheism

In opposition to the umbilicisms of religion, war and the economy, Serres himself prefers an account in which none of these domains is the origin and final truth of all the others, in which they each come and go and none of them plays the role of being the zero degree truth before which all the others must genuflect. One prominent term Serres uses to describe this refusal of all umbilicisms is the "*laïc*," the secular. This secular is quite precisely that which is not umbilical, that which does not privilege one single discourse or mode of experience at the expense of all others. It follows from this, however, that religion itself is not dismissed out of hand, but finds its place alongside the economic and the martial: "We must reconfigure the place of the religious in this secularism [laicity] that is so necessary: certainly not at the centre, dominant, but neither outside, excluded. Intimately close by."[43] Neither Jupiter nor Mars nor Quirinus should reign, but this no more leads to an absence of the divine than it does to an absence of the martial or an absence of the economic.

Serres uses a number of terms to describe the relationship between the religious and other modes of discourse and experience: Sadi Carnot "reactivates" the religions of

---

[41] Michel Serres, *Detachment*, trans. Geneviève James and Raymond Federman (Athens, OH: Ohio University Press, 1989), 78. Translation modified.
[42] Serres, *Detachment*, 78.
[43] Serres, *Andromaque*, 152.

fire in his heat engine; the religious is "displaced" from confessionals and temples into the media; and religious belief is "translated" into scientific knowledge.[44] One of the most sustained and illuminating treatments of such a reactivation, displacement or translation is the discussion, in the first chapter of *Statues*, of the relationship between, on the one hand, the ancient Carthaginian ritual of sacrificing children in the belly of a giant iron statue of the god Baal, and on the other hand the 1984 Challenger space shuttle disaster. It is an exploration of the relationship between Jupiter (Baal) and Mars and Quirinus (Challenger).

Serres' central thesis is a provocative one: Baal and Challenger can be understood as analogous models of a common structure and we can, if we are careful, elaborate a two-column table translating from the language of Baal into the language of Challenger.[45] Serres discerns sixteen such translations, including:

- The crowd: "Just as much of a crowd, on one side as on the other, forms a great crush at the tragic spectacle and gapes with horror";
- Celestial aspiration: "the Ancients and the Moderns designate the heavens as the aim and target of their aspirations or projects, space and the stars";
- Crippling cost: "the undertaking is expensive, for the Carthaginians as for us; the nation almost bankrupts itself over it";
- Repetition and ritual: "repetitions of the event, formerly like a rite returned to at a prescribed time or in the case of a pressing danger, now like on the stage or at the cinema. The event, filmed, is shown and reshown as though to assuage an unsatiated hunger in us";
- Compulsion to repeat, either in ritual re-enactment or on the television screen: "But the essential thing remains: this need to start again, to rerun, to repeat, to represent the rite, the tragedy in which the dead do not play at dying but truly die."[46]

Despite these striking similarities, Serres is very well aware of the potential objections to this translation between Baal and Challenger: the ancient rite differs from the modern accident; the ancient killing differs from the modern malfunction; the dream of reaching the heavens differs from the reality of leaving the atmosphere. Surely no one is suggesting that Baal and Challenger are strictly equivalent. Serres is sensitive to this accusation, and so chooses his words carefully: "The situations cut across and oppose each other instead of resembling one another."[47]

If an experience such as that of the Challenger disaster reactivates, displaces and translates ancient religious modes of behavior and experience then there can be no such thing, in this context at least, as an experience of pure atheism. But neither, we might conclude, can there be an experience of pure theism. Surely religion is just as liable to be reframed as a reactivation, displacement or translation of an

---

[44] Serres, *Zola*, 34; *The Incandescent*, 39; "Paris 1800," 443.
[45] Serres, *Statues*, 3.
[46] Serres, *Statues*, 3–4. For a longer discussion of the Baal/Challenger passage, see *Michel Serres: Figures of Thought*, 144–150. See also Serres and Latour, *Conversations on Culture, Science and Time* 160.
[47] Serres, *Statues*, 4.

economic or martial reality as the other way around. Can the stream of influence flow only one way?

There are, indeed, moments in Serres' work in which it appears that the religious is being co-opted as a translation of the secular. For example, Serres echoes Marcel Gauchet's argument in *The Disenchantment of the World* when he insists that, in Christian cultures, "religion secularizes religion, allowing the sacred to move elsewhere" because its rejection of any earthly temple or sacred territory leads to the universal cry according to which "Landless and tribeless, we are citizens of the world and brothers of men," a cry in terms of which the West would eventually relativize Christianity itself.[48] The Christian tradition also paves the way for the secularization of space, first restricting the pagan sacrality of every grove or forest to the single, local "Holy Land," and then locating the holy in a transcendent reality instantiated in no earthly place: "this celestial City is raised up, separated, lost for ever, leaving behind the here and now for a new state: a completely secular [*laïque*] and profane extension."[49] The homogeneous space with which Catholic, and then more aggressively Protestant Christianity replaces the local temples and territorial deities of the ancient world is a prolegomenon to the secularization of space in the work of Galileo, Descartes and Bacon.

Similarly, the debt owed by the very notion of secularity to its religious origins can also be read in terms of the secular finally fulfilling what its religious foreshadowing only dimly saw: the division into sacred and secular realms in the injunction to Give to Caesar what is Caesar's, and to God what is God's "sets up a space where unbelief, which is now possible, in a way wins its accreditation," allowing secularity to emerge for the first time, and marking the end both of the all-religious and the all-political.[50]

Most tellingly of all, in a dense passage from *The Birth of Physics*, Serres develops a fascinating reflection on the tendency of Epicurus's disciples to venerate him as a god, the same Epicurus who commended an attitude of insouciant, untroubled calmness (*ataraxia*) with relation to the gods, and enjoined his followers that the deities are far distant from us and unconcerned with our petty lives. Serres sees no irony in this worship of the anti-religious philosopher, for indeed "Epicurus is a god beyond all gods. The new god of another history, having toured all through the archaic traditions, he wrong-foots them. He abolishes the sacred by completing it."[51] This is not an idle turn of phrase for Serres. In fact, the gesture of abolition through completion (elsewhere expressed as opposition through multiplication) is one of Serres' recurring figures of thought.[52] He uses it most notably in his extended discussion of the relationship between Descartes and Leibniz in *Le Système de Leibniz*: "Leibniz crowns and completes the Cartesian method in refusing its requisites," taking what is ostensibly a universal

---

[48] Serres, "Paris 1800," 441. Serres, *The Incandescent*, 146.
[49] Michel Serres, *Habiter* (Paris: Éditions le Pommier, 2011), 206.
[50] Serres, *Andromaque*, 79.
[51] Michel Serres, *The Birth of Physics*, trans. David Webb and William Ross (London: Rowman and Littlefield International, 2018), 143.
[52] The motif is discussed throughout *Michel Serres: Figures of Thought*, with a summary table on pages 396–7.

principle and resituating it as one premise among many.⁵³ In Serres' own dense and lapidary formula, Leibniz's attitude to Descartes' system is that "he is opposed to it or generalises it."⁵⁴ To oppose by negation is to deny an affirmation, but to oppose by generalization is to show that the affirmation is one instance of a broader reality that it neither contains nor exhausts. This is the sense in which there can be an experience of atheism for Serres, not of an atheism that opposes or tries to negate theism, but an atheism that embraces theism and, in so doing, completes it by showing it to be a local translation of a larger reality it cannot control.

How does Epicurus oppose the sacred by completing it? On Serres' account, he faces down the ancient logic of sacrifice that formed the inexorable basis of justice, opposing to it the "natural contract" (*foedera naturae*) that interrupts the incessant and cyclical logic of war. The contract that founds a just peace was thought to require a sacrificial murder: every Mycenae has its Iphigenia, its "contract by blood, that of the oldest tradition, perhaps of destiny: the *foedera fati*."⁵⁵ The challenge is to break the cycle of murder and sacrifice, and whoever speaks and through speaking founds a new history does not charge a third with the sins of the earth; he takes upon himself, of his own volition, the thunder, the rumbling of the heavens, the flame at the walls of the world, the wrath of Jupiter. He freely takes on the dangerous position assigned to him by his knowledge of the laws of the universe and of human mechanisms.⁵⁶

Epicurus' *foedera naturae* have no need of a god to maintain them or to anoint them with sacrificial blood. Epicurus, like the murderers of God in the prophecy of Nietzsche's madman, now asks "[i]s the magnitude of this deed not too great for us? Do we ourselves not have to become gods merely to appear worthy of it?"⁵⁷

This leaves us in something of an impasse. Is religion secular, or is the secular religious? Is atheism theistic, or is theism atheistic? Serres remains noncommittal: "It is still a question of secularizing, but in such a way that one isn't sure who to thank for it: those who converted scientific knowledge into a religion or the religion itself which allows such a translation and such an abandonment of the religious."⁵⁸ Is atheism the truth of the experience of theism, or theism the truth of the experience of atheism? Serres' answer is—yes.

IV. Conclusion

In the case of Baal and Challenger what is the relationship between the ancient and the modern, between the religious and the technological? The question admits of no simple response. There are at least four possibilities. In the first possibility, one of the terms is subordinated to the other, giving either theism or atheism the whip hand.

---

[53] Serres, *Le Système de Leibniz*, 232.
[54] Serres, *Le Système de Leibniz*, 23–4.
[55] Serres, *The Birth of Physics*, 143.
[56] Serres, *The Birth of Physics*, 143.
[57] Friedrich Nietzsche, *The Gay Science: With a Prelude in German Rhymes and an Appendix of Songs*, ed. Bernard Williams, trans. Josefine Nauckhoff (Cambridge: Cambridge University Press, 2001).
[58] Serres, "Paris 1800," 443.

In the theological variant, Challenger is a contemporary repetition of irreducibly religious ways of thinking and behaving, instantiating indelibly religious concepts such as sacrifice. The modern event is a recapitulation of the ancient reality. In its atheistic variety, Baal is a crude foreshadowing of modern scientific realities that the Carthaginians substituted with myth, because they knew no better: the ancient sacrifice is a pale foreshadowing of the modern reality.

There are two versions of this first mode of relationship: temporal and archetypal. The temporal is the cruder version of the two: the instantiation that comes first, historically speaking, is the original, and the one that follows in time is necessarily the copy. A moment's reflection will suffice to show that this is a very unsatisfactory way of adjudicating intellectual or existential debt. This blunt instrument cannot cope with complex temporalities such as prophecy and fulfilment, in which cases it is in fact the instances that succeed in time (for example: Christ) that are taken to condition their antecedents (for example: Moses). The second version maintains the relationship of derivation and debt but allows for temporal flexibility. One instance is the model for the other, and one of the instances is in the debt of the other, but the direction of that debt must be decided with the aid of subtler calculations than temporal precedence alone. So, for example, we might hold that the fullness of the ages has come in the blossoming of modern scientific knowledge, and that all the antecedent conditions that made that knowledge possible—such as the constancy and predictable behavior of the natural world, universalism, and the claim that the book of nature is written in the language of mathematics—do not incur a relationship of debt but rather are themselves a pale foreshadowing of the fullness to which they were to lead, and therefore that theological universalism is a corrupted fore-echo of scientific universalism, and monotheism a faltering first draft of the subsequent plenitudinous understanding of the cosmological constants.

In the third possibility, both Baal and Challenger draw on schemata that neither of them owns. They both enact rhythms and patterns of experience that we label "sacrifice" and "ceremonial repetition," but these rhythms and patterns neither carry the copyright of ancient religion nor bear the indelible stamp of modern technology. Both Baal and Challenger participate in some archetypal schemata outside themselves.

A fourth possibility is that neither Baal nor Challenger own the copyright on the shapes of thought and experience they are instantiating, but neither are these shapes proper to a third instance that transcends or subtends them both. There is no structure over and above the different models, but their commonality arises in the relation between them. Modern scientific and technological knowledge is not the fullness of what religion dimly saw, nor does modern science rely on an irreducibly religious framework. They can be translated into each other, without any implication of precedence or priority.

This fourth option approximates most closely to Serres' Leibnizian outlook. As with science and literature in the cases of Zola and Verne, neither Baal nor Challenger is a controlling paradigm for the other: the Challenger disaster is not, at bottom, an enactment of an ancient rite, any more than ancient Baal worship is a modern technological enterprise. Neither Baal nor Challenger is the "literal" to the other's "metaphorical" expression, the umbilical structure to the other's model.

Serres' refusal to institute a rigid hierarchy or priority between the religious and the secular is not diffident but strategic, for any such hierarchy would represent a fall back into umbilicism. In Serres' *laïc* paradigm of translation, the only possible atheistic experience incorporates theistic experience as one possible translation among many. It must necessarily do so; to deny that possibility is to become umbilically theistic. Translational atheism is always local: Christians are atheistic about Quirinus, and atheists about Jupiter. To be universally atheistic is to be umbilical which, as we have seen, is itself a form of theism. So, the only atheism it is possible to experience is one that can always be translated into a religious experience.

Part Two

The Atheisms of Faith

7

Theism, Atheism, Anatheism

Richard Kearney

Anatheism means *ana-theos*—in Greek, after God. It is a way of thinking about God after the death of God. It means retracing the remnants, revenants, and returns of the divine after the disappearance of the old familiar divinities we thought we possessed like idols of gold. Or to be more precise, after the deconstruction of the Omni-God of dominion and delusion—philosophically formulated by Freud, Marx and Nietzsche, but already anticipated by Jesus and the prophets—whatever survives is what we could call ana-theism. Anatheism is a spirituality of the remaindered God to come: a God who may be if we let it be, a sacred promise made from the beginning of time and always still to be realized, again and again. If we remain.

I. Something lost that is found again

"Ana" is a prefix defined in the *Shorter Oxford English Dictionary* as: "Up in space or time; back again, anew." As in anamnesis, analogy, anagogy, anachronism. So understood, the term supports the deeper and broader sense of "after" contained in the expression "God after God." *Ana* opens a semantic field involving notions of retrieving, revisiting and repeating. But if it repeats, it does so *forwards* not *backwards*. It is not a matter of regressing to some prelapsarian past, but of coming back "afterwards"—returning in order to go forward again. *Reculer pour mieux sauter!*

It is in this sense that we use the term ana-theism as a "returning to God after God": a critical retrieval of sacred things that have passed but still bear radical potentialities that may be reanimated in the future. As such, anatheism proposes a future for the forgotten or still unfulfilled calls of divine history: it is an "after-faith," which is more than any "after-thought" or "after-affect." After-faith is eschatological—something ultimate in the end that was already there from the beginning. And that is why the "after" of *ana* is also a "before." A before that has been transposed, so to speak, into a second after. As Wisdom (*Sophia*) says when she plays before the face of the Lord: "Before He made the world I was there ... constantly at his side ... filled with delight, rejoicing always in his presence" (Prov. 8:26–9). This Hebraic sense of ana-chrony is aptly echoed in Jesus' startling claim: "Before Abraham was I am."

But let us be clear: anatheism is not a dialectical third term which supersedes theism and atheism in some Hegelian synthesis or final resolution. True, anatheism contains a moment of atheism within itself as it does a moment of theism. Or, to be more precise: anatheism pre-contains both—for it operates from a space and time *before* the dichotomy of atheism and theism. (As well as *after*.) The double "a" of anatheism holds out the possibility, but not the necessity, of a second affirmation once the "death of God" has done its work. But it differs from Hegel's "negation of the negation" which sees the return as an ineluctable synthesis or sublation (*Aufhebung*). Resisting the logic of theodicy, anatheism is always a wager—a risk that can go either way. It depends on us. It is a matter of discernment and decision on our part, responding to the Call of the instant. A replay of faith without cease. The return does not take place behind our backs, irrespective of our agency, like Hegel's dialectic of Absolute Spirit. There is no "Ruse of Reason" unfolding through the pretext of particulars into a Final Totality. Anatheism is not about Upper Case Divinity dictating a predetermined dialectic. *Au contraire*, anatheism has nothing to do with Alpha-Gods or Omni-Gods. It is about re-imagining—and re-living—the sacred in the "least of these." It is lower case from beginning to end.

As such, anatheism reactivates suspended or unsuspected possibilities often experienced in the a-theism of non-knowing; the "a-" marking an act of abstention and withdrawal rather than passive privation. Such a-theism is less a matter of epistemological argument *against God* than a pre-reflective lived experience of lostness and separation—a mood of *Angst* or abandon, an existential "dark night of the soul" which most people experience at some point in their lives. Even Christ on the Cross declared: "My god my god why have you forsaken me?" This "a" of atheism is indispensable to anatheism. But it is only a part, a step, a move in a larger choreography. For in "a-n-a" we have two "a"s. And the second "a" is the death of death. The death of the death of God. The yes after the no which repeats the first yes of genesis. This double A-A of anatheism signals a reopening to something always still new, strange, and ineffable. A dance of twelve steps which the AA movement calls "yielding to a higher power." A surrender which only happens when one owns one's existential "helplessness."

So, I repeat, the ana- is no guarantee of ineluctable dialectical progress. It operates by promise not predictability, by call not certainty. If anything, one could say that the end of religion brings us back to its beginning—to a fore-time preceding the division between belief and non-belief. And in this respect, we might think of the poet John Keats' famous definition of poetic faith as a "willing suspension of disbelief," a returning again to Adam's experience on the first day of Creation when everything was fresh and up for grabs, when anything could happen, for better or for worse. Keats called this originary moment of radical openness "negative capability"—"the ability to experience mystery, uncertainty and doubt, without the irritable reaching after fact and reason." And this has parallels, I believe, with Kierkegaard's famous "leap of faith" in *Fear and Trembling*. A sacred repetition—not to be understood as a regression to some original position but as a disposition of openness to the radical incoming Other.[1] In Kierkegaard's reading, Abraham had to lose his son as "given" (someone taken for granted) in order

---

[1] Cf. Søren Kierkegaard, *Fear and Trembling*, trans. A. Hannay (Penguin, New York, 1985).

to receive him back as "gift"; he had to abandon Isaac as possession in order to welcome him back as promise. Isaac does not belong to Abraham (as filial property or projection). Isaac is *other* than his father. He is himself-as-another, a gift of the Other, of God (the return gift of what Kierkegaard calls the "Absolute").

In short, anatheist faith is about something lost that is found again. It involves reiterating the before as after, the earlier as later—a replay which reconfigures the seriality of linear chronological time, where one moment succeeds another, in favor of a time out of time. A sudden lightness, if you will. An epiphanic moment (*Augenblick* or *Jetzzeit*) where Grace traverses the instant. It is this mystery of past-as-future that the verbal prefix "ana" seeks to capture.[2] This time out of time in time is what the Gospel calls the "time that remains."

II. Anatheism, atheism, and theism

To say all this is not to say that *ana* eschews historical time. Far from it. Infinite time is in-the-finite; it traverses history and cannot appear without it. As such, ana-theism consorts today with a concrete temporal situation that comes after the modern declaration of the death of God. It is indelibly marked by the secular exposés of the Enlightenment, the French Revolution, the modern critiques of Ideology as false consciousness, unconscious delusion and patriarchal hegemony. Anatheism expresses a current concern with what Max Weber terms the "disenchantment" of the world, the desacralizing of society, the general malaise of the "disappearance of God" and forfeiture of faith. In this sense, anatheism is also evidently a socio-historical phenomenon of the nineteenth to twenty-first centuries, which engages our contemporary humanist and post-humanist culture. Though not in any teleological sense which would imply we were ignorant for millennia and have now seen the light—that all faith was delusion and we are finally free at last. For anatheism, losing the illusion of God (as sovereign superintendent of the universe) offers the possibility of re-engaging with the original promise of the Stranger, the absolute Other who comes as gift, call, summons, as invitation to hospitality, love, and justice in every moment. In sum, anatheism signals an audacious embrace of the mystery that was sidelined and erased by the logic of "Western metaphysics"—a mystery that needs to be relived again and again (*ana*).

In terms of contemporary continental philosophy, several thinkers offer guiding thoughts. Paul Ricœur has acknowledged the indispensable passage through atheism on the way to what he called a "post-religious faith." But the journey from primary

---

[2] I think that several thinkers after Kierkegaard—such as Levinas (*Totality and Infinity*), Benjamin (*Theses on the Philosophy of History*), Derrida (*Specters of Marx*) or Agamben (*The Time that Remains*)—are trying to say something similar when they talk of "messianic time." Though I generally use the somewhat broader terms "kairological" or "eschatological" to express the idea that the kingdom already was, is now, and is yet to come. It is always already and still to come. Catherine Keller provides a very timely eco-eschatological reading of the Pauline "time that remains" in her *Political Theology of the Earth* (New York: Columbia University Press, 2018) 2–5, where she translates the Greek *sunestalemnos* as "gathered" or "contracted" temporality, a *kairos* moment of urgency, alertness and abiding, understood as the "right time, the time in which something can be done" (p. 3).

religious faith through atheism to a second religious faith should not, he insists, be seen as some final triumphalist summation. A-theism is, indeed, a move beyond the naïveté of first faith—one's childish certainties, facile assumptions, acquired dogmas—into an open space of possibilities; but it is for us to realize those possibilities or not. The free space may lead either to a commitment to responsible atheism or post-theism. The ana-space is always open—for no atheism or theism can presume to be certain of itself without falling back into another dogmatism (of belief or anti-belief). So, whether it is a matter of what one might call "anatheist atheism" or "anatheist theism"—a second theism or a second atheism—it is for us to choose. A hermeneutic wager. With nothing inevitable or predetermined about it. We are free to consent or dissent. In short, the anatheist moment proposes a choice between faith and non-faith "after" we have abandoned the dogmatisms of first theism or first atheism. In moving from religion through atheism to faith—if we chose to do so—a hermeneutic moment of "suspension" is indispensable. Or to put it in Ricœur's terms, unless one allows the "masters of suspicion"—Freud, Marx, Nietzsche (and one might add the mistresses of suspicion, De Beauvoir, Irigaray, Kristeva)—to unmask the religious idols, one is less likely to achieve a life-giving faith. Intellectually speaking, at least. Ricœur deems iconoclastic atheism to be a potential ally of "hermeneutic suspicion" which may lead in turn (for those so moved) to a "hermeneutic reaffirmation" of the sacred.[3]

Such talk of purgative atheism consorts with a certain deconstructive gesture in the work of Emmanuel Levinas and Jacques Derrida. Levinas talks about atheism in *Totality and Finity* as the greatest gift which Judaism grants humanity. The first step of monotheism is atheism. What I think he means by this is that Judaism serves as a prophetic prohibition against false idols—an atheistic moment of "separation" from humanity's fusion with sacral "totality" (sacrificial paganism). This separation gives the "I," the human self, a freedom and responsibility to answer the ethical summons of the Other, the Infinite, the Stranger. If there were no such atheistic separation, there would no ethical encounter with the Stranger. A Stranger who, Levinas argues, bears the face of the vulnerable and naked—"the widow, the orphan, the stranger"—in short, the "trace of God." Derrida, for his part, talks about a "religion *without* religion." And if I have a difference with Derrida here, it is the difference between the words "without" *(sans)* and "after" *(ana)*. Where I talk about religion after religion he talks about religion void of religion. In a 2001 dialogue we conducted on the question of the "God of perhaps" *(le dieu du peut-être),* Derrida surmised that there was but the "thinnest of differences" between his atheistic and my anatheistic understanding of things.[4] But a difference there is.

---

[3] See Paul Ricœur, *The Symbolism of Evil*, trans. E. Buchanan (Boston: Beacon Press, 1968) and "Religion, Atheism, Faith" in *The Conflict of Interpretations*, ed. D. Ihde (Evanston, IL: Northwestern University Press, 1974), 440–67.

[4] See our dialogue, "Terror, Religion and the new Politics," which took place in New York in October, 2001, and was published in Richard Kearney, *Debates in Continental Philosophy: Conversations with Contemporary Thinkers* (New York: Fordham University Press, 2004) 3–15. Derrida was referring to my recently published work, *The God Who May Be* (Bloomington: Indiana University Press, 2001), and my earlier book on the subject, *Poétique du Possible* (Paris: Éditions du Beauchesne, 1984). See also my related essay, which continues the dialogue, "Derrida's Messianic Atheism," in *The Trace of God: Derrida and Religion*, ed. E. Baring and P. Gordon (New York: Fordham University Press, 2014).

III. Living anatheism

Yet anatheism is more than the philosophical formulation—what comes after the disappearance of God? It is also and more fundamentally an *existential* question: how do we experience the appearing and disappearing of God in our lives? Prior to any speculative theory, anatheism bears witness to the loss and recovery of the divine. It involves attending to sacred strangers in our existence. This is why anatheism is theopraxis before it is theology. It occurs first as an act of felt abandonment followed by a turn toward something "more" (what Socrates called *periagoge*, what Augustine called *conversio*). The negative moment of letting go is, I repeat, indispensable to any genuine appreciation of anatheism, for without it we have cheap grace: God as confidence man, a supernatural peddler of comforting illusions, quick fixes, opiates for the people. Which is why we need to honor the deep experience of abandon powerfully evinced in the mystics' "dark night of the soul," or Dostoyevsky's talk of faith arising from the "crucible of doubt," or Christ's penultimate sense of dereliction on the Cross—"My god my god why have you forsaken me"—issuing ultimately in a leap of faith: "Unto thee I commend my spirit."

Read anatheistically, the Cross is not some expiatory sacrifice exacted by a patriarchal God, bent on ransoming his son for our sins. On the contrary, it harbors an "atheist" resistance to such transactional theism in favor of an "anatheistic" embrace of new life, of the gift of resurrection. The Cross is one more revelation of God after God. And I say "one more," for as Christ taught, his own death and resurrection are part of a continuous revelation from the beginning to the end of time: "Before Abraham was I am ... Now I must go so that the Paraclete can come." Christ-here-and-now is always Christ-before-and-after: ana-chronic, ana-Christ. In other words, the crucified one abandons the Omnipotent Father who has abandoned him. His final lesson is one of radical *kenosis*, letting go of lost illusions and attachments so as to affirm lovingly the future, the other, the strange. Christ's cry of forsakenness is the atheist moment of negative capability which prepares his releasement into more life, to which he boldly commends his spirit. In this anatheist return, Christ is entrusting himself to the "thee" of each God after God, each stranger who seeks and receives the bread of life—his hungry disciples at Galilee ("come and have breakfast"), Mary Magdalene at the garden tomb ("Myriam!"), his fellow travelers on the road to Emmaus ("stay and eat"). Christ keeps coming back (*ana*) to his followers after (*ana*) he has left them. He returns each time a *hospes* hosts each one of us as guest. For only as guest can we recognize the host. (The Latin term *hospes* means both host and guest.)[5]

The act of kenotic emptying triggers the wager of hospitality. This primal anatheist wager is ontological rather than merely logical (unlike Pascal's wager which was one of knowledge rather than of flesh, epistemological rather than existential). The inaugural wager to turn hostility into hospitality, death into new life, marks a moment of decisive

---

[5] See our more detailed discussion of the terms *hospes, hostis*, hostility and hospitality in "Double Hospitality," in the *Journal of the Continental Philosophy of Religion*, 1, no 1; Richard Kearney and James Taylor, eds., *Hosting the Stranger: Between Religions* (London: Continuum, 2012); and Richard Kearney and Melissa Fitzpatrick, eds., *Radical Hospitality: From Thought to Action* (New York: Fordham University Press, 2020).

conversion in most wisdom traditions. And with respect to the Abrahamic tradition, we might recall certain "primal scenes" of hospitality: Abraham and Sarah encountering the three strangers at Mamre; Jacob wrestling with his dark stranger in the night; Mary engaging with a stranger called Gabriel in Nazareth; Christ returning as a stranger (*hospes*) seeking bread and water (Matthew 25)—a sacred host to the least of these (*elachistos*). Because anatheism is a call and response it invites an endless wagering of hosting and guesting, giving and receiving. The stranger depends on humans to dwell amongst us, for word to be made flesh, for incarnation to recur as ana-carnation, again and again. The invitation is constantly, unconditionally there: it is for us to respond.

IV. Theopoetics as anapoetics

The poet, Gerard Manley Hopkins, captures the anatheist wager well in his poetry. Theology becomes theopoetics. He describes the moment of literary epiphany as an act of "aftering and seconding"—an "over and overing" of experience which replays the secular as sacred. Hopkins speaks of a retrieval of lost experience that repeats forward, proffering new life to memory, giving a future to the past. This poetic moment of "epiphany" requires a detour of distance and disenchantment *after* which we may return to our first experience in a new light, over and over. *Ana*. Or, as Freud would say, *nachträglich;* and though Freud is speaking of "trauma," the same structure of temporal repetition applies to poetic "wonder": both terms come from "wound" referring to a fright or surprise which interrupts our normal sense of time and space. Hopkins sees poetry as a sacramental re-imagining of things in three movements: (1) our initial experience of an event in first naivety; (2) the loss of innocence in the dark night of the soul, vividly depicted by Hopkins in his "dark sonnets"—"I wake and Feel the fell of dark not day" or "the mind has mountains/sheer frightful non-man-fathomed/hold them cheap may/those who ne'er hung there"; and (3) the return movement of poetic epiphany, where one sees the world as "charged with the grandeur of God ... like shining from shook foil." Hopkins, a Jesuit mystic, developed a quintessential theopoetics whereby one surrenders all presuppositions and illusions before celebrating the inherent divinity of all beings, "counter, original, spare, strange" "(Pied Beauty)". He identifies the cosmic Christ with a divine potency within all mortal things, not only human eyes and limbs, but wells, stones, dragonflies, and birds:

> As kingfishers catch fire, dragonflies draw flame;
> As tumbled over rim in roundy wells
> Stones ring; like each tucked string tells, each hung bell's
> Bow swung finds tongue to fling out broad its name;
> Each mortal thing does one thing and the same:
> Deals out that being indoors each one dwells;
> Selves—goes itself; *myself* it speaks and spells,
> Crying Whát I dó is me: for that I came.
> Acts in God's eye what in God's eye he is –
> Chríst—for Christ plays in ten thousand places,

Lovely in limbs, and lovely in eyes not his
To the Father through the features of men's faces.⁶

But this experience of holy repetition as epiphany is not confined to Christianity or any other particular religion. It extends, I believe, to any poetic movement of returning to "God *after* God." God after the loss of God. As in the replay of child's play, "gone, back again." "*Fort/Da*." We learn young that what disappears as literal comes back again as figural—that is, as sign and symbol, as a second presence in and through absence. And by symbol here we do not mean *untrue* or *unreal*. The return of the lost one—in the case of the lost God—may well be a realer presence, theopoetically speaking. A genuine second naiveté after the loss of one's first naiveté. The return may indeed be a more powerful and moving presence precisely because of the detour through separation and letting go. This involves a new notion of time—*kairological* rather than chronological—which traverses and reverses history, as in the Eucharistic formula: "we do this in memory of him until he comes again." Anatheism is about coming again, creating again, aftering again, time after time. In a word: *ana-poiesis*. Theopoetics is anapoetics.

If the examples of anatheist hospitality and epiphany I have cited here derive from the Western Abrahamic tradition, this is because it happens to be my own hermeneutic heritage, my particular spiritual tradition dependent upon the cultural time and place in which I was born and bred. But anatheist spirituality is in no way confined to the Western Judeo-Christian-Islamic tradition. It applies, in principle, to all great Wisdom Traditions and spiritualities—from Buddhism and Hinduism to Taoism and Confucianism and the many indigenous cultures of Africa, Austral-Asia and the Americas. A recent volume I co-edited, *Hosting the Stranger: Between Religions*, recounts the wagers and wonders of anatheist hospitality in five major spiritualities of the world.⁷ And let me conclude by suggesting that such interreligious hospitality is not a luxury but an imperative. To open oneself to another God after the death of the last God is an endless opportunity to rediscover not only the lost possibilities of one's own spirituality but also of other spiritualities.⁸ Hosting the stranger in one's own faith—and strange faiths other than one's own.

---

⁶ See our development of Hopkins' theopoetic notion of epiphany in "Epiphanies" in *Cyphers of Transcendence*, ed Fran O'Rourke (Dublin: Dublin University Press, 2019). For other examples of the intimate liaison between anatheism and theopoetics in works of art and literature, see Richard Kearney and Matthew Clemente, *The Art of Anatheism* (London: Bloomsbury, 2018) (in particular our "God Making: Theopoetics and Anatheism," pp. 3–28).
⁷ For more on this theme of interconfessional hospitality, see *Hosting the Stranger: Between Religions*.
⁸ See Richard Kearney, *Anatheism: returning to God after God* (New York: Columbia University Press, 2010) 175.

8

Apocalypse or Revelation?

Emmanuel Falque

"To erase everything and start again or to search for the trace of an abolished truth in the ruins, the two attitudes have this common, that we renounce finding a meaning to our nonsense itself."[1]

Discourses on the "end of a world" or better, on the "end of the world," are constantly becoming more powerful in a time of climate change and other catastrophic announcements. Of course, we could remain nostalgic for the past or predict more terrifying days than any previous time. Despite the question being primarily ecological and philosophical, however, it is also theological, or at least religious. For the Apocalypse—even if it was first "The Book of Revelation" (*apokalupsis*) in the last book of the Bible—is also, at least in its French translation ("The Book of the Apocalypse") and also in what will become of one of the uses of the word in English ("Apocalypse Now"), the book of the end of the world or the book on the end of the world. The "end times," as Günter Anders says, is no longer only today the "mortal's genre" (our own death or that of others), but also the "mortal genre" (the exhaustion of the human species).

The "end of the world" cannot be left solely to the discourses of scientists and politicians then—although objectively sounding the alarm is, to say the least, necessary. The death of the human "genre" and the possibility of its end—as it is also envisaged in the last book of the Bible if not definitively, at least as a possibility, with the emergence of the "Ten-Horned Beast" (Rev. 13:1)—has something to say in our time, not only about our past, but also and above all about our future. As long as *eschatology* (apocalypse) and *climatology* (end of the world) do not meet or dialogue, cultures will remain foreign to each other and the possibility of bringing Christianity into dialogue with all forms of atheism will not be realized.

---

[1] Maurice Merleau-Ponty, Manuscrit inédit, Automne 1958 (for the work, *Être et monde*), cited and commented on by Eugene de Saint Aubert, *Vers une ontologie indirecte, Sources et enjeux critiques de l'appel à l'ontologie chez Merleau-Ponty* (Paris: Vrin, 2006), 177–88: "Destroy and restore. Two positivisms of language" (cit. p. 178). With this twofold critique addressed directly to phenomenology and analytical philosophy by Maurice Merleau-Ponty from 1958 a few years before his death (1961): "Ruins that are being restored (the present as decadence from a mythical past [phenomenology inspired by Heidegger]. Ruins that are thrown down logical positivism [analytical philosophy]). The common premise; this none-sense has no meaning" (my emphasis, cit. p. 177).

In the Bible, the "hypothesis of the end" is initiated by God alone: "But about that day and hour no one knows, neither the angels of heaven, nor the Son, but only the Father" (Matt. 24:36). However, today it is provoked and precipitated by humanity in their *arraisonnement* or *Gestell*, as Martin Heidegger says. The apocalypse in the Book of the Apocalypse or Revelation is God's initiative, while the Apocalypse now is anthropogenic. When the Messiah's victory comes or would like to come, "capturing and defeating the ten-horned beast," and with it "the kings of the earth with their armies" and "the false prophet" (Rev. 19:11–21) (*eschatology or revelation*), perhaps it will be too late for there to still be a human race, or quite simply any human being, to save (*climatology or end of the world*). Atheism and Revelation have in common that they pronounce on the end, with a teleology that is not only that of completion, but also of the break, the crack, perhaps even of an end times that could just as easily be an end *of* time.

Will it be necessary, then, to enter into a pure catastrophism, and suddenly sound the sirens of a boat that would have run aground? Or is there still a power of "transformation" in humanity capable of holding together "apocalypse" and "revelation"? The future of the planet and our confidence (or not) in its survival and our own future with it certainly depends on the answer to this question, but also on the ability of theology itself (*Christianity and eschatology*) to join (or not) the questioning of humankind about its possible disappearance (*atheism and climatology*). The religious can no longer remain indifferent to the scientific or political. It possesses within itself resources, whether past or present [The Book of Apocalypse or Revelation] that are capable of enlightening our future.

The amphibology of the term "revelation"—apocalypse in Greek (*apokalupsis*) and revelation in Latin (*revelatio*)—is not a simple play of words. For the hazards of language, I will substitute here the necessity of the concept, even of life itself, which means that there is no manifestation or "revelation" independent of its destiny or its "apocalypse." Consideration of the end orients and requires the appearance of the phenomenon, either to thwart it (catastrophe) or to hope for it (eschatological expectation). In the first place, *Apokalupsis* certainly implies, in the Greek, "revelation" or "manifestation": *Apokalupsis Iêsou Christou*: "Revelation of Jesus Christ" (Rev. 1:1). But this first meaning must nevertheless be nuanced since the last book of the Bible is translated, at least in French, not as the "Book of Revelation" but as the "Book of the Apocalypse."

A term is defined not only by its strict translation, but also by its context and designation: the *Apocalypse* is certainly understood as Revelation, but also as the end of the world or the end times. The Omega of the Alpha, or the *Apocalypse* of a *Genesis*, marks precisely the Christian meaning of Revelation based on the book of the Bible. To deny this would be to stick to the Jewish expectation of a not yet realized messianism (*shekina*) or to the Greek world of truth waiting to be revealed (*aletheia*). Neither simply a manifested given nor a concept devoid of any historicity, the Christian Apocalypse necessitates a link between phenomenality and eschatology—conversely, at the risk of lacking "any" specificity. In this amphibology, or rather in this dual meaning of *Manifestation* and *Finalization*, the strongest part of the so-called Christian "Revelation" remains that its expectation is at least partly fulfilled. Consideration of the end times in Revelation serves as a discriminating criterion for any discourse that would like to inform it, and not to recognize it would be to confine oneself to a phenomenality that forgets the content it seeks to target: the "apocalypse" (*apokalupsis*) is both "a term that means revelation" and "a literary genre characterized by the manifestation of secrets concerning the end times and the course of history."[2]

That the Apocalypse or the Revelation "un-veils" (*apo-kalluma*) is, indeed, not only particular to the Christian apocalypse, but also relates to Greek truth—*aletheia* or "unveiling." So, in Homer, the god Hephaestus "envelops (*kalupsas*) in his night" the son of the priest Dares in order to camouflage him at the moment the enemy attacks in the *Iliad* (V, 23); or again, a "black wave covers (*kalupsen*) the goddess" in order to hide her from the eyes of Ulysses in the *Odyssey* (V, 352).[3] Nevertheless, the Christian apocalypse (*apokalupsis*) "is not identical to Greek truth (*aletheia*)."[4] One can certainly say that their modes of unveiling may be opposed—I will come back to this later—but also that in my view, we can measure the entire distance between an eschatology that is already under way, on the one hand (Saint John), and the pure neutrality of the phenomenon, on the other (Heidegger). Only consideration of the "end"—apocalypse "or" revelation in the inclusive sense of the term—makes the *apokalupsis* the place of a purely Christian and not exclusively Greek manifestation: "what is to be seen does not come from phenomena"—*me ek phainomenon to blepomenon gegonenaï*—the author of the letter to the Hebrews insists in a surprising way (Heb. 11:3).[5]

Nevertheless, in order not always to presuppose the very thing that is being sought, a methodological question poses itself. Is there a phenomenon specific to Christianity, called "apocalyptic," (*apokalupsis*), that is necessarily opposed to the *pseudo*, or the insufficient, Greek unveiling, called "phenomenological" (*ek phainomenon*)? In other words, will we still be satisfied again and again with maintaining the in principle contradiction between the Christian and the Greek (*apokalupsis aletheia*), in order to reach the myth or even the rite so often reiterated, of a "pure faith" on the one hand (demythologization), or even of a "pure philosophy," on the other hand (overcoming metaphysics). Is there no other aim of the apocalypse or the so-called "Christian" revelation than to separate the two orders to ensure a succession, the revelation of which would then be exempt from any compromise?

The question is valid here since the Christian apocalypse itself, whether it is understood in the Johannine or Pauline sense, in reality resists any reading that would not or would no longer see what is happening with respect to conversion or transformation due to the emphasis on opposition. Between the Apocalypse as the "end of time" and Revelation as "manifestation" stands, in my opinion, the "bond" or the vinculum of Conversion as the "transformation of the self" or "transfiguration." Saint

---

[2] The two meanings of *apokalypsis* are explicitly distinguished and linked to each other by Xavier Léon-Dufour, *Dictionnaire du Nouveau Testament* (Paris: Seuil, 1975) art. "apocalypse," pp. 119–20.

[3] Remark made by Jean Vioulac, "Apocalypse de la vérité, Heidegger la question de l'autre Commencement," *Revue philosophique de Louvain* 108 No. 3 (2010): 465–6. Taken from the book with the same name: *Apocalypse de la vérité* (Paris: Ad Solem, 2014), 111.

[4] Thesis developed Jean Vioulac, *La logique totalitaire: Essai sur la crise de l'Occident* (Paris: Presses Universitaires de France, 2013) § 40, pp. 486–9: "Penser l'apocalypse."

[5] I follow here the translation proposed by Jean-Luc Marion in his Préface to Vioulac, *Apocalypse de la vérité*, op. cit., p. 11. Formula cited and commented on by Vioulac, ibid. pp. 118–19.

Paul again emphasizes this in a text that is at the very least essential in the Second Epistle to the Corinthians. He invents less a new mode of "unveiling" (*apokalupsis*) than a dropping of the "veils" (*kalumma*) that in other places can still obstruct us: "we are not like Moses who would put a veil (*kalumma*) on his face ... To this day, when we read the Old Testament, this same veil remains (*auto kalumma menei*). It is not lifted (*mê anakaluppomenon*), because it is Christ who takes it away (*oti in Christô katargeitai*) ... It is only through conversion to the Lord (*epistrepsê pros kurion*) that the veil will fall (*periaireitai to kalumma*) ... And all of us who, with unveiled faces (*anakekalummenô prosôpô*), reflect the glory of the Lord, are transfigured [literally metamorphosed (*metamorphoumetha*)] in this same image" (2 Cor. 3:13–17).

Let us note well, here. If the Greek term for apocalypse (*apokalupsis*), which also means revelation, as evidenced by its Latin translation (*revelatio*), etymologically indicates the act of "throwing away" or "putting aside" (*apo*) the "veil" (*kalumma*), then the Christian apocalypse or its revelation is therefore also "unveiling," whether we refer to Jewish theophany (*theophania*) or Greek truth (*aletheia*). But Christian revelation has in its own right the characteristic that the human "and" God, Jesus "and" Christ are manifested, so that humanity and the divine are never separated. "Revelation of Jesus Christ"—*Apokalupsis Iêsou Christou* (Rev. 1:1). The first word already cited from the last book of the Bible maintains, in the unity of the same person—Christ or the Anointed One of God (*o Christos*)—his apocalypse as a manifestation and his apocalypse as a realization. In Him what "appears" (phenomenality) is, or will be at the same time, that which ends (eschatology). In the Revelation (*apokalupsis*), that which is given "to see" (manifestation) also marks the end of "history" (apocalypse).

With regard to its "unveiling" (*apo-kalupsis*), the Christian meaning of revelation thus appears to be twofold. On the one hand it is related to Hellenism, and on the other it is related to Judaism. In the first place and with regard to Hellenism, the apocalypse is "unveiling" (*apo-kalluma*) in the sense that it enters and anchors [itself] in a history that it orients. This is contrary to the pure neutrality of *aletheia*, which only manifests. The *lethê* or veil that Heidegger affixed to Heraclitus (*Aletheia*) certainly has something fascinating about it, but it always remains in the virginity of a given whole that cannot be historicized in any way."[6] And then, in relation to Judaism, apocalypse or Christian revelation (*revelatio*) is the act of "removing the veil" (*periaireitai to kalumma*) or advancing with a "revealed face" (*anakekalummenô prosôpô*) by which we are "converted" (*epistrepsê*) or "transformed" (*metamorphoumetha*) in God as soon as God is incarnate for us: "who has seen me has seen the Father" (John 14:9). Rather than opposing the traditions, Christianity transforms them from within by uniting them in him—"and" the human "and" God—and converts us in order to resurrect us.

In this sense, the masked (or even veiled) advance—"*larvatus prodeo*"—no longer only refers here to the role of the philosopher "wearing a mask" who advances on the

---

[6] Τὸ μὴ δῦνόν ποτε πῶς ἄν τις λάθοι (to mê dunon pote pôs an tis lathoi)—"From the not ever submerging (thing), how may anyone be concealed (from it)?" or "From the not ever submerging thing, how may anyone be concealed (from it)?" or "How could a human ever conceal himself from the always and forever emerging thing?" (Fgt. 16). Martin Heidegger, *Heraclitus: The Inception of Occidental Thinking and Logic: Heraclitus's Doctrine of the Logos*, trans. Julia Goesser Assaiante and S. Montgomery Ewegen (London: Bloomsbury/Athlone, 2018), 37, 49, 58, 240.

"theatre of the world" (Descartes), but also, to follow Henri Gouhier's pun, the one who advances "masked before God"—*larvatus pro Deo* (in two words this time).[7] The gap remains in relation to Judaism in the sense that the Christian does not simply veil him or herself, remaining always in the way and the veil of the *aletheia*. The Christian is called to "remove the veil" (*apo-kalumna*) as St. Paul taught us: "In the Old Testament the veil is not lifted, for it disappears in Christ" (*supra*, 2 Cor. 3:14). Therefore, contrary to Moses on Mount Horeb—"you cannot see my face; for no one shall see me and live" (Exod. 33:20), and as in Descartes in the *Cogitationes privatae*—"I advance masked in the theatre of the world" (AT, X, 212), one advances neither "masked" (Descartes) nor "veiled" (Moses) in Christianity. This is what makes it its own. The issue is first of all that of the "flesh" and "nakedness" by which the Word comes to manifests himself.

Let us note well here, however. To "remove" or "make disappear" (*katargetaï*), or even "drop" (*pariaireita*) the veil, does not give free rein to a pure demonstration (*Offenbarung*), in the Hegelian sense of the "Absolute Manifest" or the "Revealed Without Rest."[8] Rather, the act consists—and we will return to this following Saint Paul (2 Cor. 3:16–17)—in initiating a "conversion" (*epistrepsê*) in us by which we ourselves are incorporated into the One who comes to "transform" us (*metamorphoumeta*). If revelation in Christianity also emerges from the "hidden" and "unveiled" (Pascal), or even from "latency," it is only in that the Word made flesh seeks to show himself (real presence), even under the species or the "veil" of bread and wine made precisely to manifest him (Pascal, "Letter to Charlotte Roannez," late October 1656).[9] For the apostle Paul there is neither Jew nor Greek (Gal. 3:28), but assuming and converting the Jewish and the Greek, he does not advance or no longer advances "masked" but "with an open face," thus exposing himself to a transformation in which he does not know where it will take him. Using the words of Ovid, this time: *dectecta fronte prodeo*—"I advance with an uncovered face."[10]

Thus, the *apokalupsis* gives itself as "an incommensurable mode of unveiling of *aletheia*" in the face of Hellenism, as soon as the veil is unveiled or falls (apocalypse as revelation). But the *apokalupsis* is at the same time revealed as an incommensurable mode of unveiling of *Shekina*, against Judaism, in the sense that the revelation is at least partially realized (apocalypse as end times).[11] It is thus on two fronts, Greek and Jewish, that the Christian revelation stands on its own—less, however, to seek another "order"

---

[7] Cf. Emmanuel Falque, "Larvatus pro Deo: Jean-Luc Marion's Phenomenology and Theology," trans. Robyn Horner in *Counter-Experiences: Reading Jean-Luc Marion*, ed. Kevin Hart (Notre Dame, IN: University of Notre Dame Press, 2007).

[8] Cf. Dominique Dubarle, "Révélation de Dieu et manifestation de l'Esprit dans la Philosophie de la Religion de Hegel," in *Manifestation et Révélation* (Paris, Beauchesne, 1976), 81–3.

[9] The word "latency" is derived from the Latin term *latere* (to hide), to which I refer here as the Eucharistic "manence" of the Latin *manere* (to dwell [demeurer]). On the creation of this word, see F. Cassingena: "'Gloire à toi ô Caché,' Aspects du binôme caché-révélé d'Éphrem de Nisibe," in *De la Révélation* (Conference at the Institut Catholique de Paris, June 10–11, 2016).

[10] For this phenomenological and no longer only methodological interpretation of the "Laravatus prodeo," I refer to Emmanuel Falque, *The Loving Struggle: Phenomenological and Theological Debates*, trans. Bradley B. Onishi and Luke McCracken (New York: Fordham University Press, 2018), 126–40.

[11] For the debate with Hellenism or *aletheia*, see J. Vioulac, *Apocalypse de la vérité*, op. cit., p. 112 (art. p. 466), although the question of the "removed veil" is not treated as such. Development on Jewish *Shekina* is still to be conducted.

than to link and convert the orders between them. Not everything is only a matter of "unveiling" or "manifestation," nor even of the cloud and apophasis, but also and above all—I will come back this—of "conversion" by which we ourselves become the place of "transformation." In the footsteps of Saint Paul, we need to remember again that it is only through conversion to the Lord (*epistrepsê pros kurion*) that the veil will fall (*periaireitai to kalumma*)" (2 Cor. 3:16). The path from "the apocalypse to revelation" and from "the revelation to the end of time" indicates the meaning of a Christian Apocalypse that holds together in "conversion" (*epistrepsê*) the idea of the "end times" and that of its "manifestation" (the amphibology of *apokalupsis*).

I. Apocalypse

Is there truly need for a "revelation"—in Judaism certainly, but also in Christianity, even in phenomenology (*apokalupsis* in the sense of "manifestation")? It is probably only in this way that the idea of an "apocalypse" (*apokalupsis* as "end of time," this time) is also revived in philosophy today, in the determination of a certain sense of truth. At play here is the Greek root of *aletheia*, or what Heidegger will call the "completion of metaphysics," including the "*Gestell*," or the Frame of the technical world, which marks, if not its culmination, at least the most comprehensive achievement: "we take *technique* here in a sense so essential that it is equivalent to that of completed metaphysics."[12] In this single formula and even equivalence between "technology" and "metaphysics," the spearhead and the line of conduct of an entire section of contemporary phenomenology is held. Following the Heideggerian step of overcoming metaphysics, at the same time, it condemns the entire technical world, or even modernity itself, sometimes without seeing it or even knowing it. We must not be mistaken. As Hegel says in the *Phenomenology of Spirit*, if the "beautiful soul devoid of effectiveness" can believe that it is only concerned with philosophical conceptuality (the overcoming of metaphysics), it generates no less for practice, and praxis itself, consequences that it would do well to evaluate (the denunciation of any form of technicality, or even progress).[13]

Certainly, we can declare—and we have not ceased to repeat following Heidegger's analysis of *The Question Concerning Technology* (1953)—that "the revealing [unveiling] that rules throughout modern technology has the character of a setting-upon [*provocation, Heraus-forden*]" and that in this respect "the energy concealed in nature is unlocked, what is unlocked is transformed, what is transformed is stored up."[14] Certainly, it is regrettable that the Frame (*Gestell*) "dammed up [the River Rhine] into the power plant" until it lost the meaning of Hölderlin's hymn ("The Rhine") that evokes the charms of the "old wooden bridge that joined bank with bank for hundreds of years."[15] Admittedly there is, this time with "What are Poets For?" (1946) likely a

---

[12] Martin Heidegger, "Le dépassement de la métaphysique" (1951), *Essais et conférences*, op. cit., p. 92.
[13] G. F. W. Hegel, *Phénoménologie de l'esprit*, GW 9, p. 577.
[14] Martin Heidegger, *The Question Concerning Technology and Other Essays*, trans. William Lovitt (New York: Garland, 1977/1953), 16.
[15] Heidegger, "The Question."

"danger" or even a "disaster" that is constantly growing, but "where there is danger, there also grows what saves" (Hölderlin).[16] Certainly, "poets in a destitute time" could well save us and invent or reveal to us "new gods," so that *The Thing* (1950) is also expressed in the "pouring of the jug" and the act of "outpouring" or the "holding of the vessel that occurs in the giving of the outpouring."[17]

However, a crucial point remains here, which Heidegger did not see or did not want to see. There is a kind of "obsolescence of existential analytics," as Günther Anders says—wherein the author of *Sein und Zeit* sticks more to the tools of his father, a cooper in the process of "hammering" (§12), than to Auschwitz, or Hiroshima, which gave humanity the total possibility of annihilating or self-mutilating. "[I]n *Being and Time*, factories do not yet exist, the analyses are not simply non-Marxist or anti-Marxist, they are pre-Marxist and even more so pre-capitalist."[18] It goes without saying that there is no question here of claiming any return to the purity of communism against the excesses of capitalism, nor of reactivating a class struggle that Günther Anders himself acknowledges is largely outdated or obsolete. It only remains to be noted that the world has shifted, and that the "poetry of pure manifestation" leaves open gaps into which Hannah Arendt, in *The Human Condition*, has rightly been able to rush ("labour," "work," "action").

Therefore, the Heideggerian and phenomenological diagnosis of a certain nostalgia for the past cannot leave us indifferent. Can we still and always claim an "apocalypse of revelation," whose philosophical name among the Greeks would be *aletheia* or unveiling, against an "apocalypse as the end times," whose contemporary name would this time be that of the essence of technology or the end of metaphysics, according to a massive decline of the West as responsible for its decline as its completion? In other words, should we still and always be drawn to the extremes, and how far will we go with a moving pendulum according to which we always predict the worst (end of the world or of a world) in order to see the best elsewhere (another world or new world)? This is a game that is all the more crucial, and even perverse, as I have shown elsewhere, since the island of poets or the pure discourse of phenomenology sometimes joins with the prophetic arguments of some believers, whereby the announced drift will only be suspended by maintaining or returning values anchored solely in nostalgia for the past.[19] In short, and it will be understood, the "accusation of the technical world" at the same time as the "overcoming of metaphysics" replays the game, in a way, of the pure discourse of phenomenology or the separation between orders, so that a structure of sin (the *Gestell* of the technical world or the nihilism of values) responds to a salvation expected from all eternity (the word of the poet or Christian prophetism). The apocalypse as "atastrophe" or "end times" establishes, and opens the space for, the apocalypse as "manifestation" or "revelation," less within the orders than in another

---

[16] "What are Poets For?," in *Martin Heidegger, Poetry, Language, Thought*, trans. Albert Hofstadter (New York: Harper Perennial, 1971), 115.
[17] "The Thing," ibid. p. 169.
[18] Günther Anders, *Et si je suis désespéré, que voulez-vous que j'y fasse?* (Paris: Alia, 2016), 15.
[19] "Seul un Dieu peut encore nous sauver," in Claude Dagens, Guy Coq, Emmanuel Falque, *Dieu est Dieu, quête d'une humanité commune* (Paris: Cerf, 2015), 134–208.

order, less within culture (in-culturation) than being far from culture or in another culture (or even a counter-culture).

The diagnosis is severe, and yet it bounces from phenomenology to theology, even to pastoral care, and vice versa. The declared Heideggerian opposition to modernity, as well as the recourse to a pure gift of meaning (*Gegebenheit*) or a revelation that emerges more from Protestantism (Luther or Barth) than from Catholicism (Thomas Aquinas or Newman), means that the God who "alone can still save us"—and before whom "to pray," "to fall on our knees full of fear," "to play instruments," "to sing and dance" is still worth the trouble—can in no way be called causality or *Causa sui*, precisely a monster of a metaphysics to be overcome by phenomenality.[20] Still less can and should the most divine god belong to any "natural" revelation, in a way that is always reducible to an "anthropology" that supposedly locks God up. At most, God will be reserved in purity for so-called "supernatural" or even "direct" revelation, to use the three meanings of revelation that are always held together in the tradition.[21]

Everything therefore happens as if, in phenomenology at least, the twofold maintenance of the "natural light of human reason" in Vatican Council I (*Dei Filius*, ch. 2) and the knowledge of God that "can be known with certainty from created reality by the light of human reason" at Vatican Council II (*Dei Verbum*, §6), had not been heard. Henri de Lubac and Henri Bouillard's lesson that it is necessary to preserve, at the heart of the dogmatic constitution *Dei Verbum* itself, a possible access to God by reason that is not only other than reason, but also inscribed in the very nature of humanity, has found little or no place in contemporary philosophy, so well trained in "apocalyptic disaster" that it does not construct its "apocalyptic revelation" so as to counteract the "danger" (Heidegger) or the "barbarity" (Michel Henry) of an "announced ruin," or the "end of time" and of "this time."[22]

II. Revelation

Is there then a fact that would characterize our particular modernity, and that would make a "revelation" or "pure gift," whether theological or philosophical, largely justified?

---

[20] Martin Heidegger, *Identity and Difference*, trans. Joan Stambaugh (Chicago: University of Chicago Press, 1969/2002), 72.

[21] The three meanings of the word "Revelation" are distinguished in Jean-Yves Lacoste, ed. *Dictionnaire critique de théologie*, Nouvelle édition revue et augmentée ed. (Paris: Presses Universitaires de France Quadrige, 2007), art. "Révélation."

[22] Against such a trend, we will see again here in Pope John XXIII's famous Opening Address to the Second Vatican Council, which was widely commented on elsewhere (*Quête de l'humanité commune*, pp. 143–208): "In the daily exercise of our pastoral office, we sometimes have to listen, much to our regret, to voices of persons who, though burning with zeal, are not endowed with too much sense of discretion or measure. In these modern times they can see nothing but prevarication and ruin. They say that our era, in comparison with past eras, is getting worse, and they behave as though they had learned nothing from history, which is, none the less, the teacher of life. They behave as though at the time of former Councils everything was a full triumph for the Christian idea and life and for proper religious liberty. We feel we must disagree with those prophets of gloom, who are always forecasting disaster, as though the end of the world were at hand." "Opening of Vatican Contuil II (11 October 1962)," in *Vatican Council II: The Conciliar and Post conciliar Documents*, ed. Austin Flannery, new rev. ed. (Dublin/Newtown, N.S.W.: Dominican/Dwyer, 1992).

Again, Günther Anders is the guide here, but with respect to this precise point—namely, that "he draws erroneous conclusions from a right intuition."[23]

First, the right intuition with respect to the "danger" that cannot escape us today and prevents us from sinking into a blissful optimism that would understand none of the challenges of our modernity. An absolutely new fact characterizes our time, which makes it less a feature of our contemporaneity than it challenges our very ability to survive. With Hiroshima and Nagasaki, and thus the possibility and even the effectiveness of nuclear destruction, "we have passed," emphasizes Günther Anders in *Le temps de la fin*, from the "mortal's genre" to the "mortal genre."[24] Finitude is no longer that of a particular person, or of every person, as Heidegger develops it in the anxiety of death, but that of humanity in general or the human species as such, which is capable of self-destruction and thus annihilation. "If something has changed," Anders radically asserts in *L'obsolescence de l'homme*, "it is worse: today, it is humanity as a whole that can be killed."[25] The era is no longer defined by nihilism, sticking simply to Nietzsche, or even to the silent euthanasia of Christianity, but to what Günther Anders calls "annihilism" (*Annihilismus*), or the "possibility of total annihilation."[26] "[T]he possibility of our definitive destruction constitutes the definitive destruction of our possibilities," he pertinently comments, taking up the anxiety of death, but extending it this time to the whole species.[27]

We can see with Günther Anders, therefore, that things are not better, and even go from bad to worse—hence the perhaps "mistaken" conclusion of a catastrophism that is radicalized to say the least, and which leads to a despair that seems to be the only motive to philosophize. While the Heideggerian "peril" or "danger" taken from the poet Hölderlin preserved in people the capacity to save themselves, either by leaving the technical world or by discarding technology (poetry or quadripartism), Gunther's annihilism involves us ourselves and all humanity in the capacity to self-destruct. Therefore, it does not leave and never leaves this threat that is based only on human beings: "we can no longer unlearn the methods of self-destruction," the philosopher notes with regret, since all the certainly justified attempts at "denuclearization" will not mean that this new possibility can be forgotten or ensure that it will not be acted on one day.[28]

It is at this point, then, and precisely in my view, that the "Apocalypse or the Revelation" (*apokalupsis*) as it is given in the last book of the Bible, and the "military, economic or political apocalypse" (annihilism) as it is played out in the work of Günther Anders and other contemporary authors, are joined.[29] The Apocalypse "of tomorrow" declared in the title of a prophetic Revelation by Saint John on the island

---

[23] Michaël Foessel, *Après la fin du monde: Critique de la raison apocalyptique* (Paris: Seuil, 2012), 13.
[24] Günther Anders, *Le temps de la fin* (Paris: L'Herne, 2007), 13–14.
[25] Günther Anders, *L'obsolescence de l'homme* (Paris: Ed. Ivrea, 2002) t. I, p. 270.
[26] Anders, *L'obsolescence*, 338.
[27] Günther Anders, *La menace nucléaire: Considérations radicales sur l'âge atomique* (Paris: Le Serpent à plumes, 2006), 9 (my emphasis). Cf. Jean Vioulac, *La logique totalitaire*, pp. 451–89.
[28] Anders, *La menace nucléaire*.
[29] For example, Jean-Pierre Dupuy, *Pour un catastrophisme éclairé* (Paris: Seuil, 2004), in particular p. 80: "we have acquired the means of destroying the planet, but we have not changed our way of thinking."

of Patmos cannot fail to be related to the Apocalypse "Now" from the *Heart of Darkness* by Joseph Conrad, adapted to cinema and retold in the context of the Vietnam War by the American director Francis Ford Coppola.[30] The end times in the Bible (apocalypse), as in the turbulent course of history (annihilism), are not only a threat for the future but also to the horizon of our present. We would still miss its occurrence if we maintained phenomenologically that "Revelation" as Manifestation is separate from Revelation as Finalization.

Let us only recall the Ten-Horned Beast, mentioned by Saint John (or the author of the book), and let us bring it back, even if by imagination, to the tidal wave or to the "desert and empty land" (*tohu wabohu*) produced by the explosion of the nuclear bomb in Hiroshima on August 6, 1945 or in Nagasaki on August 9, 1945. *Gegonen*—"It is done!" twice emphasized in the *Book of the Apocalypse* (Rev. 16:17 and 21:6).[31] But what is being done? The first time (Rev. 16:17), there was the most total "breakage," destruction, or "clash" in the "great city" of Babylon, like—later historically—Hiroshima or Nagasaki.

> "It is done!" And there came flashes of lightning, rumblings, peals of thunder, and a violent earthquake, such as had not occurred since people were upon the earth, so violent was that earthquake. The great city was split into three parts, and the cities of the nations fell. God remembered great Babylon and gave her the wine-cup of the fury of his wrath. And every island fled away, and no mountains were to be found; and huge hailstones, each weighing about a hundred pounds, dropped from heaven on people, until they cursed God for the plague of the hail, so fearful was that plague.
>
> Rev. 16:17–21

The connection here is certainly striking, although the difference between the "technical" or "nuclear apocalypse" (Anders) and the "religious apocalypse" (Saint John) cannot, of course, reduce the last book of the Bible to a simple catastrophe. But despite their differences, to which I will return, a same community of nature nevertheless remains between the two events (Babylon or Hiroshima). Nothing remains or holds up against the destruction or outburst of anger, not even the ark of survival that will prevent the "flood" in the first book of the Bible this time (Gen. 6:1–9:17). The destruction is total and the "annihilation" of the Apocalypse, to speak like Anders, is fully realized. It is as if human beings are struck by lightning, certainly with all that there is of their humanity, but also of this earth, or of this "original ark" (Husserl), where people are supposed to live.[32]

And yet, and this is the specificity of the religious apocalypse (Saint John) over the political or military apocalypse (Anders), nothing that has not been annihilated by

---

[30] *Apocalypse Now*, American film released in 1979 (winner of the Palme d'Or at the Festival de Cannes), an adaptation of the book *Heart of Darkness* by Joseph Conrad (1899).

[31] The repetition of "It is done!" is appropriately indicated by Christoph Theobald, *La Révélation* (Paris: ed. de l'Atelier, 2001), 98–102.

[32] Cf. Edmund Husserl, *La terre ne se meut pas* (1934) (Paris: Minuit, 1989).

God can so be visited. The "It is done!" (*gegonen*) of Babylon's destruction (Rev. 16:17) is answered by the "It is done" (*gegonan*) of God always with humanity (Rev. 21:6):

> And I heard a loud voice from the throne saying, "Look! God's dwelling place is now among the people, and he will dwell with them (*meta tôn anthrôpôn*). They will be his people, and God himself will be with them and be their God (*o theos met autôn*) . . ." He said to me: "It is done (*gegonan*). I am the Alpha and the Omega, the Beginning and the End. To the thirsty I will give water without cost from the spring of the water of life. Those who are victorious will inherit all this, and I will be their God (*autô theos*) and they will be my children (*moï nios*)."
>
> Rev. 21:3–4, 6–7

In what way, then, is the religious apocalypse "revelation," to justify this well named Book of Apocalypse or Revelation (*apokalupsis*)? With all due respect to Anders himself, it is in this way: that the "being with" of God—Emmanuel *cum Deo* and not only *pro Deo* or *coram Deo*—always remains there at the cataclysmic height from which, however, on my own, I will not be able to escape. Revelation does not imply, at least from my perspective, a rescue *a maxima* where God would come to pull me out in order to eradicate definitively the Beast in me who comes to destroy me, but a "being-there," or rather a "being-with," *a minima*, where God humbly stands with me to dwell there. Certainly, salvation is definitive and given "only one time (*hapax*)" (Heb. 9:28), or "once for all (*ephapax*)" (Heb. 9:12), with respect to the forgiveness of sins. But the "Word made flesh" always remains "to dwell with us," precisely espousing our condition as humans to the point of becoming the "flesh of sin" (Rom. 8:3: "For God has done what the law, weakened by the flesh, could not do: by sending his own Son in the likeness of sinful flesh"). Nothing remains foreign to him, whether it is our animality (salvation by solidarity), or our brutality (salvation by redemption). In *Le temps de la fin*, Günther Anders criticizes the Christian Apocalypse for waiting for or even hoping for the end (the coming of the Kingdom), whereas he fears it and even wants to prevent it (from nuclear destruction).[33] I will not respond, of course, that a cataclysm is to be expected or hoped for, but that a transformation of humanity must already take place in order to prepare people for the "new heaven" (*kainon octopus*) and the "new earth" (*kainen gen*) that God wants to make for them (Rev. 21:1). As proof, the first "It's done!" regarding the destruction of Babylon (Rev. 16:17) is read imperatively as a warning of an event that is to come (*gegonen* [with an "*e*"]), while the second "It is done" of the husband's visitation (Rev. 21:6) indicates that the action, in reality, has already begun (*gegonan* with an "*a*"]).

III. Transformation

The connivance of phenomenology with a certain form of theology, either in the condemnation of the present time (*arraisonnement* or nihilism) or in the revival of

---

[33] Anders, *Le temps de la fin*, pp. 111: "we are apocalyptic only to be wrong" (whereas the believer would be so to be right).

an absolutely different discourse (overcoming metaphysics or an order supposedly "separate" from the *theo*-logy) makes it necessary not "to remain here"—neither for the exclusive deplorability of the present nor for the hypothetical rescue of the future. On the contrary, it is up to the *Apocalypse* of Saint John, or Saint Paul's revelation, to hold that there is, in reality, never any revelation without "judgment" (*krinein*), and therefore without a "an appropriate time for today" (*kaïros*) by which the imminence of what is to come can keep us awake. "Rather than being seen in terms of received knowledge," we should say with Emmanuel Levinas in *L'au-delà du verset*, "should not the Revelation be thought of as this awakening?"[34]

The phenomenologist certainly knows how to "decide"—and perhaps this is proper—but rarely "commits" (even in the sense of *praxis*—Merleau-Ponty aside). In a way, he or she sees "phenomena passing by" as cows "see trains passing by," but never stopping them or boarding them. The opinion, and even the posture of the "disinterested spectator" (Husserl), means little in reality to an apocalypse that only calculates catastrophes (the end of the world). As for appealing to *Gegebenheit* as a "manifestation" or "revelation" (Heidegger), the request is not much help if it does not at the same time give the philosopher the means to be "inserted into the painting, taken from the theatre, and thrown on the stage," or even to suspend or accelerate the course of history already initiated.[35]

Jacques Derrida already remarks on this in his book on Marx (*Spectres de Marx*, 1993) with a reading that we should listen to today, at least so that we do not flee in the "revealed" a world that we reject all the more since we accuse it of always "collapsing." "The egological conversion is not enough," emphasizes the one who was also a phenomenologist, "nor is the change in the direction of a gaze, nor a putting into parentheses, nor the phenomenological reduction; one must work—practically, actually. One must think work and work at it."[36] Jean Vioulac, who is also a recognized phenomenologist (*La logique totalitaire: Essai sur la crise de l'Occident*, 2013) but who, at the same time, has become familiar with praxis and its necessarily transforming effects (*L'époque de la technique: Marx, Heidegger et l'accomplissement de la métaphysique*, 2009), then follows suit. The warning is surprising, but it also reminds us how much the apocalypse as "end times" necessarily leads to an apocalypse as a "revelation," but most often while forgetting what is necessary for "transformation."

> "It is certainly possible that the phenomenologist, by his functions, has the latitude to pull himself away from the Technological Frame (*Gestell*) in order to enjoy the intuition of the flowers in his garden or the beauty of masterpieces, and thus gain evidence of the carnal donation of the world; this would be losing the essential," insists the author, not without pugnacity, "since it is precisely a question of thinking about what tears the subject away from this world. The 'crisis' is that of humanity,

---

[34] Emmanuel Levinas, *Beyond the Verse: Talmudic Readings and Lectures*, trans. Gary D. Mole (Bloomington: Indiana University Press, 1994), 150.
[35] This formula was first addressed by Karl Barth to the theologian. *Karl Barth, Evangelical Theology: An Introduction,* trans. Grover Foley (Grand Rapids, MI: Eerdmans, 1979/1918), lesson 7.
[36] Jacques Derrida, *Specters of Marx: The State of the Debt, the Work of Mourning, and the New International*, trans. Peggy Kamuf (New York/London: Routledge, 1994), 163.

and there are seven billion of us on this planet: it is certainly not resolved because some of us would have managed to regain the primacy of a 'life-world'—and there is, in truth, aesthetic temptation and monastic withdrawal."[37]

It will be said here that the passion is engaged, and not to say the lightning sent. Under the courtesy of a polite statement, the decision is made that we cannot bypass ourselves any longer. Praxis (Marx) waits to rival or at least to find the *epochē* (Husserl), not only in the sense of auto-affection, to which a new reading must testify (Michel Henry, for Marx), but because the imminence of an apocalypse—whether military (annihilation) or religious (Christianity)—requires us to orient ourselves differently, even to allow ourselves to "change."

In reality it is "chaos" or "descending into the abyss" at the very idea of an end of the world and of our own species that no one can imagine, let alone face. Immanuel Kant completes his booklet *What is Enlightenment?* (1784)—a kind of apocalypse as "revelation" or belief in progress—then another booklet or essay *The End of All Things* (1794), a kind of apocalypse as "end of the world" or the collapse of everything, at least for those who would neither see (counter-revolutionaries) nor manage to think that the world is in decline. Precisely between the publication of the two booklets (1784/1794) there was, indeed, the earthquake of the French Revolution (1789). The few jolts felt in our contemporary situation may pale in comparison to what was changing then. The Reign of Terror seeks to impose itself (1793–4), which according to Kant should not only be explained politically, but also considered metaphysically.[38] "[Thinking of the end times] leads us, as it were, to the edge of an abyss: for anyone who sinks into it no return is possible ... for one cannot cease turning his terrified gaze back to it again and again."[39]

The same applies here to the terror associated with the disappearance or end of a world as it does to the fascination for eternity in *The Critique of Pure Reason*: "Here everything gives way beneath us, and the greatest perfection as well as the smallest, hovers without support before speculative reason, for which it would cost nothing to let the one as much as the other disappear without the least obstacle."[40] There is not only the reversal of the phenomenon in Kant, or the inversion of the banal or the ordinary into the sublime or the saturated. There also remains—and in my opinion this is the greatest difficulty—the "*Hors phénomène*," Blanchot's "Outside," or Bataille's "Heterology," which means that sometimes, and certainly rarely, ideas or situations cannot even appear, so much so that they come to frighten us and destroy our ability to phenomenalize them. What is true of the Apocalypse as "end times" and its impossible "revelation" for lack of horizon, is also true of "evil" or the "resistance of the *il y a*" in Levinas, of the "*Cinabre*" or of the "mass of sensations" in Kant, the "destruction of the being white of all whiteness" in Plato's *Theaetetus*, the "Evil Genius" or the "piece of

---

[37] Vioulac, *Logique totalitaire*, p. 21.
[38] A hypothesis that I take, to say the least, from Michaël Foessel, *Après la fin du monde*, 57–64.
[39] Immanuel Kant, "The End of All Things," in *Religion and Rational Theology* (Cambridge: Cambridge University Press, 1994/1794), 221.
[40] Immanuel Kant, *Critique of Pure Reason*, trans. Allen W. Wood (Cambridge: Cambridge University Press), 574.

wax" before the mind's inspection in Descartes' *Méditations métaphysiques*, or the "fiction of the annihilation of the world" in Husserl's *Ideas I* (§49).[41]

The apocalypse as "revelation" (*apokalupsis*) will not be satisfied, then, or will no longer satisfied, with simple contemplation, and even less with the vision of a spectator who is all the more "uninterested" in claiming "transcendence from on high" instead of justifying a destiny in which he or she neither wants to nor can engage. On the contrary—and Saint John, as Saint Paul, requires it—there is a real "crisis" or "judgment" (*krisis*) generated by the apocalypse understood as "revelation (*apokalupsis*) of Jesus Christ" (Rev. 1:1). In view of the imminence of the end, neither the subject nor the believer can be closed in their ipseity, and even less can they take refuge in any passivity. "Fear God and give him glory, for the hour of his judgement [or even of his crisis (*ôra tes kriseôs*)] has come," proclaims and warns the angel of the Apocalypse to those who have not prepared themselves for it (Rev. 14:7). Instead of being held in subjectivity, the subject "in crisis" is thus subjected in his or her subjectivation—not only called or required, but summoned to be committed, even challenged in order to submit to transformation: "For the wrath of God is revealed (*apokaluptetaï*) from heaven against all ungodliness and wickedness of those who by their wickedness suppress the truth (*aletheia*)" (Rom. 1:18).

There is no, or no more conflict here between "apocalypse" (*apokalupsis*) and "unveiling" (*aletheia*), or between Christianity and Hellenism. Instead, it is the Apocalypse itself (*apokalupsis*)—"Revelation of Jesus Christ" (Rev. 1:1)—that integrates and converts the unveiling (*aletheia*). Far from separating the orders—the "veil" of the Jew, the "unveiled" of the Greek, and the "uncovered face" of the Christian (*supra*)—the apocalypse as Revelation therefore now expects from the believer a true "transformation," even assumption of the difference without standardization or reduction. "And all of us, with unveiled faces, seeing the glory of the Lord as though reflected in a mirror (*katoptrizomenoi*)," Saint Paul indicated to the Corinthians (2 Cor. 3:18). Far from the "trace" (Levinas) or even the "icon" (Marion), the "mirror" or speculum emphasizes visibility even more here—"mirror" because we see not only God (trace or icon), but human beings in God (Trinitarian monadology). The mirror marks the "permanent reflection" as opposed to the temporary radiance of the face, and therefore of Moses' "veil" (*kalumma*). The verb "to reflect as a mirror (*katoptrizomenoi*)" is read here in the "middle voice" precisely as it is noted in the *La traduction œcuménique de la Bible*, which notes that "[the verse] expresses the participation of the subject as personally interested in the action, and transforms passive receptivity into active receptivity."

From today, then, and well before the time of the final judgment, we do not live uniquely "as a mirror" or see exclusively "through a mirror" (1 Cor. 13:12), but "we are ourselves a mirror." *Fit speculum*, "to be" or "to become" a mirror—such is the meaning of the apocalypse as a revelation, which Saint Bonaventure testifies to as the most perfect commentator. "The soul wants the whole world to be part of it," says the

---

[41] On this point I refer to my debate with Jérôme de Gramont in *Parcours d'embûches: S'expliquer* (Paris, Éditions franciscaines, 2016), §16, pp. 115–23, and the corresponding article from Gramont in "L'arc herméneutique d'Emmanuel Falque," *L'analytique du passage*: (Paris: Éditions franciscaines, 2016), 303–14.

Hexaëmeron or *The Six Days of Creation*. "When she sees all these objects, thus returning to herself, she becomes a very beautiful and pure mirror (*fit speculum*), in which she sees everything that is bright and beautiful, in the same way that we see the image in a polished mirror."[42]

If there is, therefore, an opportune time or a divine *kairos* on the day of judgment in the Apocalypse or the Revelation—"for the time is near (*o gar kairos eggus*)" (Rev. 1:3)—it will be less about contrasting "apocalypse" or "revelation" and instead thinking about "apocalypse" and "revelation."[43] *Revelation in the apocalypse*: God himself comes to seek us, or at least to dwell "with us in the depths of our darkness." *Apocalypse in revelation*: waiting measures our days so that the gap between the "already" and the "not-yet" measures the "soon" (*tachu*) that will still not be long. "The Lord, the God of the spirits if the prophets, sent his angel to show his servant what must happen *soon* (*en tachei*). And behold I come soon (*tachu*)."[44] We will therefore stand ready and thus be "unveiled" or "without veil" (*apo-kalupsis*)—not only to contemplate or to be overwhelmed, but by letting ourselves be capable of "transformation" or literally "metamorphosed" (*metamorphoumetha*) by the Lord in "ever-increasing glory" (2 Cor. 3:18). The *thought of transformation* (resurrection) is always at the same time the *transformation of thought* (apocalypse). "Do not be conformed to this world, (*tô aiôn toutô*)," Saint Paul ultimately confides to the Romans, thus tying together the two meanings of the apocalypse (end times and revelation), "but be transformed (*metamorphousthe*) by the renewing of your minds, so that you may discern what is the will of God—what is good and acceptable and perfect" (Rom. 12:2).

Translated from the original French by Jacob Benjamins

---

[42] Bonaventure, *Works of St Bonaventure: Hexaemeron. Conferences on the Six Days of Creation: The Illuminations of the Church*, ed. Dominic V Monti, trans. Jay M Hammond, Bonaventure Texts in Translation (St Bonaventure: Franciscan Institute Publications, 2018), col. IV, 6 (V, 349b), p. 175 ["the whole world is inscribed in it"] et col. V, 25 (V, 358a), p. 204 [*"devient miroir"*]. See also Emmanuel Falque, *Saint Bonaventure and the Entrance of God into Theology: The Breviloquium as a Summa Theologica*, trans. Sara Horton, Brian Lapsa, and William C. Hackett (St Bonaventure: Franciscan Institute Publications, 2018), 242–8.
[43] In the French: "*temps presse en effet* (o gar kairos eggus)." On this point see the remarkable philosophical commentary from Manuel Dieudonné, *Le temps presse: Lectures philosophiques de saint Paul* (Paris: Vrin, 2015).
[44] On this question I am referring to "anticipation" (*attente*) in Jean-Yves Lacoste, *The Appearing of God*, trans. Oliver O'Donovan (Oxford: Oxford University Press, 2018), 112–33.

9

Atheism and Critique

Anthony J. Steinbock

Our everyday experience can be characterized as a belief posture, as straightforwardly accepting what something is, and thus as a *participation in being*. Such a participation is carried out in perception, kinesthesis, judgment, and so on, and not only concerns sensible objects like tables, glasses, pens, or intellectual objects like propositions, judgments, mathematical entities, as well as imaginary objects of phantasy, and so forth, but also beings corresponding to emotional life such as a hoped for object, something desired, a past regretted. If plants, other human beings, beings other than human, and God are understood as being susceptible to such an accepting, then such a relation with them can also be characterized as a participating in being.

As is well known, phenomenology is a kind of reflection that radically shifts postures from straightforwardly accepting what something is to how this something is given. This shift in perspective is neither a doubt, a questioning, a negating, or an asserting. Rather, it is carried out so as no longer to presuppose being in any modality, and instead to understand the *meaning* of being in which we already participate; it is a posture that suspends accepting the "whatness" (being), provoking it to come into view as the *how* of givenness or *manner* of presenting being, and thus to see the very ways of accepting of being that arise in the first place. This "how" or "manner" is another way of expressing the *sense* or *meaning* of being.

Certainly, such a postural shift allows the attitude of taking things for granted to come into view *as* the "natural," "mundane," or "naïve" attitude. It is from such a phenomenological perspective that we can identify our perceptual, intellectual, theological relations, and so on, with being *as a participation in being as* meaningful (or *as* not meaningful), *as* sense-filled (or *as* non-sensical). Because it bears on all being whatsoever, phenomenology can be understood as a necessary radical atheism as no longer participating straightforwardly in being of any kind or in any modality. Phenomenology is a critical engagement with our participation *in* being that concerns our epistemic, vital, socio-historical, and normative existence. But there is also another kind of critique that emerges within the emotional sphere, one that I call discernment. Such a discernment can take place through a diremptive experience, like shame, or through a mindful attentiveness, a discernment of the heart. Both of these presuppose and are turned toward a dynamic *participating being*—or loving.

To elucidate these kinds of critique and to suggest their relation, I investigate possible motivations of critique and suggest that phenomenology as critical, radical atheism is not motivated. In a second part, I examine possible *incitements* to critique in the emotional sphere, like shame and the mindful attentiveness as the discernment of the heart. I conclude that epistemic critique is founded in a special kind of emotional critique, a discernment of the heart. Ultimately critical participating *in* being is founded in participating being or loving, from which discernment of the heart emerges. In this way, phenomenological atheism is founded in and incited by loving.

I. Thinking, motivation, and critique

What we understand by "critique" in part depends upon its problem-field. Our English term, "critique" (and similar Indo-European and Latin forms), derives from the Greek κριτική, and is related to κρίνειν, meaning to distinguish, to discern, to arrange, to divide, to dispute, to judge, to criticize, to make a decision, and so on. In a related fashion, a *crisis* is a turning point (medically, one can have a good crisis, according to Hippocrates), and can provoke decision-making, appraisal, passing judgments.[1] Accordingly, those things evidenced for decisive decision-making are called *criteria*. In what follows, I begin by examining the problem of critique within the specific project of phenomenological philosophy.

What we can glean from these initial linguistic clues is that critique involves some manner of making distinctions and decisive discriminations. For phenomenology, it entails a reflection, *a decisive turning that redirects* the movement of experience. More specifically, this means that we decisively turn from the ordinary flow of being (natural attitude) in order to let the things themselves (all beings) appear in whichever way they give themselves.

Acceptance of being takes place within the natural attitude. It is entirely "natural" because I presuppose *what* is to come in a straightforward relation with being. But this also means that it is "mundane" or "naïve" since it is, quite "naturally," not an investigation into its *how* of givenness.[2] If we take things for granted in a motivational relation, is there anything that provokes not taking things for granted as an original shift in attitude, something sufficient to provoke a "phenomenological" reflection? In short, is there a motivation of the natural attitude (a naïve motivation, a "natural belief") to get beyond the natural attitude or belief-posture and to see it as such?

Critique can take place in an intra-mundane way. I can criticize a paper; I can compare and judge actions according to accepted social norms, and so forth. These would belong to a "natural" critical attitude. Or critique can take place as phenomenological critique. Such a critique does not want to take for granted what something is but enquires into *how* this "what" is given, that is, being *as* given. It is a

---

[1] See Hippocrates, *The Book of Prognostics*, which includes chapters dealing with "crisis" and critical days.
[2] The affective force of a particular event, say, the sight of a rock cliff, can motivate an active recollection of a former place or event of climbing.

liberation of the phenomena such that what is, its very depth, is the appearing *as* it gives itself. The inquiry into the how of givenness, initiated by a shift in attentiveness, is understood as a clarification of being in terms of its meaning or sense givenness. The how of *givenness* immediately points to the how of *giving*. As a whole, this is the relational structure called "intentionality" or the intentional relation. Thus, when God is understood as a phenomenon of religion or religious belief, phenomenology is charged with *not* straightforwardly participating in being (here, "God"), but through reflection, clarifying the meaning of God. As all encompassing, phenomenology is most radically a phenomenological atheism.

Such a reflection is not an internal *Reflexion*, but what Husserl calls a *Selbst-Besinnung*, a self-reflection of a peculiar type. It entails two things. (1) The investigation into modes of givenness or the emergence of meaning immediately points back to the *participation of the "subject"* or to the first-person (singular or plural) contribution to meaning as accepting and/or transforming that meaning. This "self-reflection" points to our constitutive responsibility for the emergence of meaning.[3] Thus, phenomenological self-reflection not only gives an account of forms of epistemic participation, but it engages in a dynamic field of interactions. (2) Taking responsibility for the emergence of meaning implies that phenomenological reflection has normative import, not only in detecting constituted norms, but directing or re-directing experience in relation to them. In both respects, the phenomenological attitude is critical, pointing to the origins of meaning; through its self-reflective distance it is *disposed* toward eventual responsible critique *as* relational participating in being (and not straightforward participation in being). Phenomenological atheism, which is neither the doubt nor the assertion of God, is a form of epistemic and normative critique.

Letting the phenomena appear *as* they give themselves, the manners of givenness immediately point to "our" contributions (and to the limits of those contributions). These contributions disclose our participation in the emergence of meaning, and the possibility of our responsible engagement in this emergence according to the normative unfolding of sense-structures, not only the *meaning* of being, but the meaning of *being*.[4]

By motivation I understand an intra-mundane provocation.[5] Motivation does not function in the way that a cause-effect relation of necessity does. Rather, motivation can be characterized as a because-so relation, suggesting an openness of what is to come on the basis of what is given. Within a motivational relation we can observe what

---

[3] Since responsibility is always already given in the execution of the reduction, it does not look for pre-established outcomes. As I try to show in another work, responsibility is already established in the vocational givenness of me as person; when I realize its gratuitousness, and I am incited to take care of it.

[4] For some, however, phenomenology needs to be supplemented by "critique" in order to reflect on those plastic structures that figure our socio-historical, political co-existence.

[5] See Edmund Husserl, *Analyses Concerning Passive and Active Synthesis: Lectures on Transcendental Logic*, trans., Anthony J. Steinbock (Dordrecht: Kluwer, 2001). *Edmund Husserl, Ideen zu einer reinen Phänomenologie und phänomenologischen Philosophie*: Zweites Buch, Husserliana, vol. 4, ed., Marly Biemel (The Hague: Martinus Nijhoff, 1952). Anthony J. Steinbock, *Limit-Phenomena and Phenomenology in Husserl* (London: Rowman & Littlefield, 2017), esp. ch. 6.

Husserl has called an open possibility and an enticing possibility.[6] What is provoked (motivated) is based on something given in the present and immediately retained, and this couplet "protends" or passively forecasts what is to come. Depending upon what has been constituted, as well as the practical context of interests, something will be affectively significant for the perceiver either as an open possibility or as an enticing possibility. Does phenomenological self-reflection as epistemic critique—or more provocatively—does phenomenological atheism as radical criticism have any motivations? Husserl seems to identify at least three possibilities: wonder, alienness, and in a qualified sense, thinking freely.

Wonder. In his *Crisis* writings, Husserl identifies θαυμάζειν (*thaumazein*), or wonder, as the origin of philosophy for the Greeks, a posture that is not practical in a customary sense of being pragmatic or rooted in psychophysical intelligence oriented toward natural interests.[7] If *crisis* alone were a motivation for phenomenological critique, it would be contained precisely by pragmatic interests, and thus not be originary critique. By identifying wonder, on the one hand, Husserl is trying to identify a shift from practical interests to *theōria*. This transition (wonder) would give philosophy as phenomenological its factual motivation in the concrete framework of historical occurrences. This is why he wants to trace out the philosophical reorientation from "mere" *thaumazein* to *theōria* as the full, genuine science. Immediately recognizing this as a historical fact (the historical emergence and motivation of wonder), he cautions that there is still "something essential" about it.[8] In order words, even though we can identify a historical situatedness of its emergence which is a quasi-motivation, ultimately, it has no motivation in it, that is, it is irreducible to its temporal location.

Seemingly unsatisfied with leaving the matter here, Husserl then distinguishes, within *theōria* itself, doxic *theōria* from epistemic *theōria*, or again, between *theōria* of the natural attitude and *theōria* of the phenomenological attitude. For me, this just pushes back the issue concerning the motivation of the phenomenological critical attitude. That is, such a formulation still begs the question concerning the motivation for what he understands as genuine philosophy: If wonder is the motivation to *theōria*, how do we get now from doxic *theōria* (natural attitude) to epistemic *theōria* (genuine science, phenomenology, and so on)?[9]

Maurice Merleau-Ponty also appealed to "wonder" before the world in his *Phenomenology of Perception* to account for a motivation of phenomenological philosophy.[10] This wonder lets the world appear as "strange," as "paradoxical," as

---

[6] Husserl, *Analyses,* part 2, ch. 3.
[7] Husserl, *Crisis,* 285. Regarding wonder (*to thaumazein*) as the beginning of philosophy, see Aristotle, *Metaphysics,* 982b 12–17. See Adam Smith, *The Early Writings of Adam Smith,* ed., J. Ralph Lindgren (New York: Augustus M. Kelly, 1967) esp. 30–1, 33, 39. Wonder is an elaboration of surprise, concerning the singularity of the succession. See Steinbock, *It's Not about the Gift: From Givenness to Loving* (London: Rowman & Littlefield, 2018), ch. 1.
[8] Husserl, *Crisis,* 285.
[9] Recall that for Husserl the philosopher (phenomenologist) is receptive only to those "motivations" of a different type, not mundane ones, but rather those that occur within this phenomenological attitude or theoretical posture. Thus, they are not motivations in the strict sense.
[10] Maurice Merleau-Ponty, *Phenomenology of Perception,* trans. Donald Landes (London: Routledge, 2012), lxxvii.

"*problem*." In defense of Husserl, he writes that phenomenology does not make use of our relation with the world, but stands in wonder before the world, in order to see the world as such and as strange. Such a rupture with our familiarity teaches us the "unmotivated" upsurge of the world. On this score, both Husserl and Merleau-Ponty agree that historically and factically, our reflections take place in the historicity and temporal flow that they, our reflections, are trying to capture. Husserl even writes that the (generative) phenomenologist stands within Generativity.[11] However, it is one thing to write of the unmotivated *upsurge of the world* (Merleau-Ponty) and the fact that this implies that (phenomenological) thinking cannot encompass all thought, and it is another to address the issue of the *unmotivated upsurge of thinking*.

Alienness. Husserl considers implicitly a different motivation of phenomenological reflection as critical. Right after he shifts the issue of motivation to the transition from doxic to epistemic *theōria*, which is an impasse of its own, he moves to the question of the plurality of lifeworlds, because such a plurality motivates the question of truth (and objectivity). But the mere plurality of lifeworlds is not sufficient to get to the issue of critique since the lifeworlds must be qualified more concretely as social, geo-historical, normatively significant homeworlds and alienworlds as they exist in a co-foundational structure, as axiological asymmetrical.[12] Thus, it is the encounter with alienworlds in relation to homeworlds that he entertains—at least implicitly—as the new motivation for phenomenological reflection.

While it is only from the home that alienness can be encountered as such, it is in the encounter with the alien that the home can be brought into relief as home. Is this the beginning of phenomenological critical reflection? In the encounter with the alien as normatively significant (for example, as not optimal for us, as not typical for us, as not familiar for us, and so on), am I not—are we not—thrown back on ourselves in normatively significant ways that institute critique, and especially responsible critique? We might ask: Why do we do things in this way when others do it in that way? Could we do better than what we do now? Could we be different? Can the encounter of the Zen Buddhist from the perspective of an Abrahamic believer, for example, motivate a phenomenological atheism as a critique of the home?

In some respect, this not substantially different from the previous consideration of wonder: It turns out to be merely a modification from a wonder at the strangeness of the world to the wonder strangeness, which is different from me or from us. The issue of alienness and the alienworld is an elaboration of Husserl's constitutive theory of normativity, since the alienworld is experienced as a constitutively abnormal lifeworld (that is, as perhaps discordant, non-optimal, atypical, or non-familiar).[13] But "rupture," discordance, or the abnormal in general (in a constitutive regard), is not sufficient to provoke critical phenomenology for the same reasons that a broken hammer cannot motivate the question concerning the meaning of being.

Encountering alienness might be the condition for constitution of home as home, but I or we can still take the home for granted as home. It does not instigate the

---

[11] See Steinbock, *Home and Beyond*.
[12] See Steinbock, *Home and Beyond*, §§ 2 and 4.
[13] See Steinbock, *Home and Beyond*, especially §§ 3 and 4.

self-reflection on how the home gets constituted as such or initiate the normative considerations of what it means to be home. Further, the matter of alienness is not the same as an interpersonal encounter, being before other persons. Thus, there is another issue at stake and only implied here that involves the "alien" because we have implicitly moved into a moral sphere entailing persons and thus the schema of the heart. I return to this in part 2.

Thinking Freely. Despite these gestures, I think we should be suspicious of trying to give an account of the motivation of phenomenological reflection—at least where motivation is understood in the "intra-mundane" epistemic sense that I have described above. Husserl was perhaps more insightful in his very initial appeal to exercising the reduction in "full freedom" as the unmotivated movement that qualifies the phenomenological attitude as the genuine critical attitude emerges.

When we become aware of the natural attitude *as* the natural attitude, we are already beyond it as not taking our everyday acceptances for granted. Phenomenological reflection is a spontaneous movement that yields the "Reduction" and that discloses the relational movement of meaning, which immediately has normative significance. This movement (a phenomenological *Selbst-Besinnung*), does not have an agenda worked out in advance, since it "sees" along with the movement given in experience as it is unfolding. We do not start analyzing in order then to make this movement happen. This comes later or after this spontaneous movement of thinking is carried out. Despite Husserl's formulation of exercising the epochē in "full freedom," or that it is a matter of our "complete freedom," the implication is less that it is a capacity, cause, or motivation, than the fact that the reduction happens *freely*.[14] I say this without taking this "freely" as a freedom or a capacity to order to suggest that this phenomenological atheism is *its own self-sufficient source,* and without identifying it as my ability-to-do (my "I can") or my ability-to-be.[15] Thus, it is not really a motivation at all because it is not intra-mundane.[16] Thinking happens freely.

If we regard the *act of thinking* in its most radical sense, then, there does not seem to be a motivation for critique. Radical thinking, or radical phenomenological atheism, is an originating movement, an upsurge, coinciding with the opening to being as an originating emergence that breaks into our participation *in* being. It does not emerge from a mundane context, a constellation of acceptances, or pragmatic concerns. What could provoke it? In this sense, not even a crisis could provoke or motivate

---

[14] Edmund Husserl, *Ideas Pertaining to a Pure Phenomenology and to a Phenomenological Philosophy: First Book, General Introduction to a Pure Phenomenology,* Trans. by F. Kersten (The Hague: Martinus Nijhoff, 1982), §31.

[15] See Steinbock, *Moral Emotions: Reclaiming the Evidence of the Heart* (Evanston, IL: Northwestern University Press, 2014), ch. 1.

[16] For a different perspective on this matter, see Tom Nenon, "Freedom, Responsibility, and Self-Awareness in Husserl," in *New Yearbook for Phenomenology and Phenomenological Philosophy,* vol. 2 (2002) 1–21; Tobias Keiling, "Phänomenologische Freiheit in Husserls Ideen," in *Frei sein, frei handeln: Freiheit zwischen theoretischer und praktischer Philosophie,* eds. Diego D'Angelo, et al. (Freiburg: Alber, 2013) 243–71; Sebastian Luft, *Subjectivity and Lifeworld in Transcendental Phenomenology* (Evanston, IL: Northwestern University Press, 2011); Van Breda, "Husserl und das Problem der Freiheit," in *Husserl (Wege der Forschung),* eds., Noack, Hermann vol. 40 (*Wissenschaftliche Buchgesellschaft,* 1973).

phenomenological critique as radical phenomenological atheism. To see this originating movement of thinking as emergent from a constellation of acceptances, for example, from habit, from a thought-situation would be to presuppose its containment, and thus be unable to break into the participation *in* being, seeing it *as such*, and intervening in *meaningful* and *responsible* ways. Thinking in this radical sense is thus not motivated by anything in the natural attitude because it is itself the very essence of the natural attitude.[17]

The phenomenological critical attitude does not have a motivation (that is, a mundane motivation) that provokes a turn from participation *in* being then to grapple critically with the meaning of being.[18] What breaks into those participations is "thinking" that aligns itself—in Husserl's later terms—with Generativity.[19] In this respect, my spontaneous thinking as phenomenological atheism is a relation of thinking with Thinking.

This would be the implication of a non-motivated, thinking freely that first emerges as critical phenomenology as phenomenological atheism. However, I suggest that it already broaches another dimension, one that belongs to the schema of the heart. Phenomenological atheism is founded in discernment of the heart.

II. Critique as discernment of the heart

It is necessary not only to consider a participation in being that is subject to radical thinking, but also what I call in another work, "participating being" or *loving* and kinds of discernment relevant to the schema of heart. When we consider the possibility of phenomenological critique, we often leave aside the schema of the heart and possible normatively significant, interpersonal sources of critique that can influence change. But just as we should not dismiss all kinds of knowing just because they might be subject to error or require correction, so should we not dismiss the schema of the heart, its distinctive kind of cognition in relation to value, just because it might be subject to deception, self-illusion or require its own kind of "critique."

In my view, there are two types of critique within the schema of the heart understood as *discernment* (κρίνειν): a spontaneous diremptive experience (for example, shame), and mindful attentive discernment of the heart. They are motivated *as incited* by

---

[17] Thus, Husserl's assertion in the Kaizo articles that freedom is an expression for a habitual critical attitude is misleading. Or in this case, it would be a natural attitude critique. See Edmund Husserl, *Aufsätze und Vorträge (1922–1937), Husserliana 27*, eds. Tom Nenon und H.-R. Sepp (Dordrecht: Kluwer Academic Publishers, 1989), 63: "*Ein Ausdruck für eine habituelle kritische Einstellung zu allem, was sich geradehin als geltend.*" (I would like to thank Mohsen Saber for calling this passage to my attention.) Thinking, phenomenological thinking, occurs in the temporal flow, but it is not from or of the temporal flow. It occurs in historical fact but there is something "essential" about it, which is not from historical fact. Wonder that arises intra-worldly cannot itself be the motivation of that movement which critically, decisively, makes distinctions and lets appear those meanings. It emerges historically in the world, but is not itself mundane.
[18] This is one of Eugen Fink's observations in his "*Phänomenologische Philosophie Edmund Husserls in der gegenwärtigen Kritik*," in *Kant-Studien*, Vol. 38, 1933, 319–83.
[19] We might even say that thinking surrenders to Generativity.

movements of the heart, ultimately, loving. This means that there is not a critique *of* loving, but a critique *from* loving.

In order to explicate these two types of discernment (κρίνειν), let me first examine those kinds of emotional experiences in which I am called into question and are therefore able to place me in a critical posture. There are certain emotional experiences in which I am (a) thrown back on an experience and, (b) thrown back on myself, and thus called into question. It is the latter that pertains to critique. Let me explain.

III. Being thrown back on myself: shame

Being thrown back on an experience is not necessarily critique or critical reflection. For example, in surprise, I am thrown back on an experience.[20] The segment of experience in question has a temporal duration that is minimally constituted from a present and retention, which provokes a protention as accepting of what is to come, fulfilling the style of that givenness. Surprise emerges in the discordance of that expectation, and for this reason is called a "disequilibrium."[21] If I am surprised, I need not examine the situation further. On the one hand, "I cannot believe it." But in order to be constituted as surprise, I have to believe what I cannot believe: I accept what I cannot (in this instance) accept. This is the inner dynamic of surprise, and even though surprise is an emotion (as distinct from a startle-reflex) it does not necessarily provoke critique. It still operates within the *participation in being as an accepting what I cannot accept.*[22]

In distinction to this, being thrown back on myself is a "diremptive" experience and is distinct from a disequilibrium. There are several types of diremptive experiences: shame, guilt, embarrassment, and so on. These are emotions in the sense that they are lived as *personal* (that is, in the dimension of personhood), and they are moral emotions in the sense that they are fundamentally interpersonal. Shame is always and fundamentally an interpersonal experience since it is always before some personal other, imaginary or real, individual or collective.[23]

As can be seen more clearly in the case of shame (but evident as well in the other diremptive experiences), a diremptive experience presupposes a personal orientation that is constituted as basic (like a spatial level is constituted in aesthetic experience), and on the basis of which another experience is given that calls this personal character orientation into question. This dehiscence, tension, or diremption is essential to shame.

To be constituted as shame, it is sufficient that the basic orientation is challenged (more than an occasional infraction, which would yield embarrassment), but not to such an extent that the basic orientation becomes something entirely different, that is, a new orientation, or from a third person perspective, "shamelessness."[24]

---

[20] Steinbock, *It's Not about the Gift*, ch. 1.
[21] Steinbock, *It's Not about the Gift*, ch. 1.
[22] On the relation of surprise and wonder, see Steinbock, *It's Not about the Gift*, ch. 1.
[23] Steinbock, *Moral Emotions*, ch. 2.
[24] Ibid.

Contrary to many theories of shame, shame is not possible without a genuine self-love and positive self-valuing. By loving, I understand the dynamic movement of givenness toward the emergence and flourishing of what is possible—an opening to all that "is" as bearer of value in all of its distinctive value-magnitude; loving is a personal movement that lets be the other (any other) of its own accord as it *is*, inciting (not provoking) it to peer out a little further in terms of its being-becoming.[25]

Our loving, then, as an act, is the improvisational, free, creative positive affirmation of this movement, as generative of this movement in a personal manner.[26] I further understand it as *participating being*. I write this "participating being" without any preposition like "in," "of," "with" where loving is concerned because of the direct, immediate presencing through which we, well, participate the other. It is how we can understand loving as "devotion."[27] By genuine self-love, I mean the self-givenness of *personal* uniqueness, and being oriented toward the depth of who I can become as person.[28]

Shame is a feeling of a fundamental *tension* that is founded in genuine self-love: shame is a response of a consciousness directed toward higher values and at the same time and on the basis of which a lower-level act is oriented.[29] (Debilitating shame has the same structure of self-love, but is a result of a disoriented heart and hating from another.) It is by virtue of the experience of the positive value of one's self that an act or event giving rise to shame can be weighted as negative and as a general experience of diremption. This movement is fundamental for other modes of shame that we might experience, be they political, moral, social, economic, or ecological, and they in their turn express this dimension of self-revelation.[30]

I am indeed called into question in the experience of shame, and it is a kind of spontaneous discernment, and therefore "critique." As Levinas writes, shame is the experience of my unbridled and unjustified freedom, my mastery, being called into question and highlighted as in need of justification.[31] If shame is not tainted by any kind of disordered heart or hating, then I am thrown back on Myself such that shame

---

[25] It is originary, responsive, participatory, normative, and limitative. Anthony J. Steinbock, *Knowing by Heart: Loving as Participation and Critique* (forthcoming, Northwestern University Press).

[26] See Anthony J. Steinbock, "Hating as Contrary to Loving," in *New Yearbook for Phenomenology and Phenomenological Philosophy*. Vol.XVII. Part 1: Phenomenology, Idealism, and Intersubjectivity: A Festschrift in Celebration of Dermot Moran's Sixty-Fifth Birthday, eds., T. Burns, T. Szanto, and A. Salice (London/New York: Routledge, 2019).

[27] "Participating the other" is an expression I take from A. R. Luther's *Persons in Love: A Study of Max Scheler's Wesen und Formen der Sympathie* (The Hague: Martinus Nijhoff, 1972).

[28] We could also say that in self-love, one is given as God's image of me with and for others, not the image I merely fashion of and for myself.

[29] See Max Scheler, "*Über Scham und Schamgefühl*," in *Schriften aus dem Nachlass*, Band 1: Zur Ethik und Erkenntneslehre (Bern: Francke, 1957), 67–154. Jim Hart, in his discussion of shame, also holds that shame always presupposes original self-love. See James G. Hart, *Who One Is*. Book 2: Existenz and Transcendental Phenomenology (Boston: Springer, 2009), 338–51.

[30] See Anthony J. Steinbock, *Phenomenology and Mysticism: The Verticality of Religious Experience* (Bloomington, IN: Indiana University Press, 2007/2009), chapter 8. That this dimension of shame is "primary" in relation to other kinds of shame, or that it is "primary" in relation to an experience like guilt does not mean that it comes first temporally, but that it is more fundamental to the person in and through its self-revelatory dimension.

[31] *Totality and Infinity* trans. Alphonso Lingis (Pittsburgh: Duquesne University Press, 1969), esp. 83–9.

reveals "me," in my depths, "Myself" as relational and as not self-grounding; I am called into question. When something emerges to elicit shame, I am moving against a more basic orientation that is sufficient to call me into question. I am not being "Myself." When it bears on my existential core, I am not being Myself as who I am in my calling (or vocation) through which I respond to the call to love or to be-love. Ultimately, this is my orientation *as beloved*, as receiving Myself from another and as toward another (the Holy, another beloved, and so on).[32]

But I am not merely called into question in shame; I am called into question as from another. In fact, only when I am as "before" some other is it possible to experience shame.[33] Thus, I am criticized from another as before another, calling me to responsibility; and I am thrown back on Myself as dynamic and relational. Thus, shame is already more than an "encounter" with alienness or strangeness, or even an alienworld.

This does not mean that shame is only something like self-critique.[34] The schema of the heart has its own structure of evidence and is not relegated to an "internal sentiment." On the basis of an insighting through loving, it is also possible to see how others, or how we as a society, are not living up to who they or we are or can be. There is no contradiction here, but it presupposes a loving-openness in and through which and according to which the other person or persons are self-revealing in their value-essence, and not for example, simply a one-sided attempt "to empathize" or worse, to dominate or manipulate.

Accordingly, the critique of the heart is not most profoundly a criticism of something, but an aid to participation: to participate responsibly in being as a calling us back to *participating being* (loving). Of course, I can critically examine this or that situation and still not return to Myself—something probably all of us have experienced.

Shame is not a rational critique of who I am according to some external norms, but a spontaneous discernment of the heart that yields a tension, a going against Myself or my "ideal" value-image as before another.[35] Shame can *incite* a return to Myself (to my deeper self or vocational self); shame can elicit this turn, but it is not itself a normative redirection.

The actual re-turning to Myself is repentance (*t'shuvah, metanoia*). Repentance is the redirection instigated, for example, by shame (or guilt, and so on), but guided by the other toward the future, and toward Myself as how I have received Myself as from another; hence, repentance is a revolution of the heart. In shame we are thrown back on ourselves, in repentance, we creatively turn back to Ourselves, renew/re-orient Ourselves as from another. I creatively return to Myself to love more deeply. Shame is one way that gives a clue to how we can redirect the situation in which we coexist so that we can live appropriately in the "center" or at the core of this movement and not lose our orientation.

---

[32] Or in Scheler's terms, my "good-in-itself-for-me," or in still other terms, my "vocational personhood."
[33] Where there is no personal other in some manner, there is no shame.
[34] Shame highlights my participation in the relation. In fact, since shame is always already interpersonal, shame concerns reorienting or readjusting our selves with and before others; it is immediately a relational (interpersonal/inter-Personal) concern, having social, political, economic, aesthetic, and so on, implications.
[35] As guilt is not a spur to a rational critique of who I am in terms of what I have done or not done.

Shame, however, is not sufficient unto itself since there can also be deceptions of the heart. We only need think of examples of debilitating shame that arise through hatred or abuse, or experiences like humiliation.[36] In these cases, even shame itself requires a critical, mindful discernment of the heart.

IV. Discernment of the heart

How do I determine that my actions or even my feelings are from loving and not, for example, a result of spite or springing from an unnoticed *ressentiment* attitude? How do I resolve that my shame or guilt is expressive of a genuine orientation to Myself from loving, and not, for example, animated by a hateful self-image that I have taken over from another or social norms? How do I recognize that my engagement with a project is done from devotion rather than from pride? Is this process different from attempting to determine if a feeling or emotion is "appropriate" at this time or that it is "justified" in this situation?

We can begin by noting that a "critical reflection" pertaining to the heart is a distinctive kind of discerning (*krinein*), namely, a mindful *discernment of the heart*. I take this discernment "of" in both the genitive and the accusative senses: discernment belongs to the heart (as from loving) and discernment's matters of concern are the matters of the heart.

Even though there are rational judgments and rational reflections on all sorts of matters, the dimension of spirit is not exhausted by rational reflection, which rational reflection is susceptible to epistemic critique. Spirit encompasses other kinds of "reflection" operative within the order of the heart. Although shame is "reflexive," since I am thrown back on Myself as being given to myself, shame is not a discerning reflection in a mindful or attentive way. If there is a critique of the heart understood as discernment, what kind of reflection is it and how is it distinct from, say, a rational reflection (which has its own properties and appropriate spheres) or for example, shame or guilt, which are immediate forms of emotional critique?

By way of initial orientation, I mean by *mindful* discernment several things. (1) It is not a reflection on experience, but an attentive reflection within experiencing, as it is happening; or rather, it is an attending to experience as it is ongoing, an intensification rather than a separate act of reflection on a passive or active experience.[37] (2) It is not a measure of experience according to external norms or expectations, but a deep resonance or dissonance that resounds as if a gift of awareness; it is a clarity that comes as if it were from without, but aligns the value-preference as from within (like in the vocational "I can't do otherwise" or "this is not me").[38] (3) It does not concern a self as isolated from others or from a situation, but bears on a personal relatedness, which is to say, it pierces the interconnectedness of personal being as within the articulated

---

[36] Steinbock, *Moral Emotions*, chs. 2 and 8.
[37] Patrick H. Byrne, *The Ethics of Discernment* (Toronto: University of Toronto Press, 2016) 81.
[38] I treat these experiences in the next work, *Vocations and Exemplars: The Verticality of Moral Experience*.

unity of being; (4) it is not a self-consciousness, but a "self"-transformation; (5) it is accompanied by spontaneous indwelling humility that becomes deeds, and is not initiated as the control over one's self with anticipated outcomes.

I am not suggesting that in different contexts we cannot gauge actions or feelings according to anticipated goals. I am not suggesting that we cannot judge whether or not, say, an experience of envy or jealousy has motivations or is (or is not) appropriate in a particular situation. There is a rich tradition in virtue ethics, for example, that takes up our discriminative ability to judge when and how right action is required for particular circumstances.[39] Some suggest that it depends on narrow or broad character traits, and/or on the concrete situations in which we find ourselves making practical decisions; others consider the possibility of growth and diminution of virtue and even stages of virtue to determine appropriate emotions (like in the case of patience); still others address questions concerning the place and efficacy of character traits, the normative status of virtues, and the significance of rule-based ethical theories.[40] Certain phenomenologists, describing the intentional and cognitive structure of emotions, consider the implications for judging related emotional experiences (like anger and indignation).[41] This is different still from accessing from objective perspectives whether an action is virtuous depending upon a target-based theory, an agent-based theory of pure motivation, or a mollified agent-based account.[42]

My main claim is that this *mindful discernment of the heart* emerges from the heart; it is not a third person arbitration of whether or not a belief is justified, having the right attitude, or, for example, adjudicating a feeling like hope or an act of trust as appropriate or inappropriate. This may seem to be similar to the example I cited above regarding shame (and debilitating shame). But discerning the difference between a shame that arises from a well-ordered or disordered heart, or even discerning between shame and humiliation (and thus a debilitating shame) is not the same as determining if that same shame is justified, even if the questions are linked.

Mindful discernment, as in the previous example, hones in on the significance of emotions that we were experiencing all along, but whose meaning was at that time perhaps opaque, confusing, or ambiguous. The judgment of the latter presupposes the process of discernment that is involved here. That is, in order to determine that this shame (a debilitating shame, say) is not appropriate or justified in this instance would mean that I (or we) have already detected that it is not oriented toward future growth,

---

[39] I would like to thank Samara Steinbock for calling these sets of issues to my attention.
[40] Rachana Kamtekar, "Situationism and Virtue Ethics on the Content of our Character," in *Ethics* (2004) Vol. 114, No.3, 458–91; Christine Swanton, "Developmental Virtue Ethics," in *Developing the Virtues: Integrating Perspectives*, eds., Julia Annas, Darcia Narvaez, Nancy E. Snow (Oxford University Press, 2016), 116–35; Jesse Prinz, "The Normativity Challenge: Cultural Psychology Provides the Real Threat to Virtue Ethics," in *The Journal of Ethics* (2009) Vol. 13/ No. 2/3, 119–44.
[41] John J. Drummond, "Anger and Indignation," in *Emotional Experiences: Ethical and Social Significance*, eds., John J. Drummond and Sonja Rinofner-Kreidl (London: Rowman & Littlefield, Int., 2018), 15–30. See too, John J. Drummond, "The Intentional Structure of Emotions," in *Logical Analysis and the History of Philosophy/Philosophiegeschichte und logische Analyse* (213) 16: 244–63 and John J. Drummond, "Having the Right Attitudes," in *The New Yearbook for Phenomenology and Phenomenological Philosophy* (2017) 15: 142–63.
[42] See, for example, Liezl Van Zyl, "Virtue Ethics and Right Action," in *The Cambridge Companion to Virtue Ethics*, ed., Daniel C. Russell (Cambridge: Cambridge University Press, 2013), 172–96.

that it is holding me in a fixed "now" that it presupposes my being made an object to myself and to another, that it is not a returning to a "deeper Myself," that my disorientation is not simultaneously revealing a deeper orientation as a way of being, and thus not even a genuine shame, and so on. On the basis of this discernment, it is "therefore" judged not to be an appropriate shame or a justified action. Accordingly, discerning whether an experience is pride, or instead, being proud of something—which are two different kinds of experiences—is not the same as determining that any pride is unjustified. Pride—in the sense that I have attempted to understand it in other works—is never "justified," even if one can attribute reasons for it. Being proud of, however, is related to a value-perception of the other and my relation to this other, so it would be subject to a discernment of the heart in a different way depending upon, for example, these or those historical or personal circumstances, my heritage, acts of preparation, bravery, violence, accomplishments, and so on.

In his impressive work on discernment within the context of Bernard Lonergan's thought, Patrick Byrne understands discernment not only as a refined kind of attentiveness oriented toward the richness, diversity, and value-differentiations of things experienced, but as also oriented toward one's own way of being attentive, as discerner. He notes that along with Aristotle, Paul of Tarsus understood discernment to be rooted in a special capacity for self-understanding, though the latter experienced this as an extraordinary gift from God.[43] But it was not until Ignatius of Loyola that the practice of discernment was linked to spiritual exercises to attain or to enhance this givenness, providing guidelines or "rules" for discriminating between subtle movements or spirits.

Discernment, then, would not "simply" be a matter of discerning between good and bad spirits, but of discerning the presences of holiness, and distinctive depths of experiences.[44] Are they genuine experiences differentiated from another? Are they deceptions, self-deceptions, maladies, and so on?[45] In Lonergan's development of this practice, Byrne asserts, discernment is conceived as "self-appropriation." Self-appropriation is the process of making myself my own (or taking up myself as Myself), the process of self-transformation through coming to know and to affirm knowing, valuing, and deciding for oneself, culminating in freely choosing to live in fidelity to that value of being a knower, valuer, and decider, as rooted in loving.[46] This self-appropriation as self-transformation entails another dimension of critique as

---

[43] See Byrne, *The Ethics of Discernment*, especially, ch. 1.
[44] Ignatius of Loyola, "Autobiography," trans., Parmananda R. Divarkar in *The Spiritual Exercises and Selected Works*, ed., George E. Ganss, S.J. (New York: Paulist Press, 1991), 71.
[45] We find in St. Teresa of Avila a distinction between what comes ostensibly of our own efforts, and infused prayer; within the latter we can discern between the prayer (or the presence of God) of quiet, the prayer of spiritual delight, the prayer of rapture, and so on. In Rabbi Dov Baer, we can discern the distinctions between the natural and divine ecstasies, and within each of them, different intensities and the presence of God (*nefesh, neshamah, ruach, chayyah, yechidah*). We find in Rūzbihān Baqlī distinctions between states and stations, and in the latter, for example, myriad stations, like the station of laughter and the station of intimacy, annihilation of self, and so on. See Steinbock, *Phenomenology and Mysticism*.
[46] Byrne, *The Ethics of Discernment*, 31–5.

discernment (*krinein*), namely, a "deciding" (in the root sense of *decisio,* from *decidere* or "determine," or parcel out, "distinguish"): a decisive movement following out the discerning of value, which is also existing morally or ethically.[47] We might want to call it a preferring according to the way in which values are presented in loving.

In a related manner, Richard Kearney understands discernment to be part of what he calls the "anatheist" wager that is not a matter of belief (Pascal), but an *existential* wager. It is existential because we are already ahead of ourselves participating the other—here the stranger—in a way that might be disorienting and puzzling, but never irrational or impossible, as if the meeting with the other person, like the divine, were a "blind date." Still, discernment is not a matter of consenting to any other just because they are other.[48]

To engage in discernment as critique, in distinction to epistemic critique, is to be enveloped by "mystery" and not simply in relation to a "problem"—to borrow a distinction from Gabriel Marcel.[49] Certainly, epistemic critique need not merely be oriented toward problems in the world with which we deal therapeutically or pragmatically; in the case of phenomenological critique, it grasps the world (or God) as a whole, as *problem*. But as problem in this sense, it is still relative to me or to us, more or less corresponding to me and correlative to my efforts to expose it *as* problem. Mystery, however, is not something relative to my efforts to disclose it; it is not object-like, *gegenständlich*, or even the horizon in which there is an object. Mystery, as Marcel puts it, is "meta-problematical" because it is, I would say, already participating being and not simply participating *in* being. As Marcel suggests, it envelops me and it comprehends me, even if it is not comprehended by me. I am already participated before I could chose (that is, already "beloved"), but in a way that *solicits* participating being: "it might even be shown that the domain of the meta-problematical coincides with that of love."[50]

If phenomenological critique can be exercised as radical atheism, discernment of the heart leads us back to Loving as vigilant movement, dis-posing or re-disposing ourselves to Loving, that is, to let be as what the other (any other) can become. Through this, we can remain attuned critically to this deeper enduring activity as vigilant, and without rendering it static. The discernment of the heart points back to Ourselves—as given from Loving in a way that distinguishes it from among all the clamorous and competing sentiments and feelings. Discerning this feeling as distinct from another so as to respond, discernment is the listening to what is an obstacle and what is a way forward, being mindful of what is from me and what is from "without," what is merely for me (pride) and what is for another.[51] This is done, however, without any pre-set path because it issues from a solicitation to unfold in the way we are, which is creative and inexhaustible.

---

[47] Byrne, *The Ethics of Discernment*, 92, 297–306.
[48] Richard Kearney, *Anatheism: Returning to God after God* (New York: Columbia University Press, 2010), esp. 44–7.
[49] Gabriel Marcel, *The Philosophy of Existentialism*, trans., Manya Harari (New York, The Citadel Press, 1968), esp. 9–46. See also the distinction between "enigma" and "noema" in Levinas.
[50] Marcel, *The Philosophy of Existentialism*, 22, 20.
[51] See Jules J. Toner, S. J., *A Commentary on St. Ignatius' Rules for the Discernment of Spirits* (St. Louis: The Institute of Jesuit Sources, 1982).

This discernment, furthermore, operates in a two-fold way. First, it is an *interpersonal process*, as seen in the mystics in relation to an exemplary figure or a mentor, confessor, or guide, whose "authority" is grounded in experience. Mindful discernment werke can also be effective like this when I see another as they love, hence they can be personally *exemplary*, since we are able to identify loving in the personal loving. It is normative in a different sense; it is not living according to pre-established norms since the exemplar (who is fundamentally personal) is founding for such norms.[52] In their own way, several of these authors in the tradition of virtue ethics appeal to the *exemplar, the model* (and emulation) as another source for gaining such insight; for Max Scheler in the phenomenological tradition, such an interpersonal source for such a discernment of the heart founds impersonal norms.[53]

Second, it is a *historical* process, suggested by their (the mystics') attentiveness to the "fruits" of their experiences understood to be from the Holy, even though they could not predict those outcomes. It is essentially tied to the moral or ethical dimension as love of stranger or love or neighbor.[54] Because I might be living in a disordered heart, I might not be able to discern well what experience is from loving or what is from *ressentiment* or even hating. This is why mindful discernment is accompanied by the interpersonal and historical dimensions, though this admittedly presupposes that the others upon whom I rely or with whom I am in dialogue have the depth of experience and well-ordered heart that can guide toward loving/Loving; it presupposes that they are able to confirm genuinely—from their depth of experience—that this is the actual experience that I am living through at this time.[55]

The point of discernment for the mystics—who are just natural human beings seeking the source of their experience as human—is not ultimately to see if they are having the experiences of God; it's not about accepting or rejecting the experiences— "*it's not about the gift*."[56] If it were, it would miss the loving. The point is to realign themselves with Loving in order to serve more deeply (as love of neighbor, as welcoming the stranger, and so on) There is an intertwining of the religious and the moral, and this founds the epistemic dimensions our lives.

The point is that critique as discernment is not just practicing a criticism of this or that thing. It brings us back to Loving. The discernment of the heart aids us in re-participating the beloved and to realign ourselves with Loving. In this regard, critique as discernment of the heart is an appropriate term. But here critique is involved in the experiencing, re-directing the participating, and not something like "critical thinking." It is loving that furnishes its own *criteria* for critique as discernment since discernment is a critique *from* loving, not *of* loving. Thus, it is not "motivated" in the intra-mundane

---

[52] See Max Scheler, *Formalismus in der Ethik und die Materiale Wertethik, Gesammelte Werke* Vol. 2. Ed. Maria Scheler. Bern: Francke, 1966. And see Scheler, "*Vorbilder und Führer*."
[53] Prinz, "The Normativity Challenge." See also Nancy E. Snow, "How Habits Make us Virtuous," in *Developing the Virtues* (ch. 6), 2016; Max Scheler, "Vorbilder und Führer," in *Schriften aus dem Nachlaß*, vol. 1 (*Gesammelte Werke*, vol. 10), ed., Maria Scheler (Bern: Francke, 1957), 255–344.
[54] See Steinbock, *Phenomenology and Mysticism*, chs. 2–4, and "Conclusion."
[55] See Steinbock, *Phenomenology and Mysticism*, chs. 1 and 5.
[56] See Steinbock, *It's Not about the Gift*.

epistemic sense but is *incited*. It is not an exercise in thought, but guided by loving to participate creatively, generatively the other.

In sum, there are two kinds of critique as discernment of the heart: a spontaneous one, shame, and a mindful discernment of the heart. The *incitement* for critique (discernment) is peculiar to the sphere of the emotions. Rather than an intra-mundane motivation, it moves from Loving (infinite Person) to loving (finite person), and as a compelling evocation that is not compelled; it is movement of loving (finite person) aligning itself with Loving (infinite Person), soliciting loving.

Insofar as I grasp being loved in any way, that loving essentially "demands" a responsive loving. Or put differently, existentially, any beloved who "grasps" or in any way awakens to generative loving is constituted as person such that this grasping is already a loving movement, a loving "response" to loving in that movement. It belongs to the essence of loving already to be *evocative* of loving without intending a loving response. Thus, to reply to the issue of motivation, I suggest that it is generative Loving that "motivates" but *in the way of inciting* critique as mindful *discernment of the heart*.

V. Conclusion

If loving as movement peculiar to the heart is "participating being," what is its relation to epistemic participating in being? What is the relation of critique as discernment to critique as phenomenological atheism?

Cognitive critique understood through epistemic thinking radically as phenomenological atheism is founded in cognitive (emotional) critique incited by loving; or again, the non-motivated critical thinking freely of phenomenological reflection as atheism is ultimately "motivated" *as incited* by loving, since thinking freely is founded in loving (holiness). This would be an atheism from loving, which coincides with Loving. No knowledge as an ontological relation, and no consciousness (as *conscientia*) as the knowledge of knowledge, is possible without loving as this most radical taking-part, this transcending movement [toward] different being as letting become.[57] Accordingly, the whole person is engaged more profoundly or participates more deeply "in" the unity of the object through loving than if it were by knowledge "alone."[58] As loving is founding for knowing, participating being for participating in (positing) being, the mindful discernment of the heart is ultimately founding for epistemic critique. It is possible to participate God (in loving) without participating in God (in belief). In fact, there are experiences that are essentially religious in terms of their structure, without intending "God." Hope is one of these experiences.[59]

---

[57] Max Scheler, *Erkenntnis und Arbeit*, in *Gesammelte Werke*, vol. 8, ed. Maria Scheler (Bern: Franke Verlag, 1960), 204; English translation by Zachary Davis, *Cognition and Work* (Evanston, IL: Northwestern University Press, forthcoming).
[58] Dietrich von Hildebrand, *The Heart: An Analysis of Human and Divine Affectivity* (South Bend, IN: St Augustine's Press, 2007), 37.
[59] See *Moral Emotions*, ch. 5.

If we understand the relation of Loving (infinite Person) and loving (finite person) as religious experiencing (not as a belief in God peculiar to a religion),[60] then phenomenological atheism as a radical epistemic critique is not only compatible with religious experiencing and the mindful discernment of the heart. Phenomenological atheism is founded in such a religious experiencing, and epistemic critique incited by critique as discernment.

---

[60] See *Phenomenology and Mysticism*.

Part Three

The Phenomenality of the Religious

10

The Death of God—Sartre against Heidegger

Philippe Cabestan

While for centuries we have wondered about the mystery of the cross, the resurrection, and the last judgment, we have to admit that these questions, today, hardly occupy people's minds. You would almost wonder how Christians ever killed each other in the past. Sacré-Coeur Cathedral, Sainte-Chapelle, and Notre-Dame of Paris are now historic monuments—"tombs and funerary monuments of God," writes Nietzsche—which are visited and photographed each year by millions of tourists, just like the Great Wall of China, the Rialto Bridge or the temple of Angkor Wat.[1] Let us ask our question without further ado: what happened? How can we interpret such an event? In response, sometimes we just repeat the madman's claim: "God is dead."[2] In fact, ordinary people today seem to believe no more in the existence of God than in that of the gods of Antiquity, even though the latter passed for that as obvious in their time—even if this evidence should not be overestimated.[3]

Yet to say that God is dead is far from satisfactory, since the claim is ambiguous. The event is, *par excellence*, the object of what Paul Ricœur calls the conflict of interpretations. One of them seems particularly significant. Indeed, some sixty years before the publication of *The Gay Science* (1882), Auguste Comte prophesied of the death of God.[4] In accordance with the law of humanity or the law of the three stages, he announces the inevitable triumph of the positivist mind, that is to say of the scientific mind over the metaphysical and theological mind. In other words, the positivist spirit

---

[1] Friedrich Wilhelm Nietzsche, *The Gay Science*, ed. Walter Kaufmann (New York: Vintage Books, 1886/1974), §125.
[2] Ibid.
[3] "For gods there are, since the knowledge of them is by clear vision." Epicurus, Letter to Menoeceus, in Cyril B Bailey, *Epicurus: The Extant Remains* (Oxford: Clarendon Press, 1926), 83/84. This assertion, which has nothing to do with a disguised atheism as has sometimes been argued, must not, however, obscure the fact that atheism proper "was already quite widespread at the time" and even before, as Plato testifies. Plato, *The Laws*, Book X, trans. Benjamin Jowett. Aristophanes echoes a certain skepticism when the first servant asks the second, "Say, do you really believe in the gods?" Aristophanes, *Acharnians Knights*, ed. Jeffrey Henderson (Cambridge, MA: Harvard University Press, 1998), 235.
[4] "Plan of the Scientific Work Necessary for the Reorganization of Society," in *Comte: Early Political Writings*, ed. Auguste Comte and H. S. Jones, Cambridge Texts in the History of Political Thought (Cambridge: Cambridge University Press, 1998). This text exposes for the first time, in 1822, the law known as that of three stages.

is called to deliver humanity from the chimeras of the imagination, specific to its childhood, so that one day animism, polytheism and monotheism will be only a vague memory, for which a new religion is called to be substituted: the positive religion of humanity.[5]

Whatever its weaknesses, let us not underestimate the importance of this concept, that has left a lasting impression. It is undoubtedly one of the sources of Max Weber when he elaborates, at the beginning of the twentieth century, the notion of disenchantment of the world (*Entzauberung der Welt*). In his text of 1919, with undoubtedly Promethean accents—"The Profession and Vocation of Scientist"— Weber maintains that, "for millennia" men are subjected to a process of intellectualist rationalization which we owe to science and scientific technique.[6] This process leads one to think that "in principle, then, we are not ruled by mysterious, unpredictable forces, but that, on the contrary, we can in principle control everything by means of calculation." With this conviction, the author can announce to the younger generation that "[its] fate is to live in an age alien to God and bereft of prophets."[7]

To tell the truth, if we evoke this interpretation of the death of God, it is because it seems to us that it should not hold our attention for long. On the one hand, far from relying on the work of historians who would give it a shadow of positive legitimacy, it has an eminently speculative character which makes the givens of history cheap. We could also show—by taking up Claude Lévi-Strauss's criticism of false evolutionism— that it rests on a form of ethnocentrism which makes it possible to take the West for a superior civilization, one that is ahead of the others.[8] On the other hand, if the philosophy of the Enlightenment has accustomed us to speak of religion in the singular, believing we have discovered behind the different religions of humanity a single, natural religion, it is undoubtedly advisable to handle this concept with caution and, as a rigorous historian, not to confuse very different spiritual phenomena from each other. We persist in ignoring their heterogeneity and singularity when we just classify them under the categories of animism, polytheism and monotheism. In short, religion is undoubtedly a convenient but dangerous abstraction and fertile with false problems.

So, in the following pages I would like to place readers in a different tradition and consider the antithetical way, so to speak, in which two figures in the history of phenomenology envisage the death of the Christian God. I think of Martin Heidegger and his essay: "The Word of Nietzsche: God is dead."[9] But first of all, I also think of Jean-Paul Sartre, a resolutely atheistic phenomenologist.

---

[5] Auguste Comte, *System of Positive Polity* (London: Longman, Greens and Co., 1875/1966).
[6] Max Weber, "Science as a Vocation" (1919), *The Vocation Lectures*, ed. David Owen and Tracy B. Strong, trans. Rodney Livingstone (Indianapolis: Hachette, 2004) 8.
[7] Weber, "Science as a Vocation," 12–13, 28. One might be tempted to include Marcel Gauchet's reflections on society outside religion as an extension of Max Weber's work. However, while using the term disenchantment, Marcel Gauchet moves away from Weberian rationalism by placing this process within the framework of a history of social relationships of which political structuring, by means of the advent of the State and democracy, puts an end to the power establishing religion. Marcel Gauchet, *The Disenchantment of the World: A Political History of Religion*, trans. Oscar Burge (Princeton, NJ: Princeton University Press, 1997).
[8] Claude Lévi-Strauss, *Race and History* (Paris: UNESCO, 1952), 13.
[9] Heidegger, "The Word of Nietzsche: 'God is Dead,'" in *The Question Concerning Technology and Other Essays* (New York: Garland, 1977).

I. Sartre, the unbeliever

Although belonging to the last century, the case of Jean-Paul Sartre seems significant for our time in many respects. Born in 1905, the same year as the passing of the French law separating Church and State, Sartre grows up in a Christian environment: his grandfather Schweitzer is Protestant; his Catholic mother and grandmother are raised by the nuns.[10] On Sundays, Sartre sometimes accompanies his mother and grandmother to mass. But the truth is that neither of them are very active. Quite simply, as Sartre writes, "the faith of others inclines them to musical ecstasy. They believe in God long enough to enjoy a toccata."[11] In *Les Mots*, Sartre reports how without warning, at the age of 12, he lost the little faith he had: "One morning in 1917, in La Rochelle, I was waiting for some schoolmates with whom I was to go to the lycée. They were late. After a while, not knowing what else to do to occupy my mind, I decided to think of the Almighty. Immediately He tumbled into the blue and disappeared without giving any explanation. He doesn't exist, I said to myself with polite surprise, and I thought the matter was settled."[12] What is remarkable in this story is the way in which the idea of God disappears: without pathos and without explanation. In other words, the idea that God does not exist is not a conclusion but an "obviousness" all the less debatable and all the more solid as it is perfectly irrational, and it imposes itself on Sartre, who feigns astonishment to hide his indifference.

In his interviews with Simone de Beauvoir, published after *Farewell to Sartre*, Sartre returns to this episode by adding some details. Above all, he returns to the way in which this "revelation" imposed itself on him: "I do not know where this thought came from, how it struck me; I suddenly said to myself: but God does not exist!" When Beauvoir, skeptical, urged him to find "the work which preceded this intuition," Sartre confirmed its suddenness even if he held it to be illusory, insofar as it is in his eyes necessarily the result of work which essentially escapes him.[13] It is thus a matter of what he calls his idealist atheism—an atheism limited to the abandonment of an idea without this abandonment affecting his relationship to the world. Simply, God is no longer part of it. It was only years later, following conversations with Paul Nizan, that Sartre realized—to use his expression—that "the absence of God must be read everywhere." In other words, Sartre is gradually moving from an idealist atheism to a materialist atheism which he defines as "the universe seen without God."[14] Such an atheism is not obvious because it requires a new conception of being, which can only be the fruit of an ascesis methodically eradicating all remains or vestiges of religion in its relation to the world. So, it is not enough to say that God does not exist in order to be completely rid of religion, and Sartre recognizes that he has long remained trapped in this promise of salvation through writing, which has been the great occupation of his life and which he

---

[10] Annie Cohen-Solal, *Jean-Paul Sartre: A Life*, trans. Anna Cancogni (New York: The New Press, 2005) 54.
[11] Jean-Paul Sartre, *The Words*, ed. Irene Clephane, trans. Irene Clephane (London: Penguin, 2000), 27.
[12] Sartre, *The Words*, 250.
[13] Simone de Beauvoir, *Adieux: a Farewell to Sartre*, ed. Jean-Paul Sartre (Harmondsworth, Middlesex: Penguin, 1985), 434.
[14] Ibid., 435, 436. Trans. modified.

holds for a form of religion. In this sense, as he writes, atheism, otherwise known as the authentic assumption of contingency, "is a cruel and long-range affair."[15]

These first considerations, however, relate only to the person of Sartre, even if what is at stake is part of the broader context of a civilization. Curiously and unless we are mistaken, Sartre rarely approaches the death of God as such. It may be objected that the death of God is at the heart of his play, *The Devil and the Good Lord*, whose action takes place during the German Peasant War (1524–6). We may recall: after having exhausted himself to do Evil in order *to be* immoral, then to do "the Good in order *to be* moral," Gœtz discovers that God does not exist.[16] He says to Heinrich: "Heinrich, I am going to make you aware of a great trick: God does not exist. He does not exist. Joy, tears of joy! Alleluia."[17] The fact remains that this awareness, which parodies the night of the memorial, remains strictly individual and that Sartre does not give it the meaning of a historic event. Additionally, the problematic of the play is much more moral than metaphysical.[18] The same is true when, recalling Dostoevsky's "if God does not exist, everything is permitted," Sartre concludes that there are no transcendent demands and that man is without excuse. In other words, he cannot hide behind any moral prescription which would be imposed upon him categorically.[19] If Sartrian existentialism acknowledges the death of God and places man face to face with his responsibilities, at the same time, he seems not to care about the event itself.

II. Relative indifference

In an article dedicated in 1943 to *Interior Experience* by Georges Bataille, Sartre evokes the death of God, on which he comments briefly as follows: "God is dead: we do not mean by that that he does not exist, or even that he no longer exists. He died: he spoke to us and he is silent, we touch only his corpse."[20] Obviously, Sartre recalls Nietzsche but, unlike the madman, the event does not "worry him more than that." No doubt Sartre is aware that it is not the same for everyone; Bataille is one of those men who has still not recovered and whom Sartre calls survivors. Like Nietzsche, Heidegger or Jaspers and like modern man, Bataille would be tormented by this silence of the transcendent and the permanence of his religious need. In *Cahiers pour une morale*

---

[15] Sartre, *the Words*, 147.
[16] *Notebooks for an Ethics*, trans. David Pellauer (Chicago: University of Chicago Press, 1992), 3.
[17] *The Devil & the Good Lord, and Two Other Plays*, trans. Sylvia Leeson, George Lesson, and Kitty Black (New York: Knopf, 1960) Act III, scene 4.
[18] Michel Contat and Michel Rybalka, eds. *The Writings of Jean-Paul Sartre*. 2 vols. Evanston, IL: Northwestern University Press, 1975.
[19] Jean-Paul Sartre, *Existentialism is a Humanism*, trans. Carol Macomber (New Haven, CT: Yale University Press, 2007), 28–9. From a similar perspective, Sartre writes: "If God does not exist, we have to decide by ourselves on the meaning of Being." *Notebooks for an Ethics*, 486.
[20] Jean-Paul Sartre, "Un nouveau mystique," *Situations*, t. I (Paris: Gallimard, 1947), 133–75, 142; "A New Mystic," *Critical Essays (Situations 1)*, trans. Chris Turner (London: Seagull Books, 2017).

(1947), Sartre again briefly mentions the death of God.[21] Then he simply notes: "The great historical change: the death of God, replacement of the eternal by the temporally infinite. During the time of God, man was inessential in relation to the Eternal unmarked by time. Today, God has fallen into time."[22] We understand that history, the idea of infinite progress, has taken over and replaced the idea of God.

How are we to understand this relative indifference? A first explanation can be drawn from Sartrian ontology and, in a sense, from divine immortality. Indeed, *Being and Nothingness*, like the *Notebooks*, gives a very special place to the idea of God as self-causing or *Ens causa sui*.[23] It goes without saying that this God is not the God of Abraham, Isaac and Jacob. This God corresponds instead to the idea of God that Descartes made his own, but that Thomas refused for the simple reason that God cannot precede himself.[24] More fundamentally and beyond the history of philosophy, this idea of a self-causing God is inscribed, according to Sartre, in the being of human-reality and finds its source in the desire to be God who haunts the for-itself. In *Being and Nothingness*, after having established that the for-itself is lacking and that this lack has for its object the impossible synthesis of the in-itself-for-itself, Sartre declares: "Let no one reproach us with capriciously inventing a being of this kind; when by a further movement of thought the being and absolute absence of this totality are hypostasized as transcendence beyond the world, it takes on the name of God."

Man is, therefore, the being who projects being God but who only succeeds in realizing a failed God.[25] Hypostasis of the desire to be of the for-itself, the self-causing God is not an invention of historically dated philosophy but an anhistoric or transhistoric idea, inscribed in the being of man. This is why, against all odds, Sartre is considering an eidetic description of God.[26] The project can be confusing: can we imagine an eidetics of Athena or Mercury? But in the case of God the project is far from absurd, even if the idea of God is contradictory and God does not exist. Thus, at the conclusion of a long analysis of the *Ens causa sui*, Sartre writes: "As soon as it *is* without having been, its concept is identified with that of Being. In this way, the *Ens causa sui* is its own nothingness. But nothingness of what? Nothing founded: he has the responsibility of having to be his being without being the foundation of this being ... So God is an inauthentic man, thrown into the vain task of founding himself and who cannot be created because he already is."[27]

---

[21] According to certain specialists, Sartre would have devoted a long study to Nietzsche (not found) within the framework of his *Notebooks for an Ethics*, of which one finds an echo in *Saint Genet*. V. de Coorebyter, *Sartre avant la phénoménologie* (Brussels: Ousia, 2005) 202; *Saint Genet Actor and Martyr*, trans. Bernard Frechtman (Minneapolis: University of Minnesota Press, 2012), 346–50. J.-F. Louette, *Sartre contra Nietzsche* (Grenoble: Presses Universitaires de Grenoble, 1996).

[22] *Notebooks for an Ethics*, 84.

[23] *Notebooks for an Ethics*, 516.

[24] René Descartes, *Réponses aux premières objections*, Œuvres philosophiques, t.II, édition F. Alquié (Paris, Garnier, 1967) 527.

[25] Jean-Paul Sartre, *Being and Nothingness: A Phenomenological Essay on Ontology*, trans. Hazel E. Barnes (New York: Pocket Books, 1978), 80, 615, 20, 22, 23, 27.

[26] *Notebooks for an Ethics*, 469.

[27] *Notebooks for an Ethics*, 520. We could add to this eidetic that God is gaze, hypostasis of the other as objectifying gaze. It is in this sense that we must understand this definition: "Religion: hypostasis of the Other who transforms us into an absolute object for a freedom that is never an object" (16).

There is another explanation for this relative indifference of Sartre which, closely dependent on the one we have just exposed, lies in his conception of history at the time of the *Notebooks*. Indeed, Sartre maintains that "Everything is in every era."[28] In other words, contrary to what Hegel maintains in *The Phenomenology of Spirit*, history is not a succession of figures of consciousness, which would find its fulfillment in absolute knowledge. For, even if bad faith hides certain aspects of his condition from him, man is immediately "absolutely aware of his condition." For example, from Antiquity, Epicureanism developed a rationalist and materialist conception which corresponded to this form of reason which Hegel projected much later in the *History* under the name of observant consciousness. Similarly, if, for Aristotle, master and slave are so by nature, for Socrates, there is "unity of the Spirit in the Master and in the Slave." Sartre concludes that "[an] era is always infinitely complex because everything is given to it and because it is instead the emphasis placed on certain aspects of the human condition." From this point of view, the communist ideal is as old as the world and "Christianity must have existed in polytheism as a personal relation of some men to some gods. And reciprocally, Christianity is polytheism for many people (the saints and the Virgin)."[29] Each epoch is thus a nebula of contradictory possibilities and is distinguished, however, by the emphasis placed on certain aspects of the human condition. We then understand that the death of God is entirely relative insofar as Christian monotheism is a possibility enshrined in the human condition, which, as such, cannot be a thing of the past.

This "conception" is, however, relatively fleeting in Sartre's work. Developed after the war, it precedes the turn made at the very beginning of the fifties in the direction of Marxism.[30] From then on, Sartre develops a philosophy of history which, without necessarily excluding the previous one, is intended to be strictly materialist. The understanding of history is based on so-called unsurpassable evidence, articulated by Marx in *Das Capital*, according to which "the mode of production of material life generally dominates the development of social, political and intellectual life."[31] From this point of view, the death of God, like Christianity or the Protestant reform, is a spiritually derived event which, like the *Declaration of the Rights of Man and the Citizen*, depends on the evolution of material conditions of social existence and class struggle. Would we go so far as to say that this is a non-event? This would undoubtedly go too far and yield to a theory of reflection that Sartre resolutely rejects.[32] But one might think that Sartre, roughly adopting the Marxist conception of religion, is led to ignore the event of the death of God as such. Because religion, as Beauvoir wrote in 1954, has long served as an ideology for the ruling class, the fact that atheism triumphs is, all in

---

[28] Ibid., 91.
[29] In *The Women's Assembly*, Praxagora proposes to "communize all the land, money, and other property that's now individually owned. We women will manage this common fund with thrift and good judgment." Aristophanes and Jeff Henderson, *Aristophanes* (Cambridge, MA/London: Harvard University Press, 2007), 323. Sartre, *Notebooks for an Ethics*, 92.
[30] *Etudes sartriennes*, N°23, "Sur les concepts d'Histoire. Sartre en dialogue."
[31] Jean-Paul Sartre, *Search for a Method*, trans. Hazel E. Barnes (New York: Alfred A. Knopf, 1963), 33–4.
[32] Sartre takes the theory of reflection as pre-Marxist. In other words, while recognizing in the theory of reflection the merit of awkwardly situating knowledge in the world, Sartre criticizes it for ignoring the negativity of thought, or rather of consciousness, which reveals the object. *Critique of Dialectical Reason*, trans. Andrew Sheridan-Smith (London: Verso, 1991/1975), 30.

all, welcome news.³³ Sartrian materialism joins in its own way the positivism of Auguste Comte whose faith it shares, if not in the order, at least in the progress of humanity.³⁴

III. Methodological atheism

We can already foresee the gulf or even the abyss that separates Heidegger from Sartre. It should be remembered, however, that for Heidegger as for Husserl, philosophy cannot be confused with faith and that both profess a methodological atheism. Indeed, a Jew converted to Protestantism and defining himself as a "non-dogmatic Protestant," Husserl subordinates phenomenology to the parenthesis of any transcendent object, including God, even if the transcendence of God would be distinct from that of the world.³⁵ However, his readers know that the figure of God reappears from the 1920s onwards in unpublished manuscripts as well as in his conference in Vienna (1935).³⁶ Husserl distinguishes between the national gods who belong to the surrounding world and the concept of God, bearer of the absolute *Logos*. It is a matter, then, of a new figure of God, who must obey the eidetic laws, who can no longer be conceived as a creative God and who announces himself indirectly in the sphere of absolute immanence.³⁷

Heidegger, for his part, is born in a Catholic milieu in Messkirch and is initially destined for the priesthood. It is in 1911, at the age of twenty-two, that he interrupts his theological studies to devote himself to philosophy. However, there can be no question of Heidegger confusing one and the other since, as he writes in 1922, philosophy is fundamentally atheistic. This is an affirmation that he reiterates in 1925 by specifying that it is "precisely in this atheism that it [phenomenology] becomes, as someone great once said, the 'gay science.'"³⁸ At the time of *Being and Time*, Heidegger therefore

---

[33] "For a long time religion has taken the place of ideology for the privileged," writes Simone de Beauvoir who qualifies her remarks a few lines below, however, by recognizing the ambiguity of Christianity: certain Christians "deny that God is in the pay of the powerful of this world" and concludes the paragraph as follows: "the fact is that the rating of God has dropped a great deal." Simone de Beauvoir, "Right thinking, today." Published in *Les Temps Modernes* in 1954, this essay is included in a collection entitled *Faut-il brûler Sade* (Paris, Gallimard, 1972) 112.
[34] "[W]e must believe in progress. And that, perhaps, is one of my last naïve ideas." Jean-Paul Sartre and Benny Lévy, *Hope Now: the 1980 Interviews*, trans. Adrian van den Hoven (Chicago: University of Chicago Press, 1996), 61.
[35] Edmund Husserl, *Ideas Pertaining to a Pure Phenomenology and to a Phenomenological Philosophy*: First Book, General Introduction to a Pure Phenomenology, trans. F. Kersten (The Hague: Martinus Nijhoff, 1982), §58, p. 134.
[36] Edmund Husserl *Grenzprobleme der Phänomenologie: Analysen des Unbewusstseins und der Instinkte. Metaphysik. Späte Ethik (Texte aus dem Nachlass 1908–37)*, vol. 42, *Husserliana* (Dordrecht: Springer, 2014). Adelgundis Jaegerschmid, "Conversations with Husserl," *New Yearbook for Phenomenology and Phenomenological Philosophy*, 1: 331–50 (2001). The Vienna Lecture is published in Engliah as an appendix in *The Crisis of European Sciences and Transcendental Phenomenology. An Introduction to Phenomenological Philosophy*, trans. David Carr (Evanston, IL: Northwestern University Press, 1970).
[37] Husserl, *Crisis*, 188ff. Françoise Dastur, *Questions of Phenomenology: Language, Alterity, Temporality, Finitude*, ed. Robert Vallier, trans. Robert Vallier (New York: Fordham University Press, 2017), 180.
[38] Martin Heidegger, *Phenomenological Interpretations of Aristotle: Initiation into Phenomenological Research*, trans. Richard Rojcewicz (Bloomington, IN: Indiana University Press, 2008); *History of the Concept of Time: Prolegomena*, trans. Theodore Kisiel (Bloomington, IN: Indiana University Press, 2009), 80, trans. modified to bring out the link with the Nietzschean text in English.

advocates a methodological atheism which requires, as he recalls in his conference of 1928, a rigorous separation of philosophy and theology.[39] However, it is important not to be mistaken about this methodological atheism. The rule, like the adjective atheist, suffers from a certain ambiguity. It does not mean that for the philosopher, God does not exist. Atheism is not, in this case, the negation of God but only a methodological principle which allows phenomenology not to be mistaken about itself and the specific task which falls to it. It is in the name of this necessary division that Heidegger takes the concept of Catholic phenomenology to be "even more inept than that of Protestant mathematics."[40]

In his 1928 lecture, Heidegger rigorously clarifies the respective places of phenomenology and theology as well as the relation of unilateral dependence of theology as a positive science *vis-à-vis* phenomenology as a primary science.[41] Indeed, Christian theology—which should not be confused with philosophical theology, which is part of onto-theo-logy—is, according to Heidegger, a positive science. Like all positive sciences, Christian theology has a pre-given—in this case Christianity (*Christlichkeit*) or the event of the cross.[42] On this subject, Heidegger writes: "that being which is primarily revealed to faith, and only to it, and which, as revelation, first gives rise to faith, is Christ, the crucified God."[43] In other words, theology has no other object than the historical event of the sacrifice of Christ as it occurs through faith. But theology as a positive science of faith is no less dependent on phenomenology in the sense that, in general, any adequate ontic interpretation necessarily rests on an ontological foundation. Thus, the theological notion of sin, for example, is understood from the being of *Dasein* and more specifically from the existential of guilt (*Schuld*) and being-guilty (*Schuldigsein*).[44] The recognition of this dependence implies no confusion and, if religion is "a fundamental possibility of human existence," it is no less for Heidegger "of a type quite different from philosophy."[45]

---

[39] "Phenomenology and Theology (1927, 1970)," in *Pathmarks*, ed. William McNeil (Cambridge: Cambridge University Press, 1998), 41. Jean Greisch, "Interlude: phénoménologie et théologie," *Ontologie et temporalité. Esquisse d'une interprétation intégrale de Sein und Zeit* (Paris, Presses Universitaires de France, 1994), 427ff.

[40] *The Basic Problems of Phenomenology*, trans. Albert Hofstadter, rev. ed. (Bloomington, IN: Indiana University Press, 1988), 20.

[41] Jean Greisch, *Ontologie et temporalité*, 436; Françoise Dastur, *Heidegger et la pensée à venir* (Paris: Vrin, 2011) 144–5.

[42] This distinction is repeated in "Nietzsche's word 'God is dead,'" where Heidegger opposes Christianity, which is "the historical, secular and political manifestation of the Church" and the Christianity of New Testament faith which corresponds to "what is Christian," in Martin Heidegger, *Off the Beaten Track*, trans. Julian Young and Kenneth Haynes (Bloomington, IN: Indiana University Press, 2002), 164.

[43] Martin Heidegger, "Phenomenology and Theology," trans. James G. Hart and John C. Maraldo in *Pathmarks*, ed. William McNeil (Cambridge: Cambridge University Press, 1998), 44.

[44] *Being and Time*, trans. John Macquarrie and Edward Robinson (Oxford: Blackwell, 1962); "Phenomenology and Theology (1927, 1970)."

[45] Letter to Elisabeth Blochmann, August 8, 1928, cited by Jean Greisch, *Ontologie et temporalité*, pp. 432–3.

IV. The dispute with Nietzsche

This articulation of phenomenology and theology is the subject of a re-elaboration during the 1930s which must be re-understood in the light of the "turning point" (*Kehre*).⁴⁶ Strictly speaking, there can be no question here of a theological turning point, in the sense that Heidegger would somehow reconnect in one way or another with Christianity.⁴⁷ It is at this time that, questioning the onto-theological essence of philosophy, Heidegger wonders what would be, consequently, an authentic understanding of the divine, that is to say, the divine God or Deity (*Gottheit*). With this term—taken from Meister Eckhart—Heidegger distinguishes between, on the one hand, the Christian God, the Almighty, the supreme being, creator of heaven and earth and, on the other hand, the Deity or god of the poets.⁴⁸ This god is then one of the four dimensions (*Geviert*) of the world understood as the unity of heaven and earth, mortals and gods.⁴⁹ And it is naturally to this god, whose absence or flight characterizes these times of distress that modern times are, that Heidegger relates when, taking up in his own way the theme of the death of God, he declares that our time "is marked by a double lack and a double negation: the 'no longer' of the gods who have fled and the 'not yet' of the god who will come."⁵⁰

The affinity with Nietzsche, "the most intimate adversary," is manifest here.⁵¹ It is hardly surprising in this regard that Heidegger, between 1936 and 1940, devotes five semesters of lectures to Nietzsche in order, as he writes, to settle his dispute with the last German philosopher who, far from all vulgar atheism, sought "God with passion."⁵² And it is on the basis of his courses on Nietzsche that he writes his essay entitled: "The Word of Nietzsche: 'God is dead,'" at the beginning of which he quotes *verbatim*

---

⁴⁶ In the title of this section, we pick up the translation of this term proposed by Michel Haar in *La Fracture de l'histoire. Douze essais sur Heidegger* (Grenoble, Jérôme Millon, 1994) 190.

⁴⁷ We recall Dominique Janicaud's formulation: "Without Heidegger's *Kehre*, there would be no theological turn." However, this theological turning point is in no way the result of Heidegger but of those whom Janicaud calls "the candidates to the theological heritage," such as Emmanuel Levinas, Michel Henry or Jean-Luc Marion. Janicaud et al., *Phenomenology and the "Theological Turn,"* 31. Françoise Dastur, *Heidegger et la pensée a venir* (Paris: Vrin, 2011), 150 n. 4.

⁴⁸ In *Contributions to Philosophy* (1936-8), Heidegger envisages "God in the extreme" or "ultimate god" (*der letzte Gott*) as a completely different god who is expected only by the small number of those who are forward-looking, at the forefront of which stands the poet Hölderlin. Martin Heidegger, *Contributions to Philosophy (Of the Event)* (Bloomington: Indiana University Press, 2012/1989), §256 pp. 324–30.

⁴⁹ "Even more sacred than any God is, therefore, the world, which the Bible—on the contrary—reduced to a divine creature," Jean Beaufret, *Dialogue avec Heidegger* (Paris, Éditions of Minuit, 1985) t.4, p. 48.

⁵⁰ Martin Heidegger, *Approche de Hölderlin*, trad. H. Corbin et al. (Paris, Gallimard, 1996). Christian Dubois, *Heidegger. Introduction à une lecture* (Paris, Éditions du Seuil, 2000) 333.

⁵¹ Haar, *La fracture de l'histoire*, p. 189; Michel Haar, *Nietzsche and Metaphysics*, trans. Michael Gendre (Albany, NY: State University of New York Press, 1996), 143–4.

⁵² From this point of view, the madman (*der tolle Mensch*), "who had started running in the public square, shouting incessantly: 'I'm looking for God,' 'I'm looking for God,'" is Nietzsche himself, thinker of the *de profundis*. Nietzsche, *The Gay Science*, §125. Martin Heidegger, "The Self-Assertion of the German University (die Rektoratsrede)," in *Martin Heidegger and National Socialism*, ed. Gunther Neske and Emil Kettering (New York: Paragon House, 1990/1933), 8–9. "The Word of Nietzsche: 'God is Dead,'" 59–60.

paragraph 125 of *The Gay Science*.⁵³ The ambition of this text is not simply to clarify but to understand "otherwise" Nietzsche's thought and to grasp in it "the unthought" from its place in the history of Western metaphysics.⁵⁴ From this point of view, it is certainly necessary, at first, to read the word of Nietzsche as Nietzsche himself understands it, that is to say as the triumph of nihilism and the correlative disappearance of the Platonic opposition of the sensible and the intelligible. This is what Heidegger calls "the metaphysical meaning of the word thought metaphysically: 'God is dead.'"⁵⁵ But according to Heidegger, this is not the ultimate meaning of this word of Nietzsche, the unveiling of which implies questioning anew the essence of metaphysics.

Actually, far from having succeeded in going beyond the metaphysics otherwise known as Platonism, Nietzsche's work would still and always come under metaphysics while ignoring its essence.⁵⁶ It would even constitute its final stage: not only because in assimilating being to the will to power, it participates in the forgetfulness of being which is the essence of metaphysics but also, because it pushes metaphysics to its completion, in the sense that once the suprasensible is discredited, metaphysics has no other way of unfolding. This is why Nietzsche's thought is, for Heidegger, the true achievement of nihilism or even the nihilist experience of nihilism, in the sense where being, in Nietzsche's thought, "is nothing."⁵⁷ To the Nietzschean interpretation of nihilism starting from the will to power, Heidegger opposes a thought of nihilism starting from being and the forgetting of being. It is therefore possible for him to identify among the murderers of God and of the suprasensible world, those who dealt them the hardest blows. It is not a question of "those who did not believe in God" but, paradoxically, of believers and their theologians who lower God to the rank of supreme value: "The heaviest blow against God is not that God is held to be unknowable, not that God's existence is demonstrated to be unprovable, but rather that the god held to be real is elevated to the highest value."⁵⁸ Let us understand, then, what now separates Heidegger from Nietzsche who, through his metaphysics of the will to power and the assimilation of being to value, appears as the ultimate murderer of God. It is that the death of God is not limited to triumphant disbelief *vis-à-vis* the Christian God nor to the dissolution of the ideas of the suprasensible world but now refers to nihilism in its Heideggerian sense, so that the murder for which we are all responsible and that we accomplish without paying attention to it is "the murder of the being of beings."⁵⁹

---

[53] Martin Heidegger, *Nietzsche*. Volume I: *The Will to Power as Art*. Volume II: *The Eternal Recurrence of the Same*, ed. David Farrell Krell, trans. David Farrell Krell (San Francisco: HarperSanFrancisco, 1991).
[54] "The Word of Nietzsche: 'God is Dead,'" 97.
[55] "The Word of Nietzsche: 'God is Dead,'" 99.
[56] "Overcoming Metaphysics" in Martin Heidegger, *The End of Philosophy*, trans. Joan Stambaugh (London: Souvenir Press, 1975), 92.
[57] "The Word of Nietzsche: 'God is Dead,'" 199.
[58] "The Word of Nietzsche: 'God is Dead,'" 105.
[59] "The Word of Nietzsche: 'God is Dead,'" 111, trans. modified. It should, however, be stressed that from 1935 to 1952, from "The introduction to Metaphysics" to "What do we call Thinking?," Heidegger's position with regard to Nietzsche evolved, and that we favor here the essay from 1943, included in Heidegger, *Off the Beaten Track*. See Haar, *La fracture de l'histoire*, p. 199.

V. Conclusion

For some unknown reason, Sartre visits Heidegger in 1952. Unsurprisingly, the discussion between the two falls short and soon turns into a Sartrean monologue on the need for engagement. At the end, says Sartre to Jean Cau, "I was talking to his hat: a green chamois hunter's hat."[60] Trying to reconcile the views of Sartre and Heidegger on the death of God would be a senseless challenge. Is a dialogue even thinkable? Certainly, Sartre is for Heidegger one of those who, as he writes at the end of his essay on Nietzsche, have become incapable of seeking God, "those standing about in the market place [who] have abolished thinking and replaced it with idle babble."[61] The Heideggerian expectation of the last God as the affirmation– untimely if there is such—that "only a god can still save us" is, it is true, inaudible for an atheist philosopher like Sartre, inhabited by this properly Promethean conviction that it is men who make their own history (in a given environment which conditions them).[62] For Sartre, as for La Fontaine, "help yourself and the heavens will help you." But we must recognize that when it comes to the death of God and, more generally, of what is called religion, the Sartrian reflection is a bit short. How can we not regret that his atheism, like his materialism, ultimately leads him to ignore an event whose importance in modern times is no less essential than the democratic revolution (Tocqueville) or the Galilean physics which are, it seems, closely related to each other. However, if Sartre does not say much about it, it is for the simple reason that the event does not seem to him in any way decisive and, consequently, does not deserve his attention.

The Heideggerian interpretation of the word of Nietzsche, at the same time, does not cease to be disconcerting, but in a completely different way. On the one hand, even if Heidegger persists in inscribing his own path within a phenomenological framework, in the name of what he calls in 1973 a "phenomenology of the inapparent," with Dominique Janicaud we can still question the solidity of the link between the phenomenological approach and the Heideggerian questioning of the essence of metaphysics.[63] We have seen that Heidegger's ambition was to understand Nietzsche, if not better, then at least otherwise than he had understood himself, and to extract the unthought from the word of Nietzsche.[64] In this perspective, even if Nietzsche is preparing to welcome a future divinity whom he provisionally gives the name of Dionysius, he nevertheless participates in this "murder of the being of beings" which is at the heart of the Heideggerian meditation.[65] However, from what hermeneutics does

---

[60] Jean Cau, "Croquis de mémoire," *Les Temps modernes* 531–3 (1990): 1127–8.
[61] Heidegger, "The Word of Nietzsche: 'God is Dead,'" 112.
[62] Conducted in 1966, the interview was, in accordance with Heidegger's wishes, published in 1976. On the reception of this word from Heidegger, cf. Pierre Aubenque, *Les Etudes philosophiques* (1976) 271. Sartre, *Search*, 166n.
[63] Janicaud et al., *Phenomenology and the "Theological Turn,"* 29–30. For Françoise Dastur, on the contrary, this link is obvious: "It is because phenomenology is already defined in Husserl as a method, a path that leads to *Sache selbst*, to the very thing that is in question, that Heidegger continues to define his thought in 1973 as a 'phenomenology of the inapparent,'" Dastur, *Heidegger et la pensée a venir*, 20.
[64] On the Heideggerian "reading strategy" of Nietzsche, cf. Haar, *La fracture de l'histoire*, 194.
[65] Because Dionysus is only a provisional name and by no means the finally definitive and ultimate Name of the god. See Haar, *Nietzsche and Metaphysics*, 143–4.

such an interpretation of the unthought in the word of Nietzsche word come? Can we still speak of a hermeneutics in the sense of a description and interpretation (*Auslegung*) of the thing itself, to use the terms of *Being and Time*? Obviously, the interpretation of Nietzsche comes from a completely different hermeneutic approach which substitutes the thing itself for speech as the house of being.[66]

Finally, it is questionable whether this Heideggerian interpretation of the word of Nietzsche grants the event of the death of the Christian God. Does Heidegger really question the event in its eventiality or, if you prefer, in its evential sense?[67] We could criticize Heideggerian hermeneutics for having erased in advance the unpredictability, the irreversibility, the singularity—or, in a word, the historicity of the event which is, as such, foundation (*Stiftung*), opening of possibilities, beginning.[68] The interpretation of the word of Nietzsche considered as the ultimate form of metaphysics, as the expectation of a God who comes to save us, shows above all the Heideggerian resistance to modernity. Modernity in this sense would be the beginning of a world from which not only the Christian God but also the deity (*Gottheit*)—as witnessed by Sartrian atheism—has irretrievably disappeared. Now, is the death of God not this historic event—we would almost be tempted to say this arch-event—by virtue of which, for better or for worse, a radically new world arises on the ruins of the old, a world without religion, without god (*Gottlos*)?

In memory of Michel Haar (1937–2003) and Dominique Janicaud (1937–2002)
Translated from the original French by Robyn Horner

---

[66] This tension between two modalities of the hermeneutic approach is present since *Being and Time* when Heidegger goes from the question of the meaning of being to the question of "being." Claude Romano, *At the Heart of Reason*, trans. Michael B. Smith (Evanston, IL: Northwestern University Press, 2015), 495.
[67] Romano, Claude. *Event and World*, trans. Shane Mackinlay (New York: Fordham University Press, 2009), 38–9. Claudia Serban, "L'Événement historique: un paradigme de la phénoménalité," *Revue de phénoménologie ALTER*, N°25 (2017) 150.
[68] We could address the same reproach to Jean-Luc Marion who, in 1976, advanced this "evidence": "What the last (or next-to-last) metaphysical word calls the 'death of God' does not signify that God passes out of play, but indicates the modern face of his insistent and eternal fidelity." There is nothing better in one and the same "evidence" than to do right and not do right to history. Marion, *The Idol and Distance*, xxxv.

11

Materialism, Social Construction, and Radical Empiricism—Debating the Status of "Experience" in the Study of Religion

Tamsin Jones

"Marley was dead, to begin with. There is no doubt whatever about that." So begins Dicken's famous Christmas parable—with a factual observation that will be repeated in many different ways in the first few pages of *A Christmas Carol*. This repetition is to heighten the surprise, both ours and dear Ebenezer's, when a non-substantial spectre resembling Marley appears before him one night. Mr. Scrooge has some options in the manner of his reception of this vision and his first instinct is to doubt, not what his senses are telling him, but their cause:

> "You don't believe in me," observed the ghost.
> "I don't," said Scrooge.
> "What evidence would you have of my reality beyond that of your senses?"
> "I don't know," said Scrooge.
> "Why do you doubt your senses?"
> "Because," said Scrooge, "a little thing affects them. A slight disorder of the stomach makes them cheats. You may be an undigested bit of beef, a blot of mustard, a crumb of cheese, a fragment of an underdone potato. There's more of gravy than of grave about you, whatever you are!"
> Scrooge was not much in the habit of cracking jokes, nor did he feel, in his heart, by any means waggish then. The truth is, that he tried to be smart, as a means of distracting his own attention, and keeping down his terror; for the spectre's voice disturbed the very marrow of his bones.[1]

The question is not whether or not Scrooge is seeing and talking with his business partner—firmly established as deceased; in question is the cause of this experience, or encounter—a bit of undigested gravy or a visitation from the grave? That is to say, the question about excessive experiences always comes down to their cause, or, to put it another way: what really happened.

---

[1] Charles Dickens, *A Christmas Carol* (London: W. & R. Chambers Ltd., 1954/1843), 1, 22.

In the invocatory materials for the *Atheism, Religion and Experience Seminar* in 2019, we were asked to consider how different people might experience the same phenomenon but receive and understand it differently. Given the phenomenological leanings of the Seminar, we were considering those phenomena given in an excessive mode, with the commanding force of an "event" (Romano) or a "saturated phenomenon" whose excessive intuition overwhelms the cognitive capacity of intentionality (Marion). But the question repeated in our invitation was how such an event or phenomenon might signify intersubjectively. How can two people encounter the same phenomenon, but one experience it as saturated and the other as common? As Jocelyn Benoist had laid down the gauntlet to Marion in 2001: "... where you see God, I see nothing."[2] In this response, I consider the question through the lens of debates on excessive experiences within the disciplines of religious studies (which, I observe, parallel the debate between Benoist and Marion) and trauma theory.

I. The materialist orientation of recent religious studies

The past couple of decades have witnessed a material turn in the study of religion. The precise elements of this turn might vary according to who is detailing them; however, all would agree that it involves, at least in large part, a rejection of the interiority, ideality, and emphasis on transcendence that long held sway in considerations of religion, in favor of exteriority, materiality, and immanence.[3] This materialist turn has at least two distinct trajectories: the first strand, which has dominated the discipline since the 1980s, is immanentist and naturalist, and deals in theories of religion that could be labeled "social constructionist." Here, as Jonathan Z. Smith has put it, *homo religious* is "preeminently *homo faber*"; all forms of religious experience are humanly constructed and their causes are primarily social, psychological, or physiological.[4] More recently, a counter claim within this materialist turn can be found in historians who insist that there is something "about human experience—and religious experience, in particular—that is excessive" and thus, "good work in religious studies does not prematurely foreclose the various (and infinite!) possibilities of religion's interpretation."[5] With this strand of scholarship in religious studies, there is a mandate to attend to whatever appears, but also to insist that whatever appears does so materially—on bodies, in communities, in ritual and performance, and so on. Robert Orsi, who leads the charge here, has borrowed from William James to call this quest a "radical empiricism."

---

[2] Jocelyn Benoist, *L'Idée de phénoménologie* (Paris: Beauchesne, 2001), 102.
[3] See Sonia Hazard, "The Material Turn in the Study of Religion," *Religion and Society: Advances in Research* 4 (2013). See also David Chidester, "Material Terms of the Study of Religion," *Journal of the American Academy of Religion* 68, no. 2 (2000).
[4] Jonathan Z. Smith, *Imagining Religion: From Babylon to Jonestown* (Chicago: University of Chicago Press, 1982), 89.
[5] Mary Dunn, "What Really Happened: Radical Empiricism and the Historian of Religion," *Journal of the American Academy of Religion* 84, no. 4 (2016): 863, 64.

This stance against foreclosing the limits of legitimate objects of study according to an enforced naturalism or positivism within the study of religion parallels fights fought by Levinas, Marion, and others in phenomenology to broaden the parameters of what might count as a possible phenomenon.[6] The argument that is made in a movement that has been referred to as "new phenomenology" is that we should not predetermine the limits of what can and cannot appear as a phenomenon, restricting the field of possible phenomena to those things that can be objectified or conceptualized adequately, because to do so would be to exclude those phenomena whose very significant impact on our lives often exceeds that which we can conceptually control.[7] As Levinas writes: "Is not the *living* of life an exceeding? Is it not the rupture of the container by the uncontainable which, precisely, thus animates and inspires?"[8] In other words, the very things that shape and determine who we are as subjects are often those things we cannot define, understand, or contain. For this reason, Marion insists: "one cannot forbid phenomenality to what claims it ... it is forbidden to forbid!"[9] Similarly, in the context of the question of the status of experience in the study of religion, the debates revolve around what is and is not a permissible source for the study.

On this point it is illuminating to compare the treatment of religious experience in two handbooks on the study of religion which bookend the last two decades: *Critical Terms for Religious Studies* from 1998 and *The Cambridge Companion to Religious Studies* from 2012.[10] To begin with the former, religious experience is notoriously disregarded by Robert Sharf as indicating nothing more than one's ideological commitments, shaped by vocation, socio-economic background, politics, sectarian affiliations, and so on.[11] In other words, the purpose of Sharf's essay on "Experience" as a critical term in religious studies is primarily to relegate it to obscurity. This is motivated in large part by Sharf's suspicions about the way in which experience functions authoritatively, and along ideological lines, most especially when talking about excessive religious, or mystical, experience: "The ideological aspect of the appeal to experience—the use of the concept to legitimize vested social, institutional, and professional interests—is most evident when we turn to the study of mysticism" because it is primarily in excessive mystical encounters that the experience is taken as "a direct encounter with the divine or the absolute" without being "affected by linguistic, cultural, or historical contingencies" (96). Otherwise expressed, when experience was "construed as an inviolable realm of pure presence," or irrefutable, as a result, it "promised a refuge from the hermeneutic and epistemological vagaries of modern

---

[6] For an overview of this debate, see Tamsin Jones, "Traumatized Subjects: Continental Philosophy of Religion and the Ethics of Alterity," *Journal of Religion* 94, no. 2 (2014).
[7] See J. Aaron Simmons and Bruce Ellis Benson, *The New Phenomenology: A Philosophical Introduction* (London: Bloomsbury, 2013).
[8] Emmanuel Levinas, *Of God Who Comes to Mind*, trans. Bettina Bergo (Stanford: Stanford University Press, 1998), 29.
[9] Jean-Luc Marion, "Metaphysics and Phenomenology: A Summary for Theologians," in *The Postmodern God: A Theological Reader*, ed. Graham Ward (Oxford: Blackwell, 1997), 289.
[10] Mark C. Taylor, ed. *Critical Terms for Religious Studies* (Chicago: Chicago University Press, 1998); Robert A. Orsi, ed. *The Cambridge Companion to Religious Studies* (Cambridge: Cambridge University Press, 2012).
[11] Robert H, Sharf, "Experience," in Taylor, *Critical Terms*, 107. Subsequent references are made parenthetically within the text.

intellectual life" (104).[12] Thus, the danger of scholarly reliance on mystical experience is its claim to be an unmediated encounter with the holy, rendering it irrefutable and hence, absolutely authoritative.

The second problem with the utilization of experience as a source of knowledge has to do with the identification and location of its referent. Sharf's concern is that when experience is employed by religious studies scholars as a source for gaining knowledge about some religious phenomenon, it is not with an understanding of experience as something one has lived through, as in "I have combat experience" or "I have experience performing heart surgery." If that were the case, Sharf would be fine with the usage as the referent of the experience appears in the social or public sphere. Instead, he argues experience is used to refer to the act of being aware or "conscious of"—that is, experience is conceptualized as a "subjective 'mental event' or 'inner process' that eludes public scrutiny" (104). This comes down to a semiotic problem for Sharf: to what do words about experiences refer? What Sharf assumes here is that for a word to have meaning, to be meaningful, it must refer to an object which is public and thus, observable. "But if," as Stephen Bush puts it in a response to Sharf, "experiences are as the rhetoric of experience takes them to be, immediate episodes of consciousness, then there is nothing public for terms such as 'experience' to refer to."[13] If we cannot locate the referent, or identify the cause of the experience in the interior, private realm of experience, we must, Sharf argues, turn elsewhere to identify the experience "on the basis of eminently public criteria." Here we will find, Sharf assures us, that experiences judged (by the experiencer) to be mystical or religious are in fact "inevitably predicated on prior ideological commitments shaped by one's vocation (monk or layperson), one's socioeconomic background (urban middle class or rural poor), one's political agenda (traditionalist or reformer), one's sectarian affiliation, one's education, and so forth"– all of which *are* publicly identifiable (107). Indeed, making such identifications of that to which an experience deemed religious actually refers is the primary role of the scholar.[14] Sharf then indicates his valuation of religious experience through a comparison with accounts of alien abductions and child abuse.

Sharf considers the fact that hundreds of Americans have claimed to have experienced some kind of alien abduction, with such consistency across the accounts— describing small hairless humanoid beings with large heads and eyes, tiny nostrils and so on—that they have persuaded "apparently reputable investigators" that something is happening to cause these experiences. Yet, as Sharf points out, not only is there no

---

[12] Here, again, we can see some parallels with what Jean-Luc Marion claims to achieve with his method of a reduction to givenness as a way of escaping the intentional strictures of the knowing "I."

[13] Stephen Bush, "Are Religious Experiences Too Private to Study?" *Journal of Religion* 92, no. 2 (2012): 203.

[14] What Sharf is advocating is a mode of scholarly "gnosticism" that is so popular in the study of religion and culture that it has become unquestioned and instinctive: when we set to analyzing texts, events, or phenomena we seek first to demonstrate our cleverness in identifying what really lies behind the account of an excessive experience: repressed desires, a struggle for power or the accommodation to power, fear or guilt, a tool of colonial oppression, a hammer of reform, and so on. The scholarly focus is on anything but the experiencer's own account of the experience. Instead, the scholar is the one in the know (*gnosis*), dispersing the mysterious mists of supernatural tomfoolery to expose the material truths of what lies at the heart of the experience.

corroborating evidence but possible folklorist material can be identified that would explain the cultural origins of central elements of the alien abduction narrative. For Sharf, however, the most worrisome point in these accounts, which he has argued are analogous to reports of religious experience, is that there is no memory of them until "recovered" by a therapist. Thus, the scholarly consensus should be, he concludes, that the abductions simply did not take place—"there is no *originary event* behind the memories" (109). Sharf then extends the analogy of such spurious experiences to the accounts of childhood trauma which, despite being the "*etiology du jour*" likewise are produced only at the hands of an analyst or therapist "whose training and institutional investments predispose him to this specific diagnosis" (109). Here the therapist plays the same role as the earlier religious confessor—both to "elicit and shape" the narrative of the excessive event—something a scholar of religion ought clearly be forbidden to do (109–10). For all these reasons, Sharf concludes that not only must we refuse the possibility of an unmediated, ahistorical, pure religious experience, but also, like the account of the alien abduction (and presumably the claim of childhood trauma), we can assume these experiences have no external cause whatsoever. They have been invented, in other words, either by the person claiming them, or by the confessor (or therapist) pre-inclined to identify them in the account. Where others see God (or an alien abduction or childhood trauma) Sharf, like Benoist in his argument with Marion, sees nothing.[15] Thus, the study of religious experience, in Sharf's hands, serves the merely critical function of unveiling the hidden biases and ideological constructions of its participants.

This approach is interestingly compared with the very different argument found in the more recent text, *The Cambridge Companion to Religious Studies*, in which Robert Orsi not only challenges the reduction of analyses of religious lives to cultural explanation, but also upends common assumptions about the ideality and subjectivity of religious experience to begin with. Through a brilliant, if unexpected, rehabilitation of Rudolph Otto's famous (and famously derided) essay translated into English as *The Idea of the Holy*, Orsi demonstrates how the English translation masks a shift of the experience of the holy from a concrete, real presence to the ideal, subjective cognition of one. Otto's own title was simply *Das Heilige*—The Holy. Thus, the translation into the English speaking world of religious studies scholars requires a shift from "the straightforward realism of 'the holy' to the psychological 'idea of the holy' [and] ... a shift from the objective to the subjective" which is precisely the opposite of Otto's intention.[16] Otto assumed this experience of the holy to be real not ideal, concrete and present, not symbolic or imagined. Orsi uses this to argue that religious experience is not subjective, ideal, private, and individual; it is material and public, manifest in sacred objects, rituals, food practices, bodily disciplines, political impacts, and so on. In a second article, "When 2+2=5," Orsi asks whether we can begin to "think about

---

[15] See Sharf: "It should now be apparent that the question is not merely whether or not mystical experiences are constructed, unmediated, pure, or philosophically significant. The more fundamental question is whether we can continue to treat the texts and reports upon which such theories are based as referring, however obliquely, to determinative phenomenal events at all" (110).

[16] Orsi, *Companion to Religious Studies*, 92.

unexplained religious experiences in ways that acknowledges their existence."[17] These two essays taken together are a major scholar of religion's articulation of an alternative vision for a materialist study of religion, one not bound to social constructivist and naturalist explanations of religious phenomena.

Orsi expresses the frustration of scholars of religion who are unsatisfied with the limitation of explanations of religious phenomena to social, psychological, and physiological processes. This frustration is not because they are erroneous explanations, or because attention to structures of social power has not been incredibly illuminating—it has. However, the problem arises because this approach "eviscerates the reality of religious imaginings and experiences, and of religious presence, as it denies the accounts religious people give of their own lives" and in the diminishment of the real force of religious experience, such "explanations are *empirically* insufficient."[18]

In order to counter the empirical insufficiency of social or psychological explanations for religious phenomena, Orsi suggests a method of "radical empiricism of the visible *and* invisible real" instead. This method would provide the scholar with an avenue to begin to respond to what he calls "abundant events"—that is, events characterized by

> "aspects of the human imagination that cannot be completely accounted for by social and cultural codes, that go beyond authorized limits; by the 'more' in William James's word (which got him in so much trouble with positivist psychologists); by the 'unthought known,' a cultural experience of *déjà vu* or uncanny awareness of something outside us and independent of us, yet still familiar to us. Abundant events are saturated by memory, desire, need, fear, terror, hope, or denial, or some inchoate combination of these."[19]

This approach is not only a disavowal of social constructivist explanations of religious experience; it is an explicit claim of a certain realism. Abundant events are not unconscious projections or fabrications of the religious subject (or, at least, *need* not be); instead, the religious subjects "experience the abundant event as something outside themselves, really in the world, and out of their control."[20] An abundant event has its own agency; takes on a "life and efficacy of its own" as unpredictable and uncontrollable, and finally as something which leaves its mark on "those who have experienced it ... [and thus] remains existentially present."[21]

---

[17] Robert Orsi, "When 2 2 = 5," *The American Scholar* 76, no. 2 (2007): 34–43.

[18] Ibid., 8. and Orsi, *Companion to Religious Studies*, 84 (emphasis mine). Tangentially, it is worth noting that Orsi positions himself as a non-theological, non-confessional historian who, nonetheless, is informed by his Catholic heritage. He is deeply invested in demonstrating the power and reality of the Catholic material phenomena and subjects of his research. Part of this research is an explicit riposte to the unspoken Protestant leaning of the study of religion which preferences interiority, ethics, and belief over materiality and ritual practices. There is an unacknowledged polemic in this history of the study of religion which Orsi, among many others, has made explicit and challenged: "It means that my religion is interior, self-determined, individual, free of authority; my religion is about ethics and not about bizarre events, and my ethics are a matter of personal choice, not of law; I take orders from no one. In the context of Western history, this means, 'I am not Catholic'" ("When 2+2=5," 4.)

[19] "When 2+2=5," 10.

[20] "When 2+2=5."

[21] "When 2+2=5," 102–3. The discussion of "abundant events" finds a certain parallel in Claude Romano's treatment of the event in Romano, *Event and World*. This is discussed below.

We return to the example of Marley's ghost. Certainly, its appearance was not foreseen or controlled by Scrooge. Furthermore, the experience had a lasting affective impact on him. But does this mean the ghost was real? On the one hand, it seems easy to say Marley's ghost was real to Scrooge. Yet does this mean that Marley's ghost was truly there? How are we to judge when the stakes are higher than here in Dicken's fictional world? In an essay on the radical empiricism of Orsi, the historian of religion, Mary Dunn, asks the same question: What really happened? For her part, Dunn considers the case of Marie Guyart, a seventeenth-century French Catholic who made the decision to abandon her young beloved son in order to enter a monastic order and travel to Canada as a missionary to eventually become *Marie de l'Incarnation*—a decision based solely on her experience of God calling her to do so. If we can be confident that Marie believed God called her thus, what is the historian to do with the jejune, yet obvious, question: yes, but did God actually ask that of her?[22] More pointedly, if one grants that the question is an understandable and legitimate one to ask, it remains to be established how one might determine the answer to such a question. It is precisely such difficulties that led many scholars in the phenomenology of religion simply to bracket the ontological question. The radical empiricist strand of scholarship in religion, however, challenges these methodological limits.

When Orsi researches the role of the worship of Saint Jude in Catholic American women's lives, for instance, he argues that to ignore the ontological question does not sufficiently account for the independence of the force or agency of the saint's intervention in the worshipper's life.[23] Moreover, according to Stephen Bush, there is another problem with the phenomenological approach which puts aside ontological questions about "what really happened" in "order to focus on the phenomenal qualities of the experience," or which refuses to "account for the *cause* of an experience in [favor of] discussing the *nature* of the experience."[24] The problem with this strategy is that it leaves the phenomenologists open to precisely the kind of critique Sharf wields: "By separating the question of the nature of the experience from the cause of the experience, the rhetoric of experience cannot but portray experiences as radically subjective. The phenomenological account—the description of what the experience is like—gets the first and last word as to the nature of the experience."[25] This is the key point; the subjective interpretation cannot be the only word about an experience for then it has no use, intelligibility, or authority beyond the subject's experience.

We return to our original dilemma—however, not quite at the same point. What both trajectories in religious studies agree on is, however you identify the cause or originary event of the experience, its outcome is more public and material than previous iterations of experience. For Sharf, this is because experiences can only point to socio-political, psychological, or physiological forces out of which the experience arises and is structured. For the radical empiricist, this is because experience is not simply a question of feeling, interiority, or consciousness: its impact is affective and

---

[22] Dunn, "What Really Happened," 882.
[23] Orsi, *Companion to Religious Studies*, 85.
[24] Bush, "Too Private," 212.
[25] "Too Private," 212.

bodily—it is performed in postures and gestures (crumpled and suppliant, confrontational and defiant, or flowing and joyous), and has a physiology rendering it wide-eyed, fainting, weeping, laughing, speaking in tongues, crying, dancing, holding and hugging, argumentative, or silent and still. All these things are publicly observable, material evidences of the experience.

Sharf and Orsi continue to disagree about how to interpret an experience such as Marley's apparition. Sharf will say this is clearly either an example of illusory thinking in which Scrooge mistakes a pile of old clothes and the noises of an old house for a ghost (due, most likely, to a combination of overworked nerves and lack of exercise, social isolation, early childhood disappointments, as well as the repressed guilt of a capitalist miser), or possibly a hallucination, brought on by that undigested bit of gravy, for instance. In contrast, Orsi, Dunn, and Bush do not want to foreclose on the possibility that Scrooge really, truly was visited by the ghost of his business partner. Despite holding open the way for such a possibility and demonstrating the appropriateness of asking the question—what really happened?—radical empiricism does not give us a way to think through how one might determine this or explain how such experiences signify intersubjectively. For insight on this point, we must turn to a different theoretical discipline: trauma theory.

By making this turn, I suggest, first, that there are significant overlaps between trauma theory and phenomenological accounts of religious experience, and second, that we might learn something from the former to shed light on the latter. However, in drawing this parallel one might object that the language of "event" is sufficient, and that to compare religious experience to traumatic experience is not necessary and may even be distracting. Certainly, it is important to be very clear that in making a claim that there are certain conceptual or structural parallels between the two, I am definitely not identifying or conflating religious and traumatic experience. However, I do claim that there is something about traumatic experience that specifically illuminates the dark aporia we face when talking about the intersubjective signification of excessive experiences more generally, including the religious. In order to do so, I will first briefly consider Claude Romano's treatment of the event in relation to traumatic experience in order to show why the theory of the event alone is insufficient to show the way beyond the aporia.

The larger aim of Romano's project of "evential hermeneutics" is to describe the phenomenality of the event without turning it into an object—that is, something whose meaning is static or determined by the subject. As has already been made clear, an event does not arise out of or depend on a self, but is, nonetheless, addressed to one. Romano defines the event "in the eventual sense" as a phenomenon which comes from elsewhere but addresses me; it necessarily surprises me, and yet demands my response, while my response determines my possibilities and transforms the shape of my own adventure as well as my own self as *advenant*.[26]

---

[26] The event taken in "its eventual sense" is to be distinguished from the "innerworldly fact" which is a kind of event that is addressed anonymously to a plurality; for example, lightening flash affects the sky, a cloud, as well as a walker and his dog. See Romano, *Event and World*, 24–31. Subsequent references are parenthetic in the text.

For Romano, while birth is the original event from which the human "ad-venes" and the human adventure begins (19), his section on "terror and traumatism" arguably focuses the heart of his argument, for trauma most perfectly resists the temptation to turn an event into an object: "Traumatism is an event that we cannot make our own. Though we are utterly exposed to it, this is as a *subject* incapable of facing it, *subjected* to the excess of what has struck us all the more painfully since it happens to us from outside, takes us by surprise, avoids any grasp, and outwits any protection" (109). However, as we've just seen, many of these qualities can be said of other events as well. Thus, the difference with a traumatism is the ongoing overwhelming intrusion of trauma due to its stubborn refusal to be integrated. Moreover, the result of being subjected to an event that I cannot integrate or make my own, results in "fascination" with the event—a compulsion or fixation with it. Indeed, the less I can understand or assimilate the event, the more I am subjected to and obsessed with it.[27] For this reason, trauma occupies a central role in Romano's "eventual hermeneutics"; it is the limit case of evential events, because it is that which disables my response, refuses integration, and hence refuses all meaning. We cannot appropriate the trauma into experience as a "source of self-transformation" as we can with a non-traumatic event: "A traumatic event, by contrast, in breaking into a human adventure and resisting an *advenant's* assimilation, is rather that which thwarts any transformation from self to self, any experience, freezing an *advenant's* very adventure and preventing him from advening" (110).

The destructive quality of traumatic experience requires that I maintain a clear distinction between it and religious experience. Thus, religious experience is not necessarily an experience of trauma, nor is traumatic experience inevitably religious. Nonetheless, I would disagree with Romano's treatment of traumatic experience in one way: that it remains, by definition, ever static and unanswerable—a kind of static event which freezes the *advenant's* adventure in time, forbidding any movement out of that moment. Certainly, in some extreme cases of Post-Traumatic Stress Disorder (PTSD), this may be what occurs, but in the majority of cases of trauma, a much messier, shifting, and non-linear journey toward (and, potentially, away from) recovery is the experience of the traumatized and this recovery will involve a variety of responses to, and interpretations of the originary traumatic event.[28]

Thus, I would argue that while distinct, there is an isomorphic relation between the structure of traumatic and religious experiences, beyond the fact that they are both excessive. This structural parallel between traumatic and religious experience lies in the following: the experience is (a) overwhelming, saturating, interruptive of the finite horizons of time and space, and thus, transgressive; (b) one does not invite it, but even

---

[27] See Romano: "Thus, the less I am able to understand myself from what happens to me—because of traumatism's excess beyond any possible appropriation—the more it holds me in its grasp, in the mode of fascination" (112).

[28] In its most extreme pathology, a number of refugees in Sweden, especially children from war-torn regions in the world, have been diagnosed with "Resignation Syndrome," a profound dissociative disorder which results in a catatonic state in which the child will remain in the same position for weeks, months, even years on end, as their bodies and minds wait to catch up with all the violence they have witnessed or experienced.

more strongly, one cannot refuse it; it happens *to* one; (c) the experience is especially marked by its ineffability, and at the same time by a compulsion to communicate it; and finally, (d) unable to be integrated—the event cannot be woven (immediately, at least) into a narrative of meaning and self-identity. Moreover, I suggest that this structural parallel may be instructive in the question of how to determine "what really happened."

II. Interventions of trauma theory

The discourses of trauma theory bring clarity on the question of the significance of excessive experience on a couple of fronts. First of all, despite the fact that the truth of the matter of trauma is not always precisely clear, there is an unquestioning simplicity about the fact that whatever the truth is, it matters. There is a need to get to the truth of a traumatic event—what actually happened—for social and ethical reasons, but also, more basically, for the survivor of a traumatic event, in order to survive.[29] Furthermore, the articulation of the difficulty in getting to the truth of the matter of a traumatic experience is illuminating in two ways: first, it confirms the materiality of excessive experience, and second, while providing an explanation of any initial disagreement over how to interpret the event, it also points forward to a way in which one might be more hopeful about *eventually* coming to the truth of an experience.

On the first point, the work of Bessel van der Kolk explores the way in which, quite materially, traumatic experience so overwhelms the brain's normal circuitry as to get "stuck" in the brain's nether regions—the amygdala, hippocampus, hypothalamus, and brain stem—which are nonverbal. Van der Kolk's theory is that the traumatic event so overloads, or over-fires, the limbic system of the brain, that it literally short circuits, it cannot re-route the impulses along the normal neural pathways. For this reason, these experiences remain stuck and never gain access to the frontal lobes, which is where not only language arises, but is also the part of the brain that reasons and understands. This interferes with "the capacity to capture the experience in words or symbols."[30] As a result, it is our bodies, not our conscious minds, that "keep the score" and dictate our response to trauma. For this reason, trauma marks its victim—whether that victim is an individual or a community—in public, observable, material ways even when its cause cannot be precisely located.

Second, the unexpectedness of an excessive event impacts one's capacity to receive (and to respond) to an event appropriately. We can imagine a scenario in which all the pertinent information—the collection of intuitive or sensible indicators—may be there but is not recognized as such because the meaning of the event is so counter to all expectation, or in the case of trauma, presents a reality one would rather not face, a

---

[29] On this point, see Susan Brison, *Aftermath: Violence and the Remaking of the Self* (Princeton, NJ: Princeton University Press, 2002).

[30] Bessel A. van der Kolk, "The Body Keeps the Score: Meaning and the Evolving Psychobiology of Post Traumatic Stress," *Harvard Review of Psychiatry* 1, no. 5 (1994). See also Bessel A. van der Kolk, Alexander C. McFarlane, and Lars Weisaeth, eds., *Traumatic Stress: The Effects of Overwhelming Experience on Mind, Body, and Society* (New York: The Guilford Press, 1996).

reality to be avoided at all cost. Dear Scrooge might prefer to avoid the implications of his partner's visitation and the subsequent judgment on his life; he might prefer to try "to be smart, as a means of distracting his own attention, and keeping down his own terror."[31] Likewise, to return to Sharf's example of childhood abuse, such an experience might happen publicly, in plain sight of other family members, or teachers, caregivers, and community members, without being recognized as such, precisely because it goes against our expectations of obligations of care for a child. Here is a situation where all the pertinent information may be public and visible and still not recognized for what it is, an experience of trauma. The dynamic of trust resulting from an expectation of care is exactly what enables an unwillingness to see, and thus a silent acceptance of violence, especially sexual violence, in families, college campuses, sports teams, charismatic yoga schools, and, of course, religious organizations such as the Catholic Church. Traumatic experience, thus, clearly illustrates the ways in which common expectations can thwart our accurate identification of "what really happened." When it comes to excessive experiences, confusion of interpretation (or the failure or delay to recognize) might also be a case of a phenomenon that is "hiding in plain sight." As a result, for the truth of the trauma to be made visible and recognized as such usually requires more than one witness to it. The hesitation to believe or the reluctance to recognize violent trauma as such implies the need for a multitude of testimonies witnessing to the reality of it in order to bring the phenomena to light.[32]

Finally, however, considering excessive experiences which are traumatic clarifies one further point which provides a kind of future hope for establishing the truth of excessive experience intersubjectively: namely, the afterlife of a traumatic experience. Because one often dissociates during a traumatic experience, it may be "experienced" first belatedly in the form of intrusive and uncontrollable flashbacks. However, these flashbacks occur with such a fixation on literal precision and sensory detail that they resist placement within an overarching narrative framework. It is important to underscore that uncertainty here does not result from lack of material evidence given by an experience, but precisely the opposite, its repeated proximity and excess—the fact that one can get no distance from the original event with which to be objective.[33] The painfulness of the truth of a traumatic experience is precisely that the subject undergoing the experience is not entirely in control of how they experience, interpret, and respond to it. However, and this is the illuminating point, the implication of this afterlife of trauma provides an example of the lasting agency of the originary event as a voice which will continue to make itself heard, correcting, augmenting, shifting, and challenging any single interpretation of it. We have seen above the way in which the determination of "what really happened" occurs intersubjectively. To this, we might

---

[31] See the opening quotation of this chapter.
[32] For an analysis of the plurality and multivocity inherent to testifying to traumatic experience see Tamsin Jones, "Bearing Witness: Hope for the Unseen," *Political Theology* 17, no. 2 (2016).
[33] See Cathy Caruth, *Trauma: Explorations in Memory* (Baltimore: Johns Hopkins University Press, 1995): "It is not, that is, having too little or indirect access to an experience that places its truth in question, in this case, but paradoxically enough, its very overwhelming immediacy, that produces its belated uncertainty" (6).

now add the element that the intersubjective signification of excessive experiences includes the signification given by the originary event itself.

How, then, do these intervening insights from trauma theory—(1) about the compulsion toward discovering the truth of the matter (what really happened), (2) about the materiality of the impact of excessive experiences, (3) about the significance of one's preparation or expectations in receptivity, and (4) about the ongoing agency of the cause of the experience—inform the previous discussion of religious experience? As I shall very briefly show, there are some remarkable parallels.

III. Returning to questions of religious experience

As the work of historians of Christian mysticism have shown, the monastery is best understood as the "schoolroom" or "military training ground" for mystical encounters, or religious experiences of a particularly acute degree; it is the place the religious learn their craft of spiritual warfare, sharpen their tools in the spiritual workshop, or learn the grammatical building blocks to mystical language.[34] Whichever metaphor one wants to use, the spiritual practices of reading scriptures, corporate and individual prayer, chanting psalms, and so on, provided the foundation within which mystical experience might emerge.[35] Such practices both prepare the ground of receptivity to excessive experiences and shape one's response to it, significantly however, without circumscribing or controlling it.

Amy Hollywood discusses this with reference to John Cassian's *Conferences*—a text all medieval monastics would have read. In Cassian, one is enjoined to:

> move through the corporate recitation or singing of the Psalms to a wordless exaltation, and then back to the measured voices of the community. Joy is engendered through practice—it is, to use Henry James's word, cultivated—and yet remains a mystery ... For the medieval monk or nun, canon or beguine, there is no contradiction between these assertions. Joy is both engendered through practice and given by divine grace; it is simultaneously recognizable and ineffable.[36]

Of course, this does not mean that a mystical experience—whether joyful or painful—is controlled or manipulated. It happens all of a sudden, unbidden, or spontaneously as a gift. But what Hollywood so acutely captures—and the mystics would have easily acknowledged—is that "spontaneity takes work; it is a cultivated habitus ..."[37]

---

[34] Amy Hollywood, "Song, Experience, and the Book in Benedictine Monasticism," in *A Cambridge Companion to Christian Mysticism*, ed. Amy Hollywood and Patricia Z. Beckman (Cambridge: Cambridge University Press, 2012), 63.
[35] Niklaus Largier, "Mysticism, Modernity, and the Invention of Aesthetic Experience," *Representations* 105 (2009): 40.
[36] Amy Hollywood, *Acute Melancholia and other Essays: Mysticism, History, and the Study of Religion* (New York: Columbia University Press, 2016), 60.
[37] Hollywood, *Acute Melancholia*, 63.

Combining these insights from mystical and traumatic experience, Patricia Dailey applies Marianne Hirsch's notion of the "postmemory" of trauma to that of a religious encounter. First, a mystical experience marks one by leaving an imprint or wound which has an affective impact felt in the soul, but also in the body. She writes, in ways that sound very reminiscent of Bessel van der Kolk, that it is "as if the body provided a mnemonic record for a memory that cannot yet be perceived or comprehended, only felt."[38] Secondly, this affective and bodily imprint compels the mystic to testify to his or her experience—whether through words or art: "Like the unassimilated memory of a traumatic event, this unlived experience continues to haunt the mystic, often in the somatic form of bodily pain" (347–8). Third, Dailey argues that such a disruptive experience is not immediately understood, and references Freud's notion of "belatedness" (*Nachträglichkeit*) to explain how the meaning of the event can only be given after some time has passed. She cites the examples of the visions of Hildegard von Bingen and Julian of Norwich, who both experience a delay before they record their experience, and when they do so, it is under some inner compulsion. Finally, in a way that coincides with what I argued above about the ongoing signifying input of the "voice" of the originary event of trauma, Dailey insists that the content of the recalled vision does not originate solely with the mystic who received it, but rather with the one who gave it, God: "It is not her memory, but the memory of God, in the strange sense of the subjective and objective genitive" (350). Thus, the belated mystical text produced in response to a vision is both an *active* and a *passive* production: "For Julian, the afterlife of the text also displays both senses of the genitive, attesting to her own spiritual practices as well as to the work of the divine in her ..." (350).

In conclusion, then, with both cases of excessive events—traumatic and religious—there is a will toward a discovery of the truth of the matter. Moreover, what is gleaned from the insights of trauma theory is that the voice of an excessively given phenomenon tends to continue to make itself heard, although not right away, but only belatedly, after some distance is gained from its original arrival. For the truth of an excessive event to be known and declared by the one who experiences it, that person must first have the capacity to bear it. In the case of trauma, there must be some distance (the establishment of basic physical and emotional safety, the re-establishment of interpersonal trust, and so on) in order to begin to cohere the original event with one's response to it. In the case of religious experience this might be thought of as a training to receive the experience as it is given, or in Gregory of Nyssa's terms, as a gracious gift to expand one's capacity to understand correctly and respond to something which remains beyond one's capacity.[39] While such preparation may control the packaging of the experience—its external structure and terminology—it cannot control the timing or

---

[38] Patricia Dailey, "Time and Memory," in *A Cambridge Companion to Christian Mysticism*, ed. Amy Hollywood and Patricia Z. Beckman (Cambridge: Cambridge University Press, 2012), 347.

[39] Gregory of Nyssa interprets Phil. 2:5–11 (in which the Incarnation is described as the kenosis of God) not as a divine self-limiting or constriction into human form, but as a filling, indeed and overflowing, of divinity into the finite vessel of humanity. Here the human is not taken over, but taken up and transformed in its ever-increasing capacity to receive the overflow of the divine being. See Lenka Karfíková, Scot Douglass, and Johannes Zachhuber, eds., *Gregory of Nyssa: Contra Eunomium II: An English version with Commentary and Supporting Studies* (Leiden: Brill, 2006).

content of the gift. Thus, in agreement with the social constructivists, as the historians of Christian mysticism have shown, mystical encounters are indeed shaped by specific spiritual practices and frameworks—they are, as Sharf put it, "affected by linguistic, cultural, or historical contingencies."[40] Yet, with the radical empiricists rather than the social constructivists, I would also argue that a scholar of religion must hold open the possibility of that truth of the experience signifying more than one's ideological commitments, socio-political status, and so on.

Such a stance of openness on the part of the scholar of religion investigating accounts of religious experience refuses the pre-determination of either a theism (requiring a supernatural explanation) or an atheism (requiring a naturalistic explanation), but instead enacts a disciplined agnosticism. Such an agnosticism needs also be distinguished from the phenomenological discipline of the *epochē*: the scholar of religion remains deeply interested in determining the cause of the experience— "what really happened"—and her scholarly discipline of openness which postpones determination is not without some hope that this will, in time, become more clear.[41]

The way in which an excessive experience is seen is dependent upon a number of subjective factors which shape the reception of the experience and one's capacity to respond to it. Yet the originary event of the experience also has an agency or a voice of its own which will not rest, or allow the subject to rest, with any one interpretation, but which acts in a corrective trajectory. Put in terms of Richard Kearney's "anatheistic" wager, the stranger at the door will eventually make itself known, friend or foe, angel or demon, visitor from the grave or the result of undigested gravy.[42]

---

[40] Sharf, "Experience," in Taylor, *Critical Terms*, 96.
[41] I am especially grateful for Christiaan Jacobs-Vandegeer (ACU) for his thoughtful response to my paper in the *Atheism, Religion and Experience Seminar*; his insights and, in particular, his questions concerning the identity of the scholar of religion, have prompted my thoughts here.
[42] See Richard Kearney, *Anatheism: Returning to God after God* (New York: Columbia University Press, 2010). I would like to thank Robyn Horner and Claude Romano for their invitation to participate in the *Atheism, Religion and Experience Seminar*, as well as all the participants of that seminar for the engaging and challenging conversations that ensued over the course of a few days.

12

Atheism, Religion, Experience (and Metaphysics?)

Patrick Masterson

In this contribution, I make a simple but much disputed point, namely, that realist metaphysics has as important a role to play as phenomenology in the philosophical elucidation of religious belief in God. They offer complementary rather than incompatible approaches to the philosophical elucidation of such belief and each plays a distinctive role in the theological presentation of the Christian religion. They are each appropriate, incomplete, and complement each other.

I. Atheism and the turn to the subject

The flight from metaphysics to phenomenology can credibly be linked to the development of modern and contemporary atheism. Until the seventeenth century, a metaphysically supported affirmation of God was almost universally accepted. It was the fool who said in his heart, "There is no God." Two great intellectual movements changed this: the modern scientific revolution and the modern philosophical revolution inaugurated by Descartes. Scientists such as Copernicus, Galileo, and Newton inaugurated a new conception of scientific knowledge –a less speculative and more practical, experimental one. Even though they were religious believers themselves, their new scientific method promoted an intrinsic understanding of the material world in terms of itself rather than an extrinsic metaphysical one in terms of a Creator. In its subsequent, extreme form, all scientific explanation—particularly of biological and mental phenomena—is to be provided in terms of basic laws of physics and chemistry. The underlying assumption that the more complex must be understood in terms of the less complex is compounded by the Darwinian claim that what comes after must be explained in terms of what comes before, the "*post-hoc propter-hoc*" assumption. This reductionist materialism finds philosophical expression in various forms of Positivism from that of Comte in the nineteenth century to that of Logical Positivism in the twentieth.

The other modern challenge to theism is the radical humanism deriving from the Cartesian turn inwards to human subjectivity rather than outwards to a divine creator for the source of all meaning and value. This approach was significantly developed in the eighteenth century by Kant, who maintained that we know things only as they appear to us and never as they are in themselves, and that not God, but we ourselves create the moral code which we adopt. This radical humanism finds contemporary expression in various forms of Existentialism, Phenomenology, and Linguistic Philosophy. Everything we know is correlative to the ecstatic intentionality of human consciousness. To claim to know about anything as it exists independently of our consciousness of it is an illusion. As Quentin Meillassoux explains:

> The central notion of modern philosophy since Kant seems to be that of *correlation*. By "correlation" we mean the idea according to which we only ever have access to the correlation between thinking and being, and never to either term considered apart from the other.... Consciousness and language enclose the world within ourselves.... We are in consciousness or language as in a transparent cage. Everything appears to be outside yet it is impossible to get out.[1]

The relationship between human consciousness and the world is thus seen as an internal one, a relation constitutive of what it relates and not one of external causality.

II. A phenomenology of "God"

Husserl makes the Cartesian innovation and its relation to his own work explicit: "Descartes, in fact, inaugurates an entirely new kind of philosophy. Changing its total style, philosophy takes a radical turn: from naïve objectivism to transcendental subjectivism—which, with its ever new but always inadequate attempts, seems to be striving toward some necessary final form, wherein its true sense and that of its radical transmutation itself might become disclosed."[2] Phenomenology, of course, is a philosophy of cognitional immanence. It suspends or brackets our allegedly naïve natural inclination to take for granted the independent existence of things in the world and our own independent existence as individual substances. This suspension of the natural attitude is called the *epochē*, or more comprehensively, the phenomenological reduction. Thus, Heidegger remarks:

> For Husserl the phenomenological reduction ... is the method of leading phenomenological vision from the natural attitude of the human being whose life is involved in the world of things and persons back to the transcendental life of consciousness and its noetic-noematic experiences, in which objects are constituted as correlates of consciousness.[3]

Many contemporary philosophers of religion abandon metaphysical speculation and take up the challenge of substituting a viable phenomenology of God and religious belief. Such phenomenological discussion addresses, in various ways, the pre-

---

[1] Quentin Meillassoux, *After Finitude: An Essay on the Necessity of Contingency*, trans. Ray Brassier (London: Continuum, 2008), 5.
[2] Edmund Husserl, *Cartesian Meditations: An Introduction to Phenomenology*, trans. Dorion Cairns (The Hague: Martinus Nijhoff, 1960), 4.
[3] Heidegger, *The Basic Problems of Phenomenology*, trans. Albert Hoftstadter (Bloomington, IN: Indiana University Press) 2008. 21.

philosophical religious belief in and worship of God and also the atheistic rejection of such worship and belief. God is envisaged, not metaphysically as independently existing Infinite Being, but rather as in an allegedly given salvific co-relationship with humanity. Through phenomenological elucidation of "natural belief" or "supernatural faith," God is affirmed as a God for humanity. This God is affirmed primarily as corresponding and giving experiential resolution to deep specifically human experiences such as those of finitude, contingency, fascination, dread, astonishment, hope, and desire. Phenomenological reflection upon what gives and manifests itself precisely as given and correlative to human consciousness is well adapted to consider philosophically the religious pre-philosophical, essentially first person and self-involving, relationship with God—a God "intended" and worshipped precisely as corresponding to and fulfilling one's deepest conscious needs and desires for meaning and value in one's life. Amongst the many philosophers of religion who have availed themselves of such a phenomenological approach, I mention a few whom I find particularly interesting: Richard Kearney, Emmanuel Levinas, Paul Ricœur, and Jean Luc Marion.

Richard Kearney, a former student of mine, escaped my metaphysical clutches and sought refuge in Paris with Levinas and Ricœur. He overcomes metaphysical speculation by resorting to a phenomenological account of the God of religious belief as an ethically enabling possibility rather than as pure act, first cause, or highest being.[4] This involves an eschatological appeal to "a possible God" experienced as an enabling ethical invocation which enables us to respond to others in a manner beyond any self-regarding consideration. He affirms that "God does not reveal himself, therefore, as an essence *in se* but as an I-Self for us ... the God of Mosaic manifestation cannot be God without relating to his other—humanity."[5] A phenomenology of religious belief and ethics is also characteristic of Levinas. "Ethics," he writes, "is the spiritual optics.... There can be no 'knowledge' of God separated from the relationship with men.... The dimension of the divine opens forth from the human face.... God rises to his supreme and ultimate presence as correlative to the justice rendered unto men."[6] Paul Ricœur questions the claim that the knowing subject has total mastery over the meaning of its experiences. There are religious feelings and dispositions, such as feelings of dependence, concern, confidence, which are experienced as ways of being absolutely affected. He remarks: "I therefore grant unreservedly that there can be a phenomenology of feelings and dispositions that can be qualified as religious by virtue of the disproportion within the relation between call and response."[7]

---

[4] Richard Kearney, *Anatheism: returning to God after God* (New York: Columbia University Press, 2010).
[5] *The God Who May Be: A Hermeneutics of Religion* (Bloomington: Indiana University Press, 2001).
[6] Emmanuel Levinas, *Totality and Infinity: an Essay on Exteriority*, trans. Alphonso Lingis (The Hague: Martinus Nijhoff, 1979), 78.
[7] Paul Ricœur, in Janicaud et al., *Phenomenology and the "Theological Turn,"* New York: Fordham University Press, 2001), 127.

III. Marion's phenomenology

Such phenomenological validation of an affirmation of God is developed profoundly by Jean Luc Marion. He challenges the unquestioned tradition of the "subject" coming down from Descartes through Kant to Husserl which sees the conscious subject as establishing rigorous pre-conditions for the emergence or manifestation of phenomena. For him, every phenomenon or manifestation that shows itself does so to the extent that it first gives itself. The "given to" does not precede the phenomenon as though constituting the pre-conditions of its appearance. The way is opened to Marion's characteristic claim that the correlative intuited given can exceed, overflow, and utterly saturate the subject's capacity to envisage, intend, or conceptualize it. A principal aim of Marion's subtle account of saturated phenomena is to delineate the possibility of a phenomenologically given intuition of God such, but not exclusively, as one finds in accounts of mystical experience. "In short," he says, "God remains incomprehensible not imperceptible—without adequate concept, not without giving intuition."[8]

But how, one might ask, can what is experienced be wholly transcendent if it is somehow calibrated with or correlative to a perceiving human subject? Would it not be more plausible to identify the allegedly dazzling experience as the pre-reflective experience of our own act of awareness rather than a perceived divine object? Perhaps what is sometimes pre-reflectively apperceived or affirmed as "saturated" or "dazzling" is our own act of perceiving rather than a dazzlingly perceived divine object or God. On some occasions our own assent and adhesion to what we claim to believe or affirm may be joyfully apprehended as a "saturating," or "dazzling," or profoundly assuring, conviction. What dazzles or saturates is not a given sacred or divine object, but the intensity and conviction of my assent to the authenticity or truth of what is affirmed or envisaged. The object thus affirmed or envisaged, however assuredly, may remain obscure, mysterious, imperceptible and incomprehensible, rather than a directly perceived, saturating, and dazzlingly evident given.

For Marion, however, it is the perceived or intuited divine reality itself which is so dazzlingly saturating. As such, it eliminates any constitutive activity of the subject. The subject is rendered wholly receptive. It is reduced to the status of a secondary or derived subject, constituted rather than constituting. It becomes a *me* rather than an *I*. I do not lay hold of the transcendent. It lays hold of me. Divine transcendence is given perceptibly and co-relatively as a structure immanent to a passively receptive human consciousness. Thus, he states: "I made it my goal to establish that givenness remains an immanent structure of any kind of phenomenality whether immanent or transcendent."[9] God's transcendent perfection is given immanently to human consciousness as beyond what we can effectively conceive. It is discovered as the instance par excellence of immanence.[10] The givenness of this transcendence and other religious phenomena is

---

[8] Richard Kearney, Jacques Derrida, and Jean-Luc Marion, "On the Gift: A Discussion between Jacques Derrida and Jean-Luc Marion, Moderated by Richard Kearney," in *God, the Gift and Postmodernism*, ed. John D. Caputo and Michael J. Scanlon (Bloomington: Indiana University Press, 1999), 40.
[9] Marion, "On the Gift," 70.
[10] *The Visible and the Revealed*. Trans. by Christina M. and others (New York: Fordham University Press, 2008), 5–6.

contained within the sphere of immanence to the exclusion of any ontological realism or metaphysical causality. As Marion explains: "When an allegedly adequate explanation is missing from them, that is to say, in fact their cause or sufficient reason, their legitimacy as phenomena is not thereby put in question, but only their objectivity beyond the limits of immanence."[11]

The phenomenological approaches to philosophy of religion which I have outlined are very appealing. They have the great merit of situating and validating discussion about God in terms which are directly relevant to its primary pre-philosophical context. This is the religious context where God is primarily affirmed, in a self-involving way as a salvific given corresponding to and resolving profound human exigencies and intentionalities such as contingency, desire, veneration, repentance, or hope. These given salvific phenomena are treated as they present and give themselves to consciousness and not subjected to any *a priori* criterion of what is rationally admissible.

Personally, I find convincing a qualified version of such an approach to an affirmation of God as correlative or, perhaps better, as co-responding asymmetrically to the rational hopes and exigencies of human consciousness. Through the exercise of our rational human subjectivity we can aspire to live under the authority of truth, beauty, goodness, and love. The hopeful affirmation of God as a personal creative principle of unrestricted truth, beauty, goodness, and love validates and makes ultimate sense of this aspiration of human subjectivity in a way that atheism does not. Such a phenomenologically oriented approach tends to reverse a traditional approach which moves from reasoned affirmation of or faith in God's existence, through the rationally grounded hope which it justifies, to love of Himself. Taking a clue from Augustine's *"Non intratur in veritatem nisi per caritatem"* this alternative approach seeks to move from love of God as infinitely desirable perfection, envisaged circumspectly as at least a possibility, through the rational hope which this evokes, to an affirmation of or faith in God's existence.

IV. A renewed appeal to metaphysical realism

However appealing—and even convincing—such a phenomenologically oriented approach to religious belief in God may be, it is not, I believe, the only valid one. It should be complemented by another similarly incomplete approach, namely, that of metaphysics or natural theology. Such an approach is characterized by realist *causal* thinking as distinct from the mutual *implication* thinking characteristic of phenomenology. The metaphysical approach to which I refer is one grounded in the "natural attitude" from which the phenomenological *epochē* abstracts, as recommended unambiguously by Husserl, who states: "*Instead now of remaining at this standpoint, we propose to alter it radically. . . . We put out of action the general thesis which belongs to the*

---

[11] Jean-Luc Marion in Richard Kearney, Jacques Derrida, and Jean-Luc Marion, "On the Gift: 70.

essence of the natural standpoint, we place in brackets whatever it includes respecting the nature of Being. I use the 'phenomenological' *epochē* which *completely bars me from using any judgment that concerns spatio-temporal existence.*"[12]

The realist metaphysical approach, abstracted from by phenomenology, originates in a primary intuition of being as "that which exists," an intuition enabled by the evidence provided by what is given immediately in perception. It rejects the fundamental presupposition of phenomenology which identifies being simply with a phenomenon given to a conscious subject. It distinguishes being and phenomena, distinguishing that which pertains to reality from that which pertains to our way of apprehending it.[13] Realist metaphysics develops through analysis of the various intelligible or knowable modalities and causal dependencies intrinsic to the analogical nature of finite being as existing independently of our consciousness of it. This reflective metaphysical appraisal culminates, by indirect argument, in the affirmation of God as infinite being, shown to exist as the creator and sustainer of the existence and activity of all finite being. It is a more detached, impersonal, and objective consideration than the self-involving dazzling impact allegedly attained by the standpoint of phenomenological givenness.

Dismissive language by either approach about the credibility of the alternative approach is not helpful. Phenomenological dismissal of moderate realism as "naïve" is likely to evoke the response from the moderate realist that the phenomenological approach is "contrived." The metaphysical approach, grounded in the natural standpoint and affirming the intuitive awareness of independently existing being, can gracefully acknowledge the psychological possibility and indeed the complementary significance of the phenomenological reduction of the natural standpoint. But the phenomenological approach appears to have difficulty in according comparable toleration and recognition to the complementary approach of realist metaphysics, as is evidenced by its endlessly repeated rejection of metaphysics, which I mentioned above.

Two separate appraisals of an identical sentence exemplify the nature of the divide. The metaphysical realist can happily endorse as a truism the phenomenological claim that: "Nothing can be *consciously affirmed* as existing—apart from a conscious subject." But she rejects as patently false the phenomenological claim that "Nothing can be consciously affirmed—*as existing apart from a conscious subject.*" The difficulty which the phenomenological approach appears to encounter with the metaphysical is grounded in its unconditional "turning away from" or "putting between brackets" the natural standpoint. It effects the reduction to immanence of all transcendent objects that present themselves as real from the natural "standpoint." In justification of this, it resorts to the claim that the natural standpoint is a trap from which human consciousness must release itself. It claims that the world which presents to the natural standpoint as existing independently is in fact somehow consciously posited. But it does not explain how that which thus presents itself naturally as existing independently is somehow an illusion and is more properly described as a posited correlate of our

---

[12] Husserl, *Ideas I*, §31.
[13] cf. Georges Van Riet, *Philosophie et Religion* (Leuven: Peeters, 1971) 267–72.

intentional subjectivity (transcendentally constituted?) and that unless this is appreciated one is involved in a snare.

It is not at all evident to me that the natural standpoint, in affirming the independent existence of the beings which it intuits, is caught in such a trap. Indeed, it seems to me that phenomenologically reduced awareness of phenomena as immanent to consciousness is more likely to find itself in a trap if it precludes as illusory or unreliable the complementary possibility and appropriateness of a metaphysical analysis of being as given in the natural standpoint. As Roger Chambon observes: "The being of the phenomenon is not its phenomenon-being but the setting it has in and from trans-phenomenal being."[14] Being and its phenomenological manifestation are always formally distinct. It is the ability of realist language to signify the existent precisely as existing independently that enables it to engage with a world that transcends it. Even in "pre-phenomenological" times, Aquinas could observe that "we must say, therefore, that concepts stand in relation to the intellect as that by which it thinks or understands and not as that of which it thinks."[15] Let me illustrate aspects of this contention and its relevance to the philosophical affirmation of the existence of the God of religious belief.

At the heart of the replacement of the moderate realist natural standpoint by the existentialist or phenomenological reduction is a replacement of the metaphysical concept of "substance" by that of "conscious subject" which exists only as a term in an internal conscious relationship with a "given" which situates it. It is an interpretation of being from the standpoint of conscious subjectivity rather than from the traditional metaphysical understanding of being from the standpoint of being itself. William Shearson argues:

> This assumption, simply stated by *every* existentialist, ... is that the Self is not a substance but a lived relation to that which situates it; that this relation is and only could be an internal relation (because only two substances could be externally related); and this in turn means that that which situates the Self—which shall be called the situating Other—enters into the very ontological constitution of the Self.[16]

For metaphysics, substance is the radical intrinsic principle or cause of being in the things that exist. It is the origin of the resources which characterize a being, its nature, its qualities, and its activity. It grounds a being in the integrity of its being as an autonomous intelligible individual self, distinct from others. In the case of a human "being," its substance as individual self possesses the required resources and causal efficacy for the emergence and exercise of its distinctive qualities, its consciousness, and its exercise of its characteristic activities of understanding and love. Consciousness

---

[14] Roger Chambon, *Le monde comme perception et realite* (Paris: Vrin, 1974), 88.
[15] Thomas Aquinas, *S.T.* I, q. 85, art.2.
[16] William A. Shearson, "The Common Assumptions of Existentialist Philosophy," *International Philosophical Quarterly*) XV (1975): 137–8.

is not what profoundly constitutes the being of the substantial self but is rather an activity distinct from and emerging from this substantial self.

My reality as existing substance precedes my phenomenological reality as intentional subjectivity and is not wholly reducible to its discourse. Such discourse implies an order prior to itself, an ontological order of independently existing substances, beyond the limited signifying capacity of phenomenological subjectivity to express adequately. Phenomenology replaces the substantial self with conscious subjectivity and the relation of intentionality is identified as the essence of this consciousness. Being itself, no longer a system of individual existing substances is only that which constitutes subject as subject and object as object in the subject-object correlation. Phenomenologically, whatever is given, including the transcendence of God, attains phenomenal manifestation and reality in virtue of a conscious and intentional correlation between given and given to. If the divine transcendence, given phenomenally in a dazzling or even terrifying perception to an utterly passive conscious subject, can, and perhaps must, be affirmed as intrinsically more than only a correlate of this subjectivity, the question arises as to how is this so. Would it not be more accurate to say that the givenness of divine transcendence experienced as a phenomenon immanent to consciousness is more appropriately described as a cipher or trace of a divine giver, an effect created and enabled in human consciousness by an ontologically distinct transcendent God?

However, phenomenologists reject such a hypothesis. They see it as a lapse into the sort of *metaphysical specialis* which the phenomenological reduction rigorously precludes. To ask of what gives itself "why does it exist?" is not to be answered by an appeal to a cause but simply with the response "there is what gives itself." Thus, Marion sees givenness as a more fundamental and rationally more illuminating consideration than efficient causation which presupposes a metaphysical outlook foreign to phenomenology. In such a metaphysical system, he insists, the possibility of appearing never belongs to what appears. A phenomenon can appear only under the condition of some sufficient reason or cause. However, far from requiring such a reason, he claims it is enough for a phenomenon to give itself through intuition. Intuition is justified *de jure* from itself by claiming to be the unconditioned origin. What is involved in phenomenology is the principle of sufficient intuition rather than the principle of sufficient reason. It is not defined extrinsically in terms of a cause or a giver. It is in no way equivalent to a production.[17] Any ontological appeal to God as the cause or giver of givenness is allegedly ruinous to the phenomenological project. More generally, Levinas remarks: "The phenomenological conception of *intentionality* consists, essentially, in identifying thinking and existing. It disputes a reference in the ontological structure of consciousness to a foundation, to any kind of nucleus which would serve as scaffolding for intention; it is a matter of not thinking of consciousness as a substantive."[18] To a realist philosopher, this sounds a bit like the problem faced by Alice

---

[17] Jean-Luc Marion, *The Visible and the Revealed*, trans. Christina M. and others Gschwandtner (New York: Fordham University Press, 2008), 100.
[18] Emmanuel Levinas, *En découvrant l'existence avec Husserl et Heidegger* (Paris, Vrin, 1967), 97.

in Wonderland. In the real world, Alice often perceived a substantial cat without a grin; only in the phenomenological Wonderland had she to perceive a grin without a cat!

It seems to me that a phenomenological approach to God which is achieved by a process of abstraction or reduction from a natural realist standpoint should be seen, precisely as such, as only one particular approach, however valuable. It precludes discussion of "being" in terms of substance and causality precisely because it has abstracted from the viewpoint or standpoint where such terminology is relevant. From this abstracted viewpoint it is enabled to make valuable observations about God as God is for humanity. But this abstraction should not eliminate the equally significant approach from the realist or natural standpoint which it evidently presupposes in order to abstract from it. This is the approach of a metaphysics of substance which elucidates the ontological conditions out of which emerges conscious subjectivity with its capacity for phenomenological reflection about the correlation in consciousness of the given and the given to. "Substance radically pre-determines the ontological conditions out of which the human conscious subject emerges as an individual conscious subject endowed with a capacity for conscious activity of a determinate kind to be exercised in intersubjectivity."[19] Substance, as the deep grounding interiority of an individual human being from which the conscious intentionality of human subjectivity emerges requires appropriate metaphysical elucidation. Perhaps metaphysics articulates the transcendent necessary conditions of those immanent necessary conditions of our phenomenological experience. The phenomenological subject is intentionally *correlated* with its phenomenological object. But individual ontological substances *participate* objectively with other such substances in the transcendent perfection of actual existence. Their existence and activity are a presupposition of subsequent phenomenological enquiry and are the ontological basis and justification of an independent metaphysical approach.

Such an approach, proceeding by way of a metaphysical analysis of the metaphysical meaning of finite being, culminates in an affirmation of infinite being as its free and self-sufficient transcendent Creator. *Pace* Hegel, without the world, God is still God! Initially, such an affirmation may not have the same intrinsically self-involving engagement as the phenomenological God allegedly given in experience precisely as corresponding correlatively to human exigencies. But it is an equally valid, even if less immediately self-involving, affirmation of God. And, I would argue that both approaches are valid but incomplete and complementary.

However existentially engaging a phenomenological confirmation of a religious affirmation of God it can give rise to certain objections. These may be addressed by reference to metaphysical considerations as an appropriate, indeed necessary, complementary approach. For example, the religious appeal of the phenomenological correlation of God as given in perception to our conscious subjectivity has been presented as a fabrication or an illusion of a tormented consciousness. Thus, Merleau-Ponty remarks that such discourse is inherently mercurial to the extent that one can never be sure whether it is God who sustains people in their humanity or vice versa,

---

[19] Desmond Connell, "Substance and Subject," *Philosophical Studies* 26 (1978): 22. My discussion is indebted to this important paper.

since his existence is affirmed only by means of their own.[20] And there is the well-known jibe articulated by Jocelyn Benoist: "What will you say to me if I say to you where you see God I see nothing?"

It seems to me that it is possible, more appropriate, and even necessary to maintain that phenomenology, metaphysics, and theology constitute three valid, but limited and complementary perspectives on the great topic of the existence and nature of God and of God's co-existence with us humans who are graced into divine friendship. Perhaps in the beatific vision it will all come together in a unified intuition. However, in the meanwhile, there is nothing disconcerting about finding that we must have recourse to different and complementary discourses. Perhaps we need such different discourses in discussing two great truths of Christian belief, namely, that God created us and that God has graced us into a loving inter-personal relationship. Whereas metaphysics can elucidate philosophically the truth of creation, phenomenology may provide a more effective account of our loving friendship with God.

Physicists are not alarmed when they find that they have to have recourse to very different explanatory discourses in terms of both waves and particles to account for physical phenomena such as light and heat! Describing the world differently does not imply that the phenomenologist and the metaphysician see different worlds or that one description is reducible to the other by translation or elimination. They retain a certain autonomy *vis-à-vis* one another; each attaining significant insights but at the expense of not considering or abstracting from the insights of the other. However, their distinctive characteristics which enable their differing stances and discourse also constitute the basis for a discussion of their compatibility and complementarity. That these two approaches to belief in God, the internal and the external, each conveying crucially important insights, do not coalesce into a unified viewpoint is a consequence of the finite nature of our knowledge of things. It is just a further illustration of the more general difficulty in every branch of knowledge of ever totally reconciling external and internal perspectives.

V. Complementarity

Granted the difference between the two approaches, how can they complement each other? Henning Tegtmeyer adverts to the importance in each approach of overlapping themes or notions such as "transcendence" and "givenness."[21] Perhaps the "being given" or *donation* of phenomenology and the "given being" or intuited *esse* of metaphysics can be helpfully interpreted as complementary accounts, inverse and obverse, of the same encompassing reality. The "being given" affirmed in our phenomenological experience is how reality appears from the immanent internal standpoint of human consciousness. The "given being" affirmed or "consented to" metaphysically is how the same reality appears from an external, objective, impersonal standpoint.

---

[20] Maurice Merleau-Ponty, *Eloge de la philosophie* (Paris, Gallimard, 1958), 38.
[21] This was a conversation that took place in the *Atheism, Religion and Experience* seminar in Rome in January 2019.

My awareness of being from the phenomenological viewpoint of its correlative givenness to my consciousness is an awareness intentionally enabled by me. Its meaning or significance presupposes, in virtue of the consciously enacted *epochē* which enables it, my prior and more fundamental realist direct intuition of being—given as existing independently of my consciousness. This is an awareness of being susceptible to subsequent metaphysical analysis of its analogical character. Such analysis is ontology, not phenomenology.

However, this fundamental affirmation of being as existing independently of my consciousness of it also involves, as part of its implicit meaning, that it can be considered differently. It can be considered from an alternative and derivative perspective as a phenomenon given to me as conscious intentional subject. Here our attention is directed not to a metaphysical analysis of being but rather to an epistemological consideration of our various ways of knowing, for example, perceiving, remembering, imagining, desiring. The two modes of givenness, one the givenness of objectively existing being to intuition, the other the givenness of phenomenologically reduced being as correlative to a conscious self or subject, are related to each other as complementary perspectives, a relationship of presupposition in the one case and of implication in the other.

The relationship of presupposition in which objectively intuited existing being stands to phenomenologically perceived being is more fundamental than the reverse relationship of implication in which phenomenological being stands to objectively intuited existing being. The objectively existing givenness is more fundamental than the phenomenological because, as indicated above, substance is more fundamental than subjectivity. Something can be considered as a phenomenon given correlatively to a conscious subject only because such consideration presupposes, as more fundamental, the existence of a human substance who can exercise her characteristically human activity of cognitional openness to and engagement with other independently existing substances.

The phenomenon which can be considered as object which gives itself intentionally to conscious subjectivity is more than a datum of consciousness. It is a reflectively considered manifestation of the being which is cognitively disclosed to intuition as an independent self-possessed being whose component principles and ultimate foundation are matters for objective metaphysical consideration beyond any subject-oriented phenomenological description of the nature of our cognitive experience. As Tegtmeyer argues, Husserl scholars maintain that his phenomenology was always meant to culminate in metaphysics although Husserl himself deferred this project. Perhaps, as Tegtmeyer contends, this aim can be elaborated by a radicalizing of the phenomenological understanding of notions such as transcendence and givenness. This suggestion would favor an approach to philosophy of religion which begins, not in abstract impersonal metaphysical argument but rather with an account of the immanent role which terms such as "transcendence" and "givenness" play in a phenomenological elucidation of religious commitment and enquiry. Such an account would respect the religious aspiration for a God who is relevant and corresponds intimately and directly to human hopes, needs, and desires—a God whose givenness and transcendence is envisaged as corresponding "correlatively" and salvifically to human exigencies.

From this initial stage of philosophy of religion one might proceed to argue that if one is to avoid an exclusively reductive and anthropomorphic absolutization of this phenomenological understanding of terms such as "givenness" and "transcendence" as applied to God, they must be complemented by a more radical realist metaphysical understanding of them. Perhaps such argument should proceed by disclosing that phenomenology's description of its immanent perception of divine givenness and transcendence as correlative to the conscious self or subject involves a performative contradiction which undermines an affirmation of the absolute and unqualified transcendence of God. The contradiction involved in the claim that God is both correlative to human consciousness and absolutely independent of this consciousness may be resolved by arguing that phenomenology's immanentist conception of divine transcendence must be complemented by one in terms of the metaphysical understanding of divine transcendence which it presupposes. Likewise, the phenomenological account of divine givenness of being as immanently correlative to human consciousness must be complemented by the metaphysical analysis of the intuition of being as intrinsically independent of this consciousness which it presupposes.

Underlying the differing approaches of phenomenological *epochē* and metaphysical realism there are two distinct guiding ideas which characterize their respective approaches to philosophy of religion. These are "correlation"—in the case of phenomenology, and "asymmetry"—in the case of realist metaphysics. Correlated terms are intrinsically related and mutually defining. In the case of an asymmetrical relationship, one term is really affected and modified by the relationship whereas the other is not. It retains a certain transcendence and independence *vis-à-vis* the other term of the relationship. Metaphysics, such as that adapted by Aquinas from Aristotle, is grounded in the affirmation of intrinsically intelligible substantial being as existing independently of my human consciousness of it. In my cognitive intuition of such being, I am genuinely modified and enhanced by knowing it. However, the being I apprehend is not intrinsically characterized or modified by my cognitive relationship to it. In phenomenology, such ontological asymmetry is reinterpreted as logical correlativity; metaphysical causality is interpreted as logical implication; external relations and distinctions are internalized. Phenomenologically, God is affirmed as existing in salvific correlation with religious sentiments of contingency, finitude and hope. In metaphysical realism the relationship between humanity and God is affirmed as an asymmetric one of radical causal dependence upon an ontologically independent and utterly transcendent Infinite Being.

What is important in the context of contemporary philosophy of religion, which as we have seen is ill-disposed to metaphysics, is to demonstrate that the correlationist epistemology characteristic of such phenomenological philosophy of religion overlaps with and ultimately presupposes as more fundamental the complementary asymmetrical ontology of metaphysical realism. The asymmetry characteristic of our intuitive realist awareness of being as existing independently of our human consciousness of it is achieves a more fundamental knowledge than the various forms in which such intuitive awareness enables this being to be subsequently considered phenomenologically as simply intentionally correlative to our conscious subjectivity.

The asymmetry involved in realist metaphysics between independently existing being and our intuition of it resembles the metaphysical asymmetry between us and God which is presupposed by the various ways in which God can be envisaged phenomenologically as correlative to our religious exigencies. But I leave the last word to Aquinas, who with customary insight hits the nail right on the head. He writes: "Now a relation of God to creatures, is not a reality in God, but in the creature; for it is in God in our idea only: as when what is knowable is so called with relation to knowledge, not that it depends on knowledge, but because knowledge depends on it."[22]

---

[22] Thomas Aquinas, *S.T*, I, q.6.

13

On Seeing Nothing—A Critique of Marion's Account of Religious Phenomenality

Christina M. Gschwandtner

Does the line between theist and atheist experience run through *what* phenomena one experiences or *how* one experiences them? Do atheists and theists have different experiences or do they rather respond to or interpret the same phenomenon differently? Can the experience distinguish between or provide a basis for a theist rather than atheist or non-theist position? What makes them different and does either have a more convincing, more coherent, more phenomenological position? This contribution will argue that Jean-Luc Marion attempts to provide such phenomenological distinctions in his work, that the positions he suggests are all recognizable, but that on his own count it ultimately proves impossible to give an account of an experience of revelation, because the (atheistic) blindness that refuses to see is indistinguishable, on phenomenological terms, from the (theistic) blindness that is bedazzled by the overwhelmingly, paradoxically saturated phenomenon. I will outline Marion's various attempts to distinguish the first kind of blindness from the second—that is, what might be called various "atheist" or non-theist experiences versus a more genuinely "theist" one, although this is not language Marion himself employs—in order to complicate his account of the first kind of blindness and challenge his assurance that the latter kind is evidence of having experienced a phenomenon of revelation.[1]

---

[1] For Marion, even the "theist" position harbors several possibilities. For example, one may see an idol rather than an icon. While this is a genuine experience of the divine, it experiences the divine in one's own image, constructs it as a mirror of oneself. While this is, indeed, a genuine experience of the divine (or some divine), it is not an experience of revelation where the conditions and parameters are all provided by the divine and we find ourselves envisioned by God rather than directing our gaze toward the divine. This may be a religious experience, but it is not a theist experience, or at least not a genuinely Christian experience (there is continual slippage between these terms for Marion). I will not be able to explore these particular dimensions in the present chapter.

I. Evidence for experiencing phenomena of revelation

Marion argues that phenomenology in the past has focused too much on what he calls "poor" or "common" phenomena, such as objects, mathematical concepts, everyday tools, and other such things that can be easily constituted by consciousness. Phenomenology has so far for the most part ignored richer phenomena, such as historical or cultural events, works of art, the immediacy of our flesh, the encounter with the face of the other, or phenomena of revelation, because all such "saturated" phenomena give more than can be constituted: they overwhelm consciousness with their bedazzling excess.[2] While maybe not always frequent, such phenomena are not esoteric but "banal"; we all encounter them: in the dazzling vision of the painting, the sensuous voice of the diva, the succulent fragrance of the perfume, the intoxicating taste of fine wine, the seductive touch of the eroticized body.[3] Marion contends that phenomena of revelation—that is to say, an experience of the divine, such as an encounter with the risen Christ—function in similar fashion: they combine all the elements of excess evident in cultural or aesthetic phenomena, inasmuch as they are experienced as overwhelming in terms of quantity, quality, relation, and modality. Although we cannot constitute such phenomena because they escape all categories, come in surprising, overwhelming, and sudden ways that cannot be predicted, foreseen, controlled, or assimilated, this very shock, surprise, or "bedazzlement" can be marked by the recipient.[4] While consciousness cannot constitute such phenomena or in any other way impose predetermined categories on them, such phenomena are still fully given and revealed or manifested in a "counter-experience," that turns the witness into someone devoted or fully given over to the phenomenon. The phenomenality of such saturated phenomena, including a possible phenomenon of revelation, can be described or unfolded through this impact and thus provide evidence (or a kind of "negative certainty") for the experience of such phenomena.[5]

Marion's account has been challenged in a variety of ways.[6] One prominent critic is Jocelyn Benoist who has written several review essays on aspects of Marion's work and

---

[2] This notion was first proposed in an essay from the 1980s, most recently included in Jean-Luc Marion, "The Possible and Revelation," in *The Visible and the Revealed* (New York: Fordham University Press, 2008). It is worked out most fully in his *Being Given: Toward a Phenomenology of Givenness*, trans. Jeffrey L. Kosky (Stanford: Stanford University Press, 2002). The different types of saturated phenomena are examined in more detail in his *In Excess: Studies of Saturated Phenomena*, trans. Robyn Horner and Vincent Berraud (New York: Fordham University Press, 2002). He addresses the idea of revelation most fully in his Gifford lectures: *Givenness and Revelation*, trans. Stephen Lewis (Oxford: Oxford University Press, 2016) *D'Ailleurs: La Révélation* (Paris: Grasset, 2020).

[3] *Visible and the Revealed*, 127–33.

[4] See especially *Being Given*, Book III, where he describes these parameters of excess of intuition in terms of anamorphosis, sudden or surprising arrival, fait accompli, incident, and event. He reiterates this in later treatments: The saturated phenomenon is "unforeseeable, irreversible, unrepeatable as such, immediately past and devoid of cause or reason." *In Excess*, 41.

[5] See especially *Negative Certainties*, trans. Stephen E. Lewis (Chicago: University of Chicago Press, 2015).

[6] These include Dominique Janicaud (most famously but perhaps least convincingly), François-David Sebbah, Shane Mackinlay, Marlène Zarader, and many others. For present purposes the critique by Anthony Steinbock is the most relevant: "The Poor Phenomenon: Marion and the Problem of Givenness," in *Words of Life: New Theological Turns in French Phenomenology*, eds. Bruce Ellis

also comments on the proposal of the saturated phenomenon in his *L'idée de phénoménologie*.[7] Marion only rarely responds to critics explicitly, so it is significant that he engages Benoist's critique in detail, arguing not only that the notion of saturation is much broader than instances of revelation, but also responding specifically to his claim that one might not see a phenomenon of revelation at all. He accuses Benoist of a "refusal to see" what is really there, fully given, but suggests at the same time that there might be various interpretations of such a phenomenon, some interpreting a phenomenon as "poor," others interpreting the same phenomenon as "saturated." Such misinterpretation or misidentification of the phenomenon—for example, by turning it into an object—also fails to see the phenomenon properly. Marion addresses this issue of whether a phenomenon of revelation can be seen or not and what it would take to identify it or make it visible also in several other places, where he offers a number of possible reasons why one might not see or experience revelatory phenomena. Sometimes he identifies such a failure to acknowledge a phenomenon of revelation as willful or self-inflicted blindness, sometimes as incomprehension or confusion, sometimes as weakness or inability to "bear" its impact, sometimes even as not having been given the proper condition by God.

We can thus distinguish between several "moments" of the phenomenon's process of phenomenalization, in which "not seeing" can be located in different places: first, not seeing because one is not even willing to approach a phenomenon or subject oneself to its phenomenality; second, not seeing because one experiences the phenomenality but cannot identify it, or experiences it in the wrong way as a different sort of phenomenality; third, not seeing because one misidentifies the phenomenon one has nevertheless experienced and experienced as the right sort of phenomenality but now gives a wrong interpretation to it, conflates the categories one nevertheless admits to exist and to be appropriate in other contexts; finally, not seeing because one experiences the phenomenon but gives up too quickly, cannot bear its phenomenality. Descriptions of these various types of "not seeing" can be found throughout Marion's work. One might suggest, then, that there are various possible (and different) types of "atheist" positions or at least positions *vis-à-vis* the theist (or believer), here taken to be the one who is able to experience the saturated phenomenon of revelation and give an account of such experience. Let us take each in turn, and then finally return to the one who sees fully, the "gifted" who responds to the saturated phenomenon as a phenomenon of revelation and is wholly given over or devoted to (*adonné à*) its manifestation.

Benson and Norman Wirzba, 120–31 (New York: Fordham University Press, 2010). Steinbock argues that Marion does not sufficiently work out the notion of "poverty" and that there are actually several kinds of poverty at work in his account, some referring to the type of phenomenon that is encountered, and some to the ways in which one encounters it. I am focusing here solely on the second dimension: the blindness or failure to see.

[7] Jocelyn Benoist, "Qu'est-ce qui est donné? La pensée et l'événement," *Archives de philosophie* 59 (1996): 629–57; "Les voix du soliloque: Sur quelques lectures récentes du cogito," *Les études philosophiques* 4 (1997): 541–55; "L'écart plutôt que l'excédent," *Philosophie*: Jean-Luc Marion 78 (2003): 77–93; *L'idée de phénoménologie* (Paris: Beauchesne, 2001).

II. Refusing to see

First, Marion suggests that such a failure of phenomenalization might consist in a willful blindness, that one would be able to see but is unwilling to look carefully, because the possible appearance or manifestation of certain kinds of phenomena have been rejected out of hand. Marion responds to Benoist's question, "What will you say to me if I say to you that where you see God, I see nothing?" by accusing him of simple denial of the phenomenon. He argues that "the force of the argument can be turned against the one who uses it, for the fact of not comprehending and seeing nothing should not always or even most often disqualify what it is a question of comprehending and seeing, but rather [disqualifies] the one who understands nothing and sees only a ruse."[8] He had already suggested as much in an earlier text: "Whatever the case might be, there is nothing astonishing in the fact that one inquires after God's right to inscribe himself within phenomenality. What is astonishing is that one should be so stubborn—and without conceptual reason—about denying him this right, or rather that one is no longer even surprised by this pigheaded refusal."[9] The "refusal to see" then sees nothing, although something is clearly there. It is blind in an obstinate or stubborn way, simply turning its eyes away, refusing to take seriously what gives itself fully, denying it, maybe even guessing that it could be there but refusing to investigate properly. This is "seeing nothing" but in a very particular way, it is the deliberate seeing nothing when there is, in fact, something to be seen. This might be called a more or less explicitly atheist position, which either maintains firmly and without further investigation that nothing can be seen or even actively tries to prove that there is nothing there to see.

After exploring some other possibilities (such as misidentification, which we will consider below), Marion returns to the fundamental accusation: "Without admitting the hypothesis of saturated phenomena, either one cannot see certain phenomena that nevertheless appear banally, or one has to deny what one nevertheless sees ... And is there a greater crime for a phenomenologist than not seeing or, worse, not accepting what one sees—in short, an inflicted or voluntary blindness?"[10] In other places, Marion gives this as the very reason for Christ's death: "And he was put to death so that one would not have to recognize him *as* this gift of God ... To recognize Jesus *as* the gift of God, one must first recognize him *as* the Son of the Father."[11] This constitutes an explicit refusal to recognize Christ as the visible phenomenon of the revelation of God. Jesus is apprehended but one turns one's eyes away and refuses to acknowledge him. In a more strictly phenomenological way, he argues in *Being Given* that the recipient of the gift or the saturated phenomenon might not want to receive it and thus refuses its manifestation.[12] Thus, one kind of blindness to revelation is the refusal to open one's

---

[8] *Visible and Revealed*, 124.
[9] *Being Given*, 243.
[10] *Visible and Revealed*, 133.
[11] Jean-Luc Marion, *Believing in Order to See*, trans. by Christina M. Gschwandtner (New York: Fordham University Press, 2017), 130.
[12] "If the gifted always phenomenalizes what gives itself to him and receives himself from it, nothing establishes that the gifted always can or wants to receive all that is given." *Being Given*, 310. We will return to the point of inability of reception below.

eyes, the unwillingness to experience the phenomenon, the deliberate turning away from any possibility of encountering the divine.

This is obviously a real and meaningful category; we might cite any number of phenomena (not only religious) that some people do not experience, because they refuse to believe that such phenomenon do, in fact, appear in any form.[13] Such "militant" atheism does not, however, ultimately respond to Benoist's contention that there is nothing to see. God's existence or the phenomenality of a possible phenomenon of revelation is not proven by the refusal of some people to engage the question. Their supposed turning away from a manifestation of the divine does not, in itself, provide evidence for such a manifestation. How would one determine that someone's inability to see is a deliberate unwillingness? It is equally possible that there has actually been no experience of a phenomenon, that such phenomena do not appear (maybe cannot appear because there simply are no phenomena of this sort) and that no dishonesty or dissembling is involved. That is to say, although we can certainly make sense of the possibility that someone might refuse to acknowledge an experience (religious or not), this provides no argument for the existence or reality or effectiveness of the phenomenon. It also does not give us any access to the potential phenomenality of such a "refused" phenomenon.

III. Confusion about what is seen

Second, it is possible that certain phenomena only appear with a very particular kind of phenomenality and if one expects a different sort of phenomenality or assumes that all phenomenality is the same, hence excluding this particular sort, one would be unable to apprehend such phenomena with their unique phenomenality. In fact, applying such incorrect categories means that nothing is experienced: "Nothing proves that experience is reducible to conditions imposed on it by the concern for objectness and objectivity nor that, when I have the experience of what does not appear as an object, I experience nothing or that nothing appears if it does not appear as an object."[14] This second category assumes that there may well be something to be seen but that it is not apprehended because the wrong approach is being used. The experience of revelation requires its own approach, its own "criteria" (to appropriate Ricœur's terms for the particularity of religious language or methodology). Here, the person's willingness or unwillingness to see is not at stake; instead, the approach to the phenomenon is misguided. There are different kinds of phenomena, each of which imposes its peculiar phenomenality and can only be experienced within that particular type of phenomenality.

In his response to Benoist, Marion goes on to elaborate this second possibility, namely that saturated phenomena display a different kind of phenomenality that has to be identified or unfolded in a different way:

---

[13] Experiences of spirits, ghosts, instances of telepathy, dreams, might constitute less explicitly religious examples.
[14] *Visible and Revealed*, 135.

Not only does admitting an insurmountable powerlessness to see or comprehend guarantee that something does indeed give itself to be seen and comprehended but the glorious claims of blindness directly and of themselves constitute a theoretical argument against this possibility of seeing or comprehending. To be sure, claiming to see is not sufficient to prove that one saw. Yet the fact or the pretense of not seeing does not prove that there is nothing to see. It can simply suggest that there is indeed something to see, but that in order to see it, it is necessary to learn to see otherwise because it could be a question of a phenomenality different from the one that manifests objects.[15]

If the correct "version" of phenomenality is discovered or applied, one will be able to experience the phenomenon. He often puts this in terms of an alternative form of knowledge in a way that parallels the claim about different kinds of phenomenality: "Faith is the mode of knowledge suitable for the saturated phenomena of the mode of Revelation."[16] More fully in the Gifford lectures, he explains: "no one can see that which is uncovered (*apokalypsis*) unless he believes it; but no one can believe if he does not will it, and *no one can will unless he loves what he believes and wills to will.*"[17]

The implication of this "different phenomenality" is obviously that these are saturated phenomena and that they do not appear as objects, but rather as events or other kinds of manifestations. Their appropriate phenomenality is not accessed through observation or strictly visual perception, but instead through love or devotion. Marion argues for the saturated phenomenon of the face: "This one alone can therefore recognize the other as the saturated phenomenon *par excellence*, and consequently also knows that it would take an eternity to envisage this saturated phenomenon as such—not constituting it as an object, but interpreting it in loving it."[18] Leaving aside the issue of interpretation for the moment, Marion clearly implies that acknowledging the face of the other in love is an appropriate response, constituting it as an object is not. Here, one might easily think that this could happen: someone might think of something as an economic phenomenon when it might have been more appropriate to apply political or ecological parameters. A cultural phenomenon might be experienced as a religious phenomenon or the reverse. People often speak of "spiritual" experiences in nature or art, which might suggest that categories are being conflated in such designation. Indeed, it might be even easier to envision phenomena that do overlap categories and that

---

[15] *Visible and Revealed*, 124.
[16] *Believing in Order to See*, 113. This is a very frequent claim in Marion's work, made in multiple essays in both *The Visible and the Revealed* and *Believing in Order to See*. He often interprets it in terms of Pascal's third order of charity. Indeed, often the appeal is to love rather than to faith: "But in this case, to see this invisible face, I must love it. Love, however, comes from charity. In consequence, one must hold that the natural phenomenon of the face of the other cannot be discovered except through the light of charity, that is, through the 'auxiliary' of Revelation. Without the revelation of the transcendence of love, the phenomenon of the face, and thus of the other, simply cannot be seen." *Visible and Revealed*, 74.
[17] *Givenness and Revelation*, 45. He concludes from this that for apprehending phenomena of revelation, knowing and loving are the same.
[18] *In Excess*, 126-7.

someone might reduce the phenomenon to only one of them. This is possibly the more common mistake: something is identified as a purely religious phenomenon when it is also social, political, economic, and so on; something is identified as a purely aesthetic phenomenon when it also has religious and social dimensions. This might be a kind of atheism that does not deny that people have religious experiences but attributes such phenomena instead to hysteria, mental confusion, psychological complexes, or other such categories. They attribute the "wrong" phenomenality to them.

One might suggest, then, that one should be able to learn such phenomenality or be able to prepare for recognizing it, hence applying the correct "lens" or vision, the correct type of phenomenality. Yet it is not entirely clear that this will work for Marion, because he insists so strongly that the phenomenon comes entirely on its own terms and that it imposes its own modes of appearing (in fact, this is of a piece with the previous claim, namely that categories of phenomenality cannot be imposed but that the phenomenon defies all such categories). For example:

> I cannot have vision of these phenomena, because I cannot constitute them starting from a univocal meaning, and even less produce them as objects. What I see of them, if I see anything of them that *is*, does not result from the constitution I would assign to them in the visible, but from the effect they produce on me. And, in fact, this happens in reverse so that my look is submerged, in a counter-intentional manner... In this way, the phenomenon that befalls and happens to us reverses the order of visibility in that it no longer results from my intention but from its own counter-intentionality.[19]

Thus, one does not switch phenomenalities, does not choose to move from poverty to saturation, the constitution of objects to immersion in events, but the phenomenon imposes this upon me. In another context he contends even more strongly: "Appearance no longer imposes itself on the phenomenon with the status of an object coming from a transcendental authority but, rather, erupts at its own initiative. The phenomenon appears in and by itself. It owes the crossing of gap between the invisible and the visible only to itself."[20] If, however, the phenomenality of these phenomena is, indeed, something imposed solely by the phenomenon itself rather than a category we choose to apply to it, how would a switch from one sort of phenomenality to another actually become possible? How would we "learn to see otherwise" (as he contends Benoist must do)? Can one choose to apply or recognize a different phenomenality if one does not already recognize it, if it is not already overwhelmingly provided by the phenomenon in apparently unmistakable fashion? It is clear that Marion thinks of this as a confusion of categories, but it is not clear that one must not always already up front be open to the unique category of revelatory phenomenality. His account seems to forbid "learning" it or preparing for it in some fashion that would then, subsequently, enable one to recognize and perceive the phenomena in that category, the ones that come with this

---

[19] *In Excess*, 113.
[20] *Believing in Order to See*, 110.

sort of phenomenality.[21] Indeed, Marion says quite clearly that "from the perspective of objectivity, one can and should say—without any contradiction—that the saturated phenomenon gives nothing to see."[22] How, then, can this switch of perspectives occur? The phenomenon itself seems unable to effect it.

IV. Misinterpreting the seen

Third, Marion suggests that a particular hermeneutic might be needed in order to "see" phenomena and contends that anything could become a saturated phenomenon if seen in the right way. He concludes the essay that responds to Benoist by stressing that "in each case [whether poor or saturated], attentiveness, discernment, time, and hermeneutics are necessary."[23] Although at first glance, this kind of blindness seems similar to the previous one, there is an important difference: in the earlier case the assumption is that the phenomenon appears as saturated but is perceived or identified as an object and therefore misidentified in terms of its phenomenality. In this case the same phenomenon could be appropriately experienced as poor in some cases and as rich in others.[24] Indeed, Marion suggests several times—albeit fairly briefly—that it may depend on our reception whether something appears as a poor or saturated phenomenon and thus that the hermeneutic determines the category or type of phenomenality. A phenomenon can appear as either poor or saturated, depending on how it is interpreted: "I have the possibility of passing from one interpretation to the other, from a poor or common phenomenality to a saturated phenomenality."[25] In *Negative Certainties*, he suggests that there might be a "hermeneutic variation" that involves interpreting a phenomenon in two different ways that attribute different kinds of phenomenality to it based on the interpretation.[26] By seeing something *as* something, a hermeneutic variation is introduced:

> the distinction between the modes of phenomenality (for us, between object and event) can be joined to the hermeneutical variations that ... have (ontological) authority over the phenomenality of entities. That even a stone could sometimes appear as an event depends only upon my gaze ... or, inversely, that even God might sometimes appear as an object.[27]

---

[21] Tamsin Jones advances this critique in regard to religious phenomena in her *A Genealogy of Marion's Phenomenology of Religion: Apparent Darkness* (Bloomington: Indiana University Press, 2011), 155–60.
[22] *Being Given*, 244.
[23] *Visible and Revealed*, 136.
[24] In practice, however, Marion often conflates these two replies, partly because he thinks of hermeneutics in fairly arbitrary terms. I have explored this in much more detail in my *Degrees of Givenness: On Saturation in Jean-Luc Marion* (Bloomington: Indiana University Press, 2014). Shane Mackinlay provides a similar critique in his *Interpreting Excess: Saturated Phenomena, and Hermeneutics* (New York: Fordham University Press, 2010).
[25] *Visible and Revealed*, 126.
[26] *Negative Certainties*, 194–200.
[27] *Negative Certainties*, 199.

This clearly implies that the manifestation of the phenomenon depends on the phenomenality attributed to it hermeneutically.

Yet, Marion almost immediately takes back this claim and argues, as he also does in other contexts, that the phenomenon imposes its "own" hermeneutic and hence that to interpret a saturated phenomenon as poor is simply wrong, one has not interpreted it correctly. This is of a piece with his frequent emphasis that "correct" hermeneutics is given by God or by the giver of the phenomenon, rather than the recipient:

> Recognizing the gift *as* such requires seeing it *as* given, that is to say, aiming across the minimalist transparency at the one who gives it. In this way one can, in turn, see the gift from the point of view of its giver, according to the abandon granted by him, all the way to the essential contingency of givenness, and not, as is often the case, from the point of view of its recipient, who is unable not to make himself its owner, cutting it off from its giver, removing any trace of givenness from it, and finally making it an object without reference to anything other than itself. In all these cases, recognizing or not recognizing the gift *as* gift depends on the capacity of the gaze to see, through the transparency of the given thing, the giver from whom it comes forth and the givenness that determines it with contingency (or rather makes it indeterminate). In the end, recognizing the gift *as* gift accordingly depends on the proper hermeneutical decision—on the hermeneutics of givenness.[28]

There is, thus, a "proper" interpretation—namely, the one that identifies the gift or the saturated phenomenon as abundant givenness—rather than interpreting it as an object or poor phenomenon. We are consequently returned to a failure of identification, only that here, the "failure" lies not in the type of phenomenality with which the phenomenon appears but with the particular interpretation given to it. So, this person might recognize that there are indeed saturated phenomena and might be able to apply the category correctly in some cases but misses it in this particular case. This person is not confused about the category, but only about this specific instance. This stance would not deny that a phenomenon appears, but by applying the "wrong" hermeneutic, one perceives it as "poor" when really it is rich or saturated. One turns the phenomenon of revelation into a rock or some other object, mistakes it for something other than as it presents itself. Indeed, "without the hermeneutic decision, there is nothing to see, nothing to believe, and nothing revealed."[29]

We might think of concrete examples for this category as well. For instance, a person might admit that there are religious experiences but mistake a particular experience as

---

[28] *Believing in Order to See*, 135. This quote actually pulls together (or conflates) several of the categories: appropriate category, capacity, and hermeneutic decision. With regard to a correct hermeneutics being given by God, he argues this most forcefully in his essay on eucharistic hermeneutics in *God without Being*, trans. Thomas A. Carlson (Chicago: University of Chicago Press, 1991), 139–58, especially 149–52. The one who does not move over to God's point of view is simply blind. See also *Givenness and Revelation*, 64–70.

[29] *Givenness and Revelation*, 42. He continues: "Revelation happens to me through hermeneutics, which is to say, through the conversion of one intentionality into another" (ibid.).

aesthetic rather than religious or as hysteria rather than religious rapture. While the level of saturation should suggest a phenomenon of revelation, the recipient experiences "only" aesthetics. Non-religious examples might also be given: someone might interpret a phenomenon as a magnificent or moving work of art, while someone else might experience the phenomenon as junk or as disharmonious cacophony. Something might be experienced as a generous gift when it was meant as a subtle form of bribery. A different hermeneutic is applied in each case, and the music critic might well argue that the person who does not appreciate the recently commissioned piece of music fails in interpretation, either through lack of training or bad taste. John Caputo suggests something like this, albeit in reverse, by arguing that Marion is mistaking a literary or aesthetic phenomenon for the divine and that those two types of inspiration cannot be distinguished.[30] This particular response may well be an "honest" mistake; this "atheist" is a potential theist. If he or she could be shown the proper interpretation or be taught to be more open to the interpretation as it imposes itself, the phenomenon would be recognized and identified correctly. At the same time, it is also possible that this "false" interpretation is given deliberately; in this case the person deceives himself or herself (and maybe others). In the latter case, this category may well collapse into the first one, although the refusal to look at all is more fundamental and presumably more egregious than the refusal to interpret "correctly."

Is this "only" a hermeneutic interpretation of the phenomenon and can one really claim that "anything" can become a saturated phenomenon if one just looks at it in the right way? If that is the case, then nothing is "really" a saturated phenomenon, but it always depends on our reception. At the same time, as we have seen and will see again shortly, Marion wants to say that the one who doesn't see "anything" is simply wrong; there is something to see but the person is blind to it or unwilling to receive it or unable to bear its weight. Yet, we cannot have both: on the one hand, it cannot be a personal failure if one does not see, as well as a matter of how one sees, a matter of interpretation, on the other. In fact, Marion often says the opposite, namely, that the phenomenon comes with such force that one has no choice but to phenomenalize it: "Such an event gives *itself*, in effect, all at once: it leaves us without a voice to speak it; it leaves us also without any other way to avoid it; and it leaves us finally without a choice to refuse it or even to accept it voluntarily. Its *fait accompli* is not discussed, is not avoided, is not decided either."[31] If Marion's claim is that the hermeneutic is ultimately *false*, that the person interpreting the phenomenon as aesthetic really *should* experience it as religious, then this category of blindness to some extent collapses into the previous one, it becomes a matter of misidentification or confusion of categories. If, however, his claim is that a phenomenon is *appropriately* interpreted as poor or rich—that is to say, that what sort of phenomenon it is depends on how it is experienced and the description given to its experience, that what is a phenomenon of revelation for some may only be an everyday phenomenon to others, not because they misinterpret it, but because it does actually manifest in these different ways—then his account of saturation collapses,

---

[30] John D. Caputo, "Marion's Line," paper presented at the Annual Meeting of the Society for Phenomenology and Existential Philosophy, 2006.
[31] *In Excess*, 44.

at least in its strong sense. No phenomenon is "as such" saturated, if its level of saturation depends entirely on the hermeneutic with which it is interpreted.[32]

V. Lacking the strength or capacity to see

Fourth, certain phenomena (especially the beautiful or the divine) require a special strength or fortitude—one must "bear up" under them, as Marion stresses repeatedly especially in regard to the "unseen" that inspires the work of art. A phenomenon of revelation similarly can "only be manifested to believers themselves to the extent to which they can 'bear' it."[33] He suggests that one might be *unable* to see for several reasons, although he does not always distinguish them carefully. First, the person may just be too weak. These recipients want to see but are unable through no fault of their own. In fact, Marion insists that phenomenality always "runs up against the finitude of the devoted (of the 'subject'), who undergoes it without possessing the power to objectify it."[34] Such weakness might have a variety of reasons: perhaps the person is too young and will grow into perceiving such phenomena later. Perhaps one has to look many times—the phenomenon is obscure and difficult to detect—and thus training or talent are required.[35] It is possible that recipients in these cases have not developed the capacities to see: perhaps they are unable to develop such capacities, perhaps they are only sometimes too weak but are able to see in other cases. We can easily envision a small child unable to apprehend a phenomenon in all its profundity or an ill person unable to bear a particular experience because it overwhelms the fragile and limited resources that can be mustered in this case.

In fact, Marion often suggests that the saturated phenomenon might be positively dangerous or, at least, have a great weight.[36] It is so overwhelming and bedazzling that

---

[32] This is precisely why Marion usually rejects this route and argues that the saturated phenomenon itself provides the "correct" hermeneutic. An infinite number of interpretations is needed to unfold the richness of the phenomenon, but these come only afterwards and are always profoundly inadequate: "And, therefore, I will only be able to bear this paradox and do it justice in consecrating myself to its infinite hermeneutic according to space, and especially time ... The face of the other person requires in this way an infinite hermeneutic ..." *In Excess*, 126.

[33] *Believing in Order to See*, 150. The title of this book obviously makes a similar point.

[34] *Visible and Revealed*, 136.

[35] "The greater the resistance to the impact of the given (therefore first of the lived experiences, intuitions), the more the phenomenological light shows itself ... The more the intuitive given increases its pressure, the more a great resistance becomes necessary in order for l'adonné still to reveal a phenomenon there ... Before such phenomena, which are in fact partially non-visible (except in the mode of being dazzling), it solely depends on the resistance of l'adonné to manage to transmute, up to a certain point, the excess of givenness into a monstration to an equal extent, that is to say, unmeasured. This opens the way for a phenomenological theory of art: the painter renders visible as a phenomenon what no one had seen before, because he or she manages, being the first to do that every time, to resist the given enough to get it to show itself—and then in a phenomenon accessible to all." *In Excess*, 51.

[36] "By saturating phenomenon I mean that which the manifest given surpasses—not only what a human gaze can bear without being blinded and dying, but what the world in its essential finitude can receive and contain." *Believing in Order to See*, 99. "For if the given only shows itself in being forced up against and spread out on the screen which, itself, becomes l'adonné, if l'adonné must and can alone in this way transform an impact into visibility the extent of the phenomenalization depends on the resistance of the l'adonné to the brutal shock of the given." *In Excess*, 51.

most of us turn away, unable to bear it. Thus, "the ordeal of excess is actually attested by the resistance, possibly the pain, that it imposes itself on the one who receives it."[37] There is real danger here, and not only in the case of phenomena of revelation: "Resistance can go so far as to expose me to a danger, the danger of seeing too much, hearing too much, sensing too much, tasting too much, smelling too much. This resistance imposes itself as suffering, and what does one feel more than one's pain?"[38] One can respond to such danger either by "recoiling" from its excess or by "repressing" it, "because this affection becomes an unbearable suffering."[39] Marion often contemplates the possibility that one might not be able to bear such weight:

> Instead of the saturated phenomenon still being inscribed within phenomenality because the gifted still receives it, the gifted might no longer be able or might decide not to bear the given, to no longer convey it to the visible. In short, the gifted might no longer put intuitive excess into operation in a phenomenon, not even in a saturated phenomenon.[40]

Indeed, in *Being Given* he identifies a variety of possible failures or denials, through fainting, idle talk, denegation, or contempt.[41] He often stresses that it requires strength, talent, great endurance—maybe even genius—to see properly: it takes "an immense effort of resistance to the given, in order to phenomenalize as far as *l'adonné* can bear it. Genius only consists in a great resistance to the impact of the given revealing itself."[42]

Second, on occasion Marion suggests that the inability to see depends on our sinfulness. Here also, the phenomenon becomes the very measure of my finitude, but in a way that implies at least some censure:

> My idol defines what I can bear of phenomenality—the maximum of intuitive intensity that I can endure while keeping my look on a distinctly visible spectacle, all in transforming an intuition into a distinct and constituted visible, without weakening into confusion or blindness. In this way my idol exposes the span of all my aims—what I set my heart on seeing, and thus also want to see and do. In short, it denudes my desire and my hope. What I look at that is visible decides who I am. I am what I can look at. What I admire judges me.[43]

Not seeing is our failure; it is a weakness for which we are to be blamed, a weakness we should not have: "We can never exclude some cases in which a given would not succeed in showing itself because the gifted could or simply would not receive it; we need only imagine those arrivals in which the gifted fails before the excess of the given or remains

---

[37] *Visible and Revealed*, 138.
[38] *Visible and Revealed*, 139.
[39] *Visible and Revealed*, 139.
[40] *Being Given*, 313.
[41] These are denials, respectively, of the types of saturated phenomena: of event, idol, flesh, and icon. *Being Given*, 314–19.
[42] *In Excess*, 52.
[43] *In Excess*, 61.

idle in its shortage."⁴⁴ While in the first place, the weakness might be excusable, part of the frail and finite human situation, in this case, the weakness is entirely one's own fault. This second kind of failure again comes closest to the "refusal" to see, but here it constitutes the refusal to bear the phenomenalization as it occurs, to undergo it fully, rather than the refusal to approach it at all, to look carefully. For example, one might not experience Eucharist as an overwhelming phenomenon because one is too tired or has not fasted or has a major sin on one's conscience; in these cases, one does not come to liturgy with the proper preparation or posture and thus becomes unable to experience it in its fullness.

Finally, and in a more troubling way, the person may want to see, greatly desire to see, but is barred from seeing by God, is not given the condition for seeing, the desire is frustrated: "For in order for a gift to be seen as given, it is not enough that it really appear; it is also necessary that it appear *as* given, hence be recognized *as* such. Yet this very recognition of the gift as gift itself has to happen as a gift. For only those to whom it has been given to see it as given will recognize it." Drawing on a biblical verse, he continues: "To see the gift, one must double the gift of the gift by the gift of its recognition."⁴⁵ God provides the condition for seeing the gift; this condition itself is a gift that comes to us entirely without our doing. God supplies the intuition that enables the seeing of the phenomenon:

> Indeed, they will not truly recognize him until his "words," and thus his own significations and concepts, allow them at last to constitute the intuition, maddening for as long as it remained bare, into a complete phenomenon. And here, as on the road to Emmaus, the point is to replace all the intuitions into the significations of God; for all the intuitions that we receive from the *gesta Christi* can only be understood according to their final intention.⁴⁶

Christ provides the intuition, the concepts, and the proper interpretation. This seems to imply that God is selective in who is given the capacity for seeing. Marion does not want to draw these implications—God gives to everyone—but he does stress this need for God to provide the conditions repeatedly in ways that suggest that there might be situations where God does not provide the conditions.

Marion explicates this position the most fully in his Gifford lectures on revelation, suggesting that this is implied in the very notion of revelation: "Revelation assumes a plot, in which the attraction acts first on the will, which then makes the reason choose to see what it would otherwise not will to see." Here he tries to maintain the tension between my decision to see and God's giving of the capacity or impetus for seeing: "Seeing is the result of the decision to see, and this decision, made by me, nevertheless

---

⁴⁴ *Being Given*, 310.
⁴⁵ *Believing in Order to See*, 129. See also the two chapters on the gift in *Negative Certainties*, 83–154.
⁴⁶ *Believing in Order to See*, 143. Marion frequently insists that the witness does not have the correct categories for interpretation and that these must be provided by the phenomenon itself: "Yet the witness precisely does not have available the concept or concepts that would be adequate to the intuition unfurling over him." *Visible and Revealed*, 143.

comes to me from elsewhere. I must make the decision to make a decision, will to be willing, in order to arrive at seeing. Revelation comes to me *from elsewhere*."[47] He returns in this context to the idea that we must pass over to God's point of view, because "only God uncovers God" and therefore "in order to see the uncovered *mysterion*, it is thus necessary to pass from our spirit to the Spirit of God, so as to see it as God sees it."[48] Even if we might be able to set this category aside for Marion specifically, it is a possible and recognizable category.[49]

Although Marion has recourse to these explanations of weakness or lack of capacity frequently, they are perhaps the ones that trouble his account the most. If the phenomenon appears or is manifested only if its weight can be borne and if its weight is such that no one can ever bear it, that it is so utterly overwhelming that no one has the capacity for phenomenalizing it, then no phenomenon ever appears: "The excess can saturate the capacity of the concept, therefore the reception of the gifted. As a result, the given that the gifted cannot stage cannot show itself."[50] Marion admits that "to be exposed unwillingly to all that which emerges that is visible does not yet allow us to see anything, but only to let us be affected by the extravagant rhapsody of the accident as it happens." In this case, he concludes:

> To see does not require any choice or decision; it is enough to be exposed to the wave always recommenced from the visible. In order to see, it is enough to have eyes. To look demands much more: one must discern the visible from itself, distinguishing surfaces there in depth and breadth, delimiting forms, little by little, marking changes, and pursuing movements.[51]

It is not enough to "see"—one must "look" properly. Thus, the phenomenon becomes entirely dependent on the recipient's ability to receive or phenomenalize it: "in order nevertheless to receive it, the *I* must allow itself to be constituted, 'revealed,' and stunned by this paradoxical phenomenon."[52] This is why Marion concludes the final section of *Being Given* by calling the one given over to the phenomenon "in the end the sole master and servant of the given."[53] On the one hand, Marion insists so strongly on the utter weight and bedazzlement of the phenomenon that ultimately no one can truly bear it, and on the other hand, he so forcefully insists on the need for it to become phenomenalized by the recipient, that the question remains whether any phenomenalization would actually be possible.

---

[47] *Givenness and Revelation*, 41.
[48] *Givenness and Revelation*, 64.
[49] Namely, the one Jeff Bloechl examines in his contribution to this volume.
[50] *Being Given*, 313.
[51] *In Excess*, 55.
[52] *Believing in Order to See*, 100. Or: "Screen, prism, frame—*l'adonné* takes the impact of the pure, unseen given, holding back the momentum of it in order in this way to transform its longitudinal force into a slack, even, open surface." *In Excess*, 50.
[53] *Being Given*, 319.

VI. Bedazzled blindness

The incapacity for any phenomenalization to take place at all is what we discover when we consider the last position more closely. While Marion posits these different ways of not seeing against the possibility of seeing and phenomenalizing correctly, on his own terms, this is actually highly unlikely. There are at least three aspects of Marion's description of the saturated phenomenon that make its identification as saturated difficult, if not impossible. All three of these aspects are crucial or even essential dimensions of the saturated phenomenon and, at least for Marion, there cannot be saturated phenomenality without them. The notion, therefore, implies its own erasure. I will mention the first two briefly and then focus more fully on the third.

The first issue is Marion's consistent insistence on the utterly unpredictable and excessive nature of the saturated phenomenon that causes blindness; it is so bedazzling that it cannot, in fact, be seen (or even really experienced).[54] It is defined, precisely, by this overwhelming nature that makes any constitution (indeed, any seeing) impossible. Its very phenomenality as surprising, excessive, without cause or reason, sudden, arriving in pure facticity, defies recognition. The phenomenality cannot be phenomenalized, because any phenomenalization would immediately "tame" the phenomenon and impose parameters upon it. The second (and related) issue is the fact that his distinction between types of saturation (in terms of quantity, quality, relation, modality) collapses and that, more importantly, each of the types ultimately becomes indistinguishable from the phenomenon of revelation, which is supposedly saturated in all of these respects.[55] Already, in *Being Given*, not only the phenomenon of revelation but even the face combines all the other elements of saturation and both are ultimately impossible to see. The face "incontestably saturates phenomenality, since it reverses intentionality and submerges my gaze with its own; and yet this counter-gaze comes to meet me only while remaining invisible, at least as object or being—strictly speaking, there is nothing to see."[56] Later, he will make such claims of the other types as well: the work of art and the event similarly combine all aspects of saturation.[57] It is also telling that Marion almost always speaks of "the" saturated phenomenon and rarely maintains the distinction into types explicitly. He makes no such distinctions for his account of negative certainty: we are simply certain that the phenomenon cannot be constituted; there are not different kinds of certainties for different types of saturated phenomena.[58]

The third issue is that Marion speaks of the saturated phenomenon in general and especially of the supremely religious phenomenon, the Eucharist, in particular, as an

---

[54] Marion tries to make sense of this in terms of disappointment: "I always see, but what I see no longer attests anything; rather, it measures the range of my disappointed vision. I no longer achieve any vision, but I experience the limits of my sight." *Visible and Revealed*, 137. But how is this kind of disappointment to be distinguished from other kinds, such as nothing being encountered at all?

[55] I address this issue several times in my *Degrees of Givenness*.

[56] *Being Given*, 243.

[57] Cf. *Negative Certainties*, 200. He makes similar claims about the flesh in his interview with Dan Arbib, *The Rigor of Things* (New York: Fordham University Press, 2017).

[58] See my critique of this in "Marion and Negative Certainty: Epistemological Dimensions of the Phenomenology of Givenness," *Philosophy Today* 56.3 (2012): 363–70.

"erased" phenomenon that is so fully "abandoned" that it cannot appear; its "givenness" becomes identical to and indistinguishable from a "non-givenness," because any trace of it is immediately erased. The Eucharist is such a fully abandoned gift, so intense and so utterly kenotic that it becomes erased (*raturé*) rather than saturated (*saturaté*): "To define the phenomenality of the sacrament, one must see that within it the invisible is translated, delivers itself up, and abandons itself to the visible to the point of appearing in it as the invisible that it remains."[59] It is given so fully that its very givenness becomes erased. In other places, Marion claims this not only of the Eucharist but of all saturated phenomenality: "This abandon marks only one of the intrinsic possibilities of phenomenality—for if every phenomenon appears because it first gives itself, it belongs to phenomenality that this gift can be exposed to abandon, to what no gifted would succeed in receiving in order to render it visible."[60] It is not only that we are blinded and bedazzled by it, something that might still be marked as a sort of "negative" experience, but that the phenomenon erases itself, no longer has "being," is entirely abandoned to its recipient. Yet, if that is true, can we still speak of phenomenon, phenomenality, experience, or reception here?[61]

The phenomenon of revelation, then, abandons itself so absolutely, with such abandon, that it humbles itself to such a point as to become essentially unrecognizable. What we are left with here is that one can ultimately never really see. There is no genuine way of distinguishing the blinding bedazzlement of the overwhelming saturated phenomenon from the simple blindness of the refusal to see. The only way in which we can "detect" the phenomenon's impact is through the ways in which it transforms the recipient into a witness (where Marion is explicit that the phenomenon remains anonymous and is identified by the witness without confidence or proof) or an *adonné*.[62] While this latter clearly has been transformed more permanently, the devotion and abandonment called for in response is so extreme that the abandoned self can no longer serve as a reliable witness and his or her testimony cannot be trusted. Indeed, any sort of testimony would exercise some sort of control over the phenomenon, would have to constitute it to some extent. The only way in which the saturated phenomenon can be phenomenalized is through the practical annihilation of the recipient *as recipient*. If he or she retains any ability to respond, to define, to provide a description, then some control or constitution or interpretation is at work and thus it cannot have been a saturated phenomenon, certainly not a phenomenon of revelation. Any attempt at description of a phenomenon of revelation (indeed, of any saturated

---

[59] *Believing in Order to See*, 108.
[60] *Being Given*, 314.
[61] Ultimately (in the Gifford lectures), phenomenon, phenomenality, and reception become identified with Christ: Christ is the true phenomenon of revelation, he alone phenomenalizes it, and Christ is also its only adequate recipient of the phenomenon. *Givenness and Revelation*, 72–3.
[62] See *Being Given*, 216–19; *Givenness and Revelation*, 52–5. He raises the question explicitly: "But if my gaze, encompassed and saturated, cannot phenomenalize the overabundance of what is given, and if, in the milieu of charity there remains for me no central point of observation from which to receive and see the fullness of that which shows itself, then how can the *mystērion* genuinely (*nyn*) manifest itself?" (ibid., 72). His response: "The only gaze and the only point of view that can make the infinite hyperbole of the charity that gives itself show itself is found in Christ: the only infinite phenomenological gaze, yet in our flesh" (ibid.).

phenomenon) must necessarily fail. Only silence can function as a response that is not always already a betrayal.[63] For Marion, then, even the profoundly theist experience must in some manner remain atheist, because identifying it as theist would always already impose some sort of parameter or constriction. To use more theological terms, one might call this a combination of radical apophasis and equally radical kenosis.

Marion consistently stresses this apophatic or kenotic invisibility. He often insists that even the manifestation of Christ ultimately remains invisible: "It is the eternal linking of the visible to the invisible as such, which remains invisible even to its manifestation. In this way the transition from the invisible to the visible—precisely what phenomenology knows how to think as such—determines the very person of the Word assuming flesh in Christ."[64] One might also argue that "seeing nothing" is an essential part of religious experience. Can this "nothing" of the "dark night of the soul" be distinguished from the "nothing" of contemporary uninterest in religion? Might this suggest something about different types of experiences, different types of "atheism" (or agnosticism), if we want to use this kind of language, or is it simply that Marion has not distinguished sufficiently? Are the types of failure illuminative of something? Is the "dark night of the soul" in Mother Teresa or John of the Cross different from atheism or does it point to an essential (or at least frequent/common) "atheist" dimension within religious experience? Must the most intense type of religious experience always be accompanied by such drought? One should note that such drought, such absence of the experience of the divine, is not necessarily the same as doubt, though presumably the former could lead to the latter (and maybe the latter also to the former).

In a different context, Marion roots this essential invisibility in God's glory and holiness: "God's glory, that is to say, God's holiness, is manifested as such and consequently is manifested as invisible. Holiness marks the realm of God's very phenomenality as unreachable invisibility."[65] Invisibility is absolutely crucial to the very nature of the divine phenomenon:

> What is called the messianic secret does not consist in a voluntary concealment, which would retain a possible visibility, reserved for a privileged few and denied to the crowd. It results from the fact (by right) that holiness cannot give itself to be seen to what is not (yet) itself holy: manifestation can only be fulfilled to the extent of what the eyes can bear.[66]

He concludes: "Thus holiness, even that of Christ, even that of the resurrected, remains by definition invisible."[67] Indeed, "it goes without saying that Revelation, in the sense of the irruption of God into that which is finite, limited, and without holiness, by definition cannot make itself received, conceived, or seen there."[68] Yet, this is true not only of

---

[63] Cf. the final chapter of *In Excess*. He also makes this claim in *Givenness and Revelation*, 50.
[64] *Believing in Order to See*, 111.
[65] *Believing in Order to See*, 149.
[66] *Believing in Order to See*, 149.
[67] *Believing in Order to See*, 150.
[68] *Givenness and Revelation*, 57. He continues: "The conditions of possibility of Revelation not only are not and never shall be brought together, but they must never be, if this revelation is to merit the title of the Revelation of God by himself" (ibid., 58).

Christ, but of any gift. He calls it an "eidetic law" that "the gift can never be seen. We are not talking here about a gift that would not be truly given or given only ambiguously, but about a gift that is clearly and indisputably accomplished. The gift becomes all the *more* invisible the *more* effectively it gives itself. It disappears precisely in direct proportion to its appearing."[69] It seems, then, that despite all of Marion's protestations to the contrary, certainly the divine and perhaps *any* saturated phenomenon cannot be phenomenalized at all. "God" just cannot appear as a phenomenon, because any phenomenality would reduce the absolutely saturated to the particular and concrete. Or, at least, if "God," appears, maybe even becomes incarnate, what appears as a phenomenon can no longer experienced as "divine" in any sort of straight-forward fashion, but the "divine" dimension of such a phenomenon, so to say, would have to remain entirely hidden.[70] Ultimately, for Marion, it is always a matter of "seeing nothing."

---

[69] *Believing in Order to See*, 125.
[70] If Kierkegaard's Climacus had been a phenomenologist, presumably this is the route he would have taken (cf. the *Philosophical Fragments*). This seems to be the path Lacoste often chooses, albeit not entirely. For Lacoste, the divine does not come to experience; being-before-God is, in fact, a non-experience. It is so liminal that it is simply impossible to experience before the parousia. We can speak of phenomenology here only in the tiny cracks or fissures where a little light seeps through and that only in the radical effect of dislocation, abnegation, utter kenotic displacement it effects—and that only for moments and fragments. Marion's notion of bedazzlement actually comes close to this. Lacoste and Marion share an utterly apophatic position that for both leads to a completely kenotic abnegation on the part of the self. Thus for both, non-seeing is also possible in the sense that the divine is so overwhelming and utterly blinding, so absolute, that it is experienced as nothingness, as non-presence, as non-experience. Although they express this in different language—for Marion always in terms of excess, for Lacoste usually in terms of abnegation or liminality—the outcome is similar if not identical in both cases. And both seem to promise more fulfilment in the parousia. This is a very different sort of "atheist" experience, if that term even still makes sense there.

14

Doubling Metaphysics

Jean-Luc Marion, of the Academie Française

I. Inversion

What function can we recognize in the philosophy of religion? Do we even have to recognize one anymore?

We could doubt it, if only by considering its origin, which is actually modern. Strictly speaking, there can be no philosophy of religion because it cannot intervene without the constitution, or rather the reconstruction of a concept of "religion." This concept has a modern origin, made possible by the breakup of Western Catholicism. It is true that, from the beginning, philosophy had inquired about the divine, the gods, and then God. But the concept of "religion" implies something else: the comparison of religions and of religious doctrines, taken in their particularity, therefore in their divergences, their contradictions and their aporias. To understand them, it was therefore necessary to suppose an abstract model, capable of comparing them, of unifying or hierarchizing them in order to recognize them or deny them a status in the productions of culture, if not knowledge and science. Thus understood, "religion" could give rise to a "philosophy of religion," and then to "religious studies." This is what seems to confirm the first appearance of the *Philosophy of Religion* under the pen of the Jesuit S. von Storchenau, in 1780.[1] But this undertaking remains dependent on and contemporary with the constitution of the *metaphysica* itself, the critical empire of which it extends into the field that natural theology had already challenged to revealed theology. This situation, which still dominates today, makes philosophy of religion (like the history of religions or even, for the most part, "religious studies") an extension of the philosophical project, and therefore actually metaphysical, in a peripheral field,

---

[1] Sigismund von Storchenau, *Zugaben zur Philosophie der Religion*, Augsburg, 1772 (first volume, followed by several others), according to Jean Greisch, who specifies that "... notwithstanding the brilliant predecessors such as Hume, Pascal and Spinoza, it is difficult to speak of 'philosophy of religion' prior to the 18th century, which, from a lexical point of view alone, is characterized by a veritable profusion of publications dealing with religion." *Le Buisson ardent et les Lumières de la raison*, vol. 1, Inheritance and heirs of nineteenth century (Paris, Cerf, 2002) p. 31. See L. Wallner, *Der Verfasser der Religionsphilosophie Sigismund von Storchenau (1711–1797)* (Innsbruck, 1963); and, more generally, Konrad Feiereis, *Die Umprägung der natülichen Theologie in Religionsphilosophie. Ein Beitrag zur deutschen Geistesgeschichte des 18* (Leipzig: Jahrhunderts, 1965); and James Collins, *The Emergency of Philosophy of Religion* (New Haven, CT: Yale University Press, 1997).

comparable to others (philosophy of science, political philosophy, philosophy of art, and so on). The philosophy of religion consists, then, in a philosophy applied to "*the religion*" (amongst other *objects*) that it tries to lead back *to reason*.²

This model, which Hegel positively accomplished (and which Marx and Nietzsche simply turned around), is today in crisis. Not, first of all, as a result of an improbable and unprovable crisis of the divine, of the gods or of God—as we make ourselves believe without fully understanding what we are saying—but due to the indeterminacy of the very concept of "religion" (and still more of *the* religion) that is presupposed in all philosophy of religion. There is more: at the basis of the indeterminacy of the concept of "religion" is the even more uneasy indeterminacy of the philosophy which claims to deploy this concept; more precisely, the indeterminacy of the metaphysical determination decided by and for philosophy. The imprecision of the best recent attempts—although they were made by the best minds—even only to sketch the principles and contours of a philosophy of religion, results essentially either from the impotence of the metaphysical project which underlies them, or from its total absence. What philosophical (or metaphysical) reason can be recognized as apt to account for a reality as undetermined for philosophy and in itself as *religion*? What logic, what principles and what *a priori* can legitimately claim to bring back to intelligibility a field—the divine, the gods or God—about which our theory admits to not knowing anything and even often *having* not to know anything? The crisis of the philosophy of religion suddenly appears as the index and the symptom of the crisis of philosophical reason itself, that is to say, of the metaphysical determination of the latter. Schelling, when he tried to free philosophy from the *metaphysica* (in his language, to reverse negative philosophy into positive philosophy), did not hesitate to invert the stakes of the question: "Even with Christianity, one should not ask 'how do I have to think?' in order to match Christianity with any philosophy; one must ask oneself instead: 'what kind of philosophy must be in order to be able to absorb and understand Christianity (*in sich aufnehmen und begreifen*)?'"³

It could be now that the success of any serious attempt to sketch a non-metaphysical philosophy is measured by its ability to speak properly and with dignity of the sacred, of the gods and God. This question no longer offers a peripheral, possibly optional region to rationality, like a distant colony or even a *terra incognita* for the exportation—not without violence sometimes—of the certainties of rationalism well established on the mainland. This question becomes the advance party of rationality, where it tests its strengths, its weaknesses and always its limits by putting them to the test under the most extreme conditions, the conditions of the *unconditioned*. Unconditioned indeed, and of a new type, since it is an exception to what *we* condition, by imposing itself as what we no longer condition. We make experience of this *x* not conditioned *by us* by

---

² [Hereafter, Marion's references to "*la religion*" will be translated as *religion* except when the article is clearly needed—Trans.]
³ "Auch bei dem Christentums soll man nicht fragen, wie habe ich zu denken, um es mit irgend einer Philosophie in Uebereinstimmung zu setzen, sondern umgekehrt, von welcher Art muß die Philosophie sein, um auch das Christentum in sich aufnehmen und begreifen zu können." FWJ Schelling, *Philosophie der Offenbarung*, Werke, vol. 6, ed. M. Schröter (Beck: Munich: 1979 3), p. 34.

the conditions that it imposes *from elsewhere*, whatever name we give to that elsewhere.[4] Thus, the posture of philosophy of religion is reversed: it no longer provides, in the name of the *metaphysica*, the court of a rationalist critique on the dissident, regional, and allegedly ontic territory of *religion*; it means—in still imprecise terms—putting rationality, and its claim to draw limits according to *a priori* concepts, in crisis.

Terms that are still imprecise, indeed. For this critical function cannot be exercised by an instance so badly defined as *religion* (even less understood in the plural, from a common denominator which is not adequate to any of them), especially as any possible definition of *religion* precisely puts to work *a priori*, or at least decisions that build on them without the concept. This critical function can only come by hypothesis from *elsewhere*. All the difficulty consists here in determining from whence this *elsewhere* can arrive. In any case, it should be a fact of reason, in the sense in which moral law is *de facto* imposed on practical reason, from the outside, with no other condition of possibility than its own possibility, as impossible as it appears *to us*—to the point that it "humiliates" us. Yet since what is at stake here is not practical reason, but what is still hidden under the inappropriate term *religion*, we must look beyond that for the fact, which is missing for non-metaphysical reason, or else that non-metaphysical reason is still looking for. This term, or rather this aim point, can be specified by theology, particularly Christian theology insofar as it still retains today its resources that are not originally metaphysical: it is a matter of Revelation, as the *a priori* fact coming from a radical *elsewhere*. Philosophy of religion today will conquer or reconquer a decisive role only to the strict extent that it focuses on the struggle between the *metaphysica* and Revelation.

II. Situation

The relationship between Judeo-Christian theology and what is called metaphysics has always been problematic. Today it is becoming confrontational and crucial. This is why it arouses controversy, a controversy that is always renewed and disappointing. This is for two main reasons.

The first is easy to find out: neither of the two extreme figures that could define their relationship is adequate. It cannot be maintained that Christianity can and must today, more so than in the past, identify itself absolutely with a doctrine of being [*l'être*], even if only because, in one way or another, if God is, it is not, thus, in the same sense that things are, or because it is not obvious that metaphysics still remains fit today to address the question of being. It cannot be claimed either that Christianity should only conceive the radical otherness of God by renouncing conceptual thought, or at least, by renouncing to conceive of it at the level of reason. These two extremes—unequivocal rationalism or conceptual Manicheism—would confirm an equal defeat of rationality and faith.

---

[4] [*D'ailleurs* can mean both "besides" and "from elsewhere." While we have chosen to use the latter, it is important to keep this polysemy in play—Trans.]

But another reason—less visible perhaps, but more coercive—is added to the first. For can we admit as evidence, today, that the *metaphysica* has such a decided meaning and offers such principles of rationality that it could found the discourse of theology? None of us, probably, could subscribe wholeheartedly to the statement Francisco Suarez inscribed in the prologue of his *Metaphysical Disputations*. It deserves to be read again:

> While divine and supernatural theology is based on principles revealed by God in the divine light, it also rests on the truths known by the light of nature and uses them like servants and as if instruments to improve her reasoning and to clarify divine truths.... For, since, when we discuss the divine mysteries, these metaphysical dogmas (*haec metaphysica dogmata*) intervene without the knowledge and the intelligence of which one can hardly—or even not at all (*vix, vel ne vix quidem*)—treat these most high mysteries according to their dignity, I was often forced to mix ... divine and supernatural things with inferior questions.... For these *metaphysical* principles and truths form such a coherent whole with the conclusions and theological reasonings (*principia et veritates metaphysicae cum theologis conclusionibus ac discursibus ita cohaerent*) that, if we removed the science and the perfect knowledge of the former, it would also be necessary for the science of the [latter] certainly to collapse (*nimirum*).[5]

Indeed, far from being a sure landmark for us, which can unreservedly offer a solid foundation—even less founding principles—to theological rationality, the *metaphysica* would provide us instead with an obstacle and an aporia, which are added to what constitutes its complex and disputed relation to Christianity.

This situation, to which neither the divorce nor the union seem to apply, opens a theatre for all discussions and even all disputes. This indicates, by way of contrast, the need to redefine the terms of the question. And for this, let us start with the distinctions that are, so to speak, formal, and as such are admissible for all, if not indisputable.

III. Distinctions

First, from a historical point of view, it should be noted that the *metaphysica* does not incorporate all philosophy. No one, or almost no one before Thomas Aquinas—who, himself, does not formalize the *metaphysica* as such—attempted to articulate metaphysics to philosophy in general. It is to John Duns Scotus that we owe the emergence of the *metaphysica,* elevated to the rank of *scientia transcendentalis*; it is especially to Suarez that we owe its domination as the "system of metaphysics," as it unfolds until Baumgarten and Kant, and even, in another sense, until Fichte and Hegel.[6]

---

[5] Suarez, *Opera Omnia*, vol. XXV (Paris, 1856), p. 1.
[6] Hence the importance of the publication of the *Quæstiones super Metaphysicam*, recently started by Olivier Boulnois and Dan Arbib, *Jean Duns Scot. Questions sur la métaphysique*, volume 1, Books I to III (Paris, Presses Universitaires de France, 2017).

But from Schelling onwards (Schelling puts it in question as negative philosophy), it enters a period of conflict; metaphysics is all the more reaffirmed that it is constantly redefined and remains pressured by the increasingly powerful critiques of Kierkegaard, Marx and Nietzsche. The possibility of a non-metaphysical philosophy therefore survives during all the nineteenth century up to phenomenology and the Vienna Circle. The recent attempt to identify a plurality of "rebellious metaphysics [*métaphysiques rebelles*]" confirms *a contrario* this *de facto* historical uniqueness.[7] For, among the three originally conflicting models in the Middle Ages—the *science* of God, the articulation of ontology to theology, and transcendental science (to simplify Bonaventure, Thomas Aquinas and Duns Scotus), only the last, as the *scientia transcendentalis*, used and imposed the term *metaphysica*. And it is only in its wake, taken up in the Cartesian school, but especially in the Calvinist scholasticism of the seventeenth century, that the late neologism of *ontologia* was born—a neologism that is unknown to medieval thinkers as much as to Aristotle and his commentators. Metaphysics, in other words what used to be named the *metaphysica*, therefore only results in a hesitant and recent genealogy.

To this fragile genealogy, a narrowness of usage is added. Indeed, during the modern age, the very time when the *metaphysica* dominated, many philosophers—and not the least—were reluctant to claim it, even if, in one way or another, modern interpretations can (following Heidegger) include authors like Descartes, Spinoza, Locke, Hume, and even Leibniz under the figure of its onto-theo-logical constitution. Starting from Fichte, even more than from Kant, the term is already under suspicion and tends to be replaced by other names—*transzendentale Philosophie*, *Wissenschaftslehre*, *Erkenntnistheorie*, and so on. As for the contemporary era, hesitation and indecision, or even about-faces are not lacking: Husserl waited until the *Cartesian Meditations* to admit the term, with reluctance and caution besides. Heidegger, who had frankly assumed it in *Kant and the Problem of Metaphysics*, then in the *Introduction to Metaphysics* and even in "What is Metaphysics?," ended up being opposed to it and even "leaving metaphysics to itself." Levinas did not decide clearly, standing himself opposed to totality, but in the end saving metaphysics by infinity. Derrida deposed it very explicitly, but some (of whom I am one) are not sure he remained ultimately indemnified from it. Finally, exemplary of this move is the reversal of the initial position by analytic philosophy: while Carnap challenged Heidegger understood as metaphysician *par excellence* (*"The Elimination of Metaphysics through Logical Analysis of Language"*), his contemporary successors (Armstrong, and so on) restored the metaphysical program, at the same time as they restricted it to an ontology of the object and attenuated the foundational requirements of its principles. "Metaphysics" today only benefits from a foundation as fragile and shifting as that of the *metaphysica*.

Once noted, from the simple point of view of the historian, this genealogical narrowness and this fragility of foundation must in the end be explained by conceptual reasons. Several of these reasons appeared with an obviousness which does not call, here, at least, for a developed commentary. (a) The *metaphysica* does not consider being

---

[7] Olivier Boulnois, *Métaphysiques rebelles: Genèse et structures d'une science au Moyen Âge* (Paris: Presses Universitaires de France, 2013).

[*l'être*], but only the being [*l'être*] of beings [*l'étant*], or even in fact the entity [*l'étant*] alone and as such, *ens ut tale*—or, to deserve the title of the science of being (as its contemporary supporters would like), it would have had to consider not the *ens in quantum ens*, but precisely the *ens in quantum esse* (such was the diagnosis of Heidegger, but also of Gilson, in his way). And it has precisely ignored or missed the question of *esse*. (b) Further, in considering the entity alone, the *metaphysica* did not consider it either uniquely or at length, or first as a being (*ens in quantum ens*), but as a knowable and representable being (*ens ut cognitum, ut intelligibile, ut cogitabile*), according to the canonical decision of the founders of the *ontologia*:

> This Metaphysics, as it is usually called, but which should more precisely be called Ontology or catholic science, is called a universal science and universal philosophy ... [I]t denotes all that can be cogitated (the *intelligible*, some say for the sake of distinction).... [T]hus omitting some traits of being taken in the first two meanings [*something* and *substance/accident*], we will begin the universal philosophy by *cogitable* being, just the same as when it starts with the singular, first philosophy does not consider anything before the *cogitant spirit*.[8]

One will note straight away that this reduction of being [*l'étant*] to being [*l'étant*] as *cogitabile* makes Kant's all-too-solemn declaration banal and obvious: "the proud name of ontology, which claims to give synthetic knowledge *a priori* of things in general in a systematic doctrine (for example, the principles of causality), must give way to the more modest claim of simple analysis of pure understanding."[9] In fact, without waiting for Kant's criticism, *ontology* had henceforth reduced the *ens* to what the pure understanding could conceive of it *a priori* (in this case, its possibility, fixed by the *a priori* conditions of experience). And it is not surprising either that the *ontologia* of metaphysics thus ends, always and still today, in an ontology of the object, since the conditions of experience are also and at the same time the conditions of the objects of

---

[8] "Ea vulgo Metaphysica, sed aptius Ontologia sive scientia catholica, eine allgemeine Wissenschaft, and Philosophia universalis nominatur.... [D]enotat omne quod cogitari potest (distinctionis causa nonnullis vocatur Intelligibile) ... nonnulla de Ente in prima et secunda acceptione [aliquid & res/substantia] praetermittimus, inchoaturi universalem philosophiam ab Ente cogitabili, quemadmodum a singulari incipiens prima philosophia nihil prius considerat Mente cogitante." Johannes Clauberg, *Metaphysica de Ente* [Amsterdam, 1664], §§1, 2 & 4, *Opera omnia Philosophica*, [Amsterdam, 1691 1] (Olms: Hildesheim, 1968), vol. 1, p. 283. See also M. Savini, *Johannes Clauberg: Methodus cartesiana et ontologie* (Paris: Vrin, 2011) and the work of J.-F Courtine. Likewise: "Essentia definiri potest per id, quod primum de ente concipitur et in quo ratio continetur sufficiens." Christian Wolff, *Ontologia*, 1730, §168. Hence the definition of metaphysics by Alexander Gottlieb Baumgarten logically follows as "scientia primorum in humana cognitione principiorum." *Metaphysica*, [1739], §1, ed G. Gawlick & L. Kreimendhal (Stuttgart: Frommann-Holzboog, 2011), 52, anticipant on the transformation, in fact quite banal, of ontology into knowledge by Kant. And further Fichte: "Das Wort Sein bedeutet unmittelbar immer schon ein Objekt des Denkens, ein Gedachtes Nun kommt ihm entweder auch eine Existenz, der Bestehen und Dauern, außer dem Denken zu, in der sinnlichen Wahrnehmung; dann ist ein reelles Sein bezeichnet, und man kann vom Gegenstande sagen: is ist. Oder es kommt ihm außer dem Denken kein anderes Sein zu; da ist die Bedeutung des Seins bloß die logische." (Rückerinnerungen, Fragen: Antworten, §28, 1799, ed. F. Medicus, *Fichtes werke*, Leipzig, Bk. III, p. 105 = *Sämtlichen Werke*, éd. Fichte, 1845) Bk. V, p. 359.
[9] Immanuel Kant, *Kritik der reinen Vernunft*, A 247/B303.

experience. The success of metaphysics was only made real by restricting itself to the knowledge of objects, which it constituted precisely in order to know them. (c) The privilege accorded to being [*l'étant*] over the being in it [*l'être en lui*] can finally confer to it a privileged function with respect to all beings: it has the privilege, instead of being reduced to silence and in the place of it, to deploy all other beings. It actually performs this task under the guise (also strictly ontic and epistemic) of explanation and foundation. Being [*l'étant*] is thus changed into supreme being (*ens supremum*), whose function is to found all beings (as *principium, causa*, and thus in elevating itself finally to the rank of *causa sui*). In this way, onto-theology allows, amongst other consequences, an idolatrous determination of God (hence the denunciations of Nietzsche and already of Pascal). Consequently, these bankruptcies seem so massive that almost all contemporary supporters of a return to a metaphysics do not want to remain hostages of it. Or, if there must still be a metaphysics (for example, a "metaphysics of the Exodus"), this will only be in rupture with the *metaphysica*, as it was historically achieved. For, as Gilson first noted, "Everything happens as if the history of metaphysics was that of a science which is continually mistaken about its object."[10]

If there is, therefore, and according to its supporters themselves, a crisis of metaphysics, what resources remain to replace it by another metaphysics? Another metaphysics—which will have to be understood not as other than metaphysics, but as a *metaphysica* thought otherwise, merely rectified and better recommended. Indeed, these improvements were all attempted, and by the best philosophers. We can distinguish at least three types. (a) The corrections taking place within a metaphysical horizon, which lead us to consider the *ens* according to a transcendental other than that of being, for example, the one (Stanislas Breton), the good (Emmanuel Levinas, and more recently Rémi Brague), or the beautiful (Hans Urs von Balthasar). (b) Regressive amendments, which persist in remaining in the unquestioned horizon of objectity and decidedly restore an ontology of the object, which presupposes not only the maintenance and extension of logic, but the choice of never questioning its essence or its function.[11] (c) Or else, the last posture, sigetics: the *metaphysical* demand is only attested to in the silence maintained on its territory and its project. It can be an explicit silence (Ludwig Wittgenstein), or a silence itself, so to speak, reduced to silence by the noise of deconstruction (Jacques Derrida).

There remains, finally, a last rectification, but one that encompasses all those preceding it: to reduce the metaphysical undertaking to its transgressive dimension of *scientia* trans*physica*, such as it is claimed to be opened by the "*meta*-function" (Breton, Paul Ricœur, Jean Greisch, and so on). Such a "*meta*-function" would indicate henceforth the proper character of metaphysics: according to these authors, in contrast to the specific horizon of any particular science, metaphysics signals itself by its power of *trans*-gression—the power to go beyond the specific horizon of each science toward

---

[10] Etienne Gilson, *L'Etre et essence* (Paris: Vrin, [1948 1], 1962 1), 316.
[11] See the solemn and inaugural declaration by Fréderic Nef: "These different mutations lead to a very general definition: ontology is a formal discipline that deals with the objects and the content of models that allow us to grasp the reality of the most general and abstract." *Traité d'ontologie pour les non-philosophes (et des philosophes)* (Paris: Gallimard/Tel, 2009), 20.

an unspecified horizon, in other words (since by definition any horizon delimits or is determined by a limit)—toward a non-horizon; metaphysics should think of itself as a science of being as *x*, neither being [*étant*], nor nothing, nor being [*être*], nor otherwise than being: a science of the *as*, as such, for and by an endless hermeneutics. The illimitation of the *meta*-function, therefore, implies the indeterminacy of its *non*-horizon. But then an objection arises, precisely by virtue of this re-interpretation of the *metaphysica*: if "metaphysics" ends up in all cases a "*meta-métaphysique*," and if, thus, the restoration of metaphysics implies its continuous transcendence and its repeated erasure, why keep the name that one wants it precisely to delete and transgress—that of the *metaphysica*, the only one historically achieved?[12] Why keep the name, if we must transcend the thing? What do we gain, still to name "metaphysics" what we agree it is necessary to discard?[13]

Hence, this first conclusion: in general, and therefore in particular for Christian thought, it is necessary to *double metaphysics*, to double it as a sailor doubles a cape—in order to challenge it, to free oneself from it, to open the horizon to another ocean with no apparent limits.[14] To exceed metaphysics and the question of the being [*l'être*] of entities [*l'étant*] would thus mean to pass by metaphysics (and the privilege it bestows on entities [*l'étant*], objects and the thinkable), or even to go beyond the *Seinsfrage* (and the privilege that it concedes to the persistence of presence) as one passes, bypasses and goes beyond Cape Horn. Besides, how can we not admit that in fact none of us practices metaphysics any longer, in the only precise historical sense we know of, that of the *metaphysica*? Under the name of "metaphysics," even and above all its most resolute supporters have for a long time been aiming at something quite different from what was and remains the historical achievement of it.

IV. Limits

By definition, the undertaking of the *metaphysica* implies limits, and this, *a priori*. To leave behind metaphysics [*doubler la métaphysique*], if only to redouble its *meta*-function, it is therefore necessary to move or to cross boundaries. And to cross them, one must first identify them. Now, it is clear that the extension of the front and the field of experience ends, in strict metaphysics, at the bounds of the possible and the impossible and their originary distinction. A *meta*-move, a step outside the possible as

---

[12] According to Kant's brilliant formula in the Letter to Marcus Herz, after May 11, 1781, *Correspondence*, tr. Fr. (Paris: Gallimard, 1986), 181.

[13] Thus: "The interpretive model of metaphysics is quite different from that of modernity.... [H]e [St. Thomas] concedes a metaphysics of another type, different from many points of view, including in its autonomy from the architecture of science and the role of theology, but consistent ... Even restored to its naturalness, Thomas is presented as one of the possible cases of interpretative models. A metaphysics is possible, not modern, specified anyway by another kind of precision." Thierry-Dominique Humbrecht, in Philippe Capelle-Dumont, ed., *Philosophie de Jean-Luc Marion: Phénoménologie, theologie, métaphysique* (Paris: Hermann, 2014), 79 and my responses (pp. 131–3).

[14] [To say that a sailor doubles a cape means that he or she passes beyond a cape or a headland and then doubles back, effectively reversing the original direction, but on the other side of the promontory—Trans.]

metaphysics understands it and colonizes it (to stick to the index provided very early on by metaphysics itself in its modern foundation) confronts the polemic on miracles—a polemic all the more violent that it bears precisely on the putting in play of the possible and the impossible as the *border* of the *a priori*—undeclared, but nevertheless inevitable. Hume defines a miracle as what, very precisely, cannot be thought of metaphysically, since it consists only of "a violation of the laws of nature."[15] This exclusion benefited, at the time, from the apparent evidence of its assumptions: there are laws of nature, certainly not yet all established, or not governing all phenomena, but nevertheless supposedly achieving this, in the end. And this, even more so that one could also assimilate them to the alleged "laws of order" [*lois de l'ordre*], in which Malebranche recognized the divine Word itself. But the history of science has since well-established that, strictly speaking, there are no "laws of nature," except as hypotheses that are always revisable. And this, especially since there is no "nature," except what the technological frame unmakes and remakes according to its measure. Consequently, for better or for worse, the contemporary view cannot and can no longer claim to set the limits of the possible. Criticism of the miracle belongs, therefore, to the history of the *metaphysica*, and disappears in the contemporary horizon of nihilism. Philosophy, today no longer able to assume acquired the difference between the possible and the impossible, must confront it as a question. A question for philosophy, of course, but not only for philosophy.

Now, it turns out that this question—to leave behind [*doubler*] the limits of possibility—also concerns Christian thought, or at least, it should concern it first and foremost, if Christianity really thought through what it should rather incarnate, instead of eluding it, as Charles Péguy noted: "When will we have the disestablishment of metaphysics?"[16] It is this disestablishment that no doubt Simone Weil also aimed at under the title of the "philosophical cleansing of the Catholic religion."[17] But if Christian (and Jewish) theology was resolved to double the Cape of the *metaphysica*, it would still need to determine the limit in question, and to specify the one who would have the quality to leave it behind [*pour la doubler*].

---

[15] David Hume, *An Enquiry concerning Human Understanding*, X, 12, ed. Tom L. Beauchamp (Oxford: Oxford University Press, 1999), 173. Should we emphasize that the rejection of the miracle does not depend on a rejection of Christianity? The example of Malebranche (the most eminent of a large troupe), who challenges the miracle to found Christianity in reason, proves the opposite.

[16] "When will we finally have the separation of metaphysics and the state; but for good this time; the true, the good separation; not always the separation of metaphysics electorally, politically weakest, in parliamentary politics, for the profit and for the governmental establishment of metaphysics electorally, politically strong, in electoral policy, but definitively the separation of metaphysics, strong or weak, without acceptance and without exception, same electoral, same political, and even parliamentary.... We have the de-establishment of the Churches. When will we have the disestablishment of metaphysics?" Charles Péguy, *De la situation faite au parti intellectuel dans le monde moderne*, in *Œuvres en prose*, ed. Robert Burac (Paris: Gallimard, 1988) vol.2, pp. 563ff. Certainly directly linked to the controversial history of France at the time of the law of separation, this remark nevertheless deserves to be taken seriously in theory.

[17] "The philosophical cleansing of the Catholic religion has never been done. In order to do it, it would be necessary to be inside and outside." Simone Weil, *Gravity and Grace*, trans. Emma Crawford and Mario von der Ruhr (London: Routledge, 2002), 133. But rightly, who knows the border and the boundary between the inside and the outside?

The answer to this question could be outlined on the basis of two observations, one philosophical, the other theological, and their comparison. (a) In philosophical terms, we have seen that the initial decision of the *metaphysica* consists in defining the *ens* by possibility:—either negatively ("What is impossible cannot exist")—or very positively— ("Only what is possible can exist")—being understood that possibility itself is defined by the non-contradictory representation *for us*.[18] "The not-nothing is something. The representable, namely that which does not include any contradiction, that which, whatever it is, is not A and not-A—this is possible."[19] Kant confirms and doubles this principle by leading back the couple possible/impossible to the supreme concept of the object: "The highest concept, by which it is customary to begin a transcendental philosophy, is generally the division between the possible and the impossible. But, as all division supposes a divided concept, we must admit in it still another, higher one, and this is the concept of an object in general."[20] In fact, Kant shows clearly that possibility, conceived as the condition for all representation for a finite mind within the *a priori* limits of experience, can *only* relate to *objects*. To transgress the boundary between the concepts of possible and impossible means, therefore, also to challenge the irreducible priority of the concept of the object. Philosophically, the limit to be crossed as a border coincides with the line that separates the possible and the impossible.

Now, (b) it turns out, this time in biblical and therefore theological terms, that the nature of God also and equally (which does not mean univocally) consists in not depending on the distinction or the opposition between the possible and the impossible: "for nothing with God will be impossible."[21] This is unlike human beings, for whom, precisely, the possible always comes up against the impossible in the last instance (even if only in death): for the mortal, the possible is always defined on principle as the not-yet-impossible, which will necessarily end up becoming it—impossible. As the prophets announced and as Jesus Christ reveals, God is characterized instead by removing the limit of the *metaphysica:* for God, possible and impossible are not distinguished (even if the extremes of the [im-]possible do not coincide, for God, with what they seem to be for us). It is this coincidence that Nicholas of Cusa, one of the few contemporary thinkers of the establishment of the *metaphysica* not to have subscribed to it, had admirably seen and stressed: "Hence, since nothing is impossible for God, we should look for Him (in whom impossibility is necessity) in those things which are impossible in this world. Just as in this world infinity is actually impossible, so endless

---

[18] "Quod impossibile est, existere nequit" and "Quod possibile est, illud existere potest." Christian Wolff, *Ontologia*, §§132 & 133). See also "Ens dicitur, quod existere potest, consequenter cui Existia non repugnat" (§134).

[19] "Nonnihil est aliquid. Repraesentabile, quidquid non involvit contradictionem, quidquid non est A et non-A, est possibile." Alexander Gottlieb Baumgarten, *Metaphysica*, §8, p. 56.

[20] Kant: "Der höchste Begriff, von dem man eine Transzendentalphilosophie anzufangen pflegt, ist gemeiniglich die Einteilung in das Mögliche und das Unmögliche. Da aber alle Entteilung einen eingeteilten Begriff voraussetzt, so muß noch ein höherer angegeben werden, und dieser ist der Begriff von einem Gegenstande überhaupt." Immanuel Kant, *Kritik der reinen Vernunft*, A290/B346.

[21] Luke 1:37 = Gen. 18:14 (on the birth of a child from a sterile woman); Luke 18:27 = Matt. 19:26 (on the dependence of the rich on their wealth); Mark 14:36 (about the agony at Gethsemane).

magnitude is the necessity which necessitates the existence of not-being, or nothing."[22] Or again:

> I thank You, my God, for disclosing to me that there is no other way of approaching You than this way which seems to all men, including the most learned philosophers, altogether inaccessible and impossible. For You have shown me that You cannot be seen elsewhere than where impossibility appears and stands in the way (*ubi impossibilitas occurrit et obviat*).[23]

Thus the space which could, *perhaps*, make sense of the question of God as revealed in Jesus Christ is only opened once the possible and the impossible are *exceeded* (therefore, once objectity is also surpassed), in short, once *our* domain is exceeded, that which we are sufficient to govern (at least we can claim so). The space where God is manifest opens, for us, there where the impossible becomes, or rather *can* become possible, that is to say where we—we cannot take a step, because "the place on which [we] are standing is holy ground" (Exod. 3:5).

We have probably reached the point where it becomes *reasonable* to work (to let ourselves be worked by) the impossible. We therefore have to listen seriously to Heidegger's warning: "*Das Unmögliche ist des Menschen höchste Möglichkeit*" (the impossible is the highest possibility for man), and the watchword of Stéphane Mallarmé: "only the impossible is achievable!"[24]

---

[22] "Unde cum deo nihil sit impossibile, oportet per ea quae in hoc mundo sunt impossibilia nos ad ipsum respicere, apud quem impossibilitas est necessitas. Sicut infinitas in hoc m undo actu est impossibilis, sic magnitudo cuius non est finis est necessitas ilia, ouae non-ens seu nihil ut sit necessitat." Nicholas of Cusa, in Jasper Hopkins, *A Concise Introduction to the Philosophy of Nicholas of Cusa* (Minneapolis, MN: University of Minnesota Press, 1978) 59/134, 135.

[23] "Quapropter tibi gratias ago, Deus meus, quia patefacis mihi, quod non est via alia ad te accendendi nisi illa, quae omnibus hominibus etiam doctissimis philosophis, videtur penitus inaccessibilis et impossibilis, quoniam tu mihi ostendisti te non posse alibi videri quam ubi impossibilitas occurrit et obviat." Nicholas of Cusa, *De Visione Dei*, in Jasper Hopkins, *Nicholas of Cusa's Dialectical Mysticism: Text, Translation, and Interpretive Study of De Visione Dei* (Minneapolis, MN: The Arthur J. Banning Press, 1985) 39/697. This can be transposed into the necessary incomprehensibility of the infinite:"Apparuisti mihi Domine aliquando, ut invisibilis ab omni creatura, quia es Deus absconditus infinitus. Infinitas autem est incomprehensibilis omni modo comprehendendi." Cusa, *De Visione Dei*, 48/702. We then find Descartes' thesis: "Idea infiniti, ut sit vera, nullo modo debet comprehendi, quoniam ipsa incomprehensibilitas in ratione formali infiniti continetur" (AT VII, 368). On all these points, see a more detailed analysis in Jean-Luc Marion, *Negative Certainties*, trans. Stephen Lewis (Chicago, University of Chicago Press), chapter 2.

[24] Martin Heidegger, *Ponderings. Volume 3, XII-XV Black notebooks, 1939–1941*, trans. and ed. Richard Rojcewicz (Bloomington, IN: Indiana University Press, 2017) 37/217. "If the impossible—that which is withdrawn from calculation—has become impossible, then humans have falsely turned their smallest smallness into greatness." Martin Heidegger, *Ponderings. Volume 1, I-VI Black notebooks, 1931–1938*, trans. and ed. Richard Rojcewicz (Bloomington, IN: Indiana University Press, 2016), 116 (132)/360. To Henri Cazalis, May 29, 1867, *Œuvres Complètes*, ed. Bertrand Marachal (Paris: Gallimard, 1998), "Pléiade," t. 1, p. 721. Declaration which arose in "the black, humid and freezing climate of Besançon" (p. 714), where it entered "into Supreme Disappearance" (p. 715), but where "Poetry [takes its place] love" (p. 715).

V. Orders

But it is not impossible to reach the impossible. For the *metaphysica* defined it very easily in opposition to what it thinks as possible—to the possibility of an essence, according to the criterion of logical contradiction of A toward non-A; correlated, the definition of the impossibility of an existence by the impotence of actuality (it is not possible that A becomes effective) merely declines this contradiction from essence to existence; or more precisely, it notes the insufficiency of cause to produce an effect, and so, it confirms the inadequacy of sufficient reason to produce such an existence. Christian theology certainly cannot purport to change or dispense with these logical laws, which precisely define finite thought: it envisages instead circumventing them and bypassing the cape [*doubler le cap*] in overdetermining this very logic. Not toward an absence of logic (a situation inconceivable in principle), but toward a redefinition of what the *logos* implies and deploys as far as logic is concerned. For Christian theology is characterized, amongst other particularities, by the denomination of God as *Logos*; this denomination allows us to consider doubling one *logos* by another, eventually doubling one logic by another—so that some impossibilities are reverted into possibilities, according to another logic than that of metaphysical formality. How to thematize this crossing and this reversal? How to identify the limit where, like on a watershed, the possible and the impossible divide? By seriously considering the formula which designates the foundation of biblical revelation: "God is *agapē*" (1 John 4, 8, 16) and formalizes the fact that Jesus Christ, "having loved (*agapēsas*) his own who were in the world, he loved them to the end (*eis telos hēgapêsên autous*)" (John 13:1). The question, therefore, becomes clearer: to reach the point from which we could double the cape of the impossible (thus also of objectity), we must double the logic of the *metaphysica* by a logic of *agapē*.

We owe it to Pascal, confronted both with the Cartesian foundation of the *cogitatio* in the *ego* and (through controversies over grace) with the first consequences of the establishment of the system of the *metaphysica*, brilliantly and without doubt definitively to have emphasized this gap and fixed the only way to overcome it. The doctrine of the three orders shows that *agapē*, here named love [*charité*], constitutes at once the proper basis of Christian thought and the only means of acceding to it.[25] Let us reread the text which redoubles the distinction between Cartesian extension and the *cogitatio* (and thus the *ens ut cogitabile*, under the custody of the possible) by the immeasurable gap between this very *cogitatio* and love:

> The infinite distance between body and mind symbolizes the infinitely more infinite distance between mind and charity, for charity is supernatural. / All the splendour of greatness lacks lustre for those engaged in pursuits of the mind. / The greatness of intellectual people is not visible to kings, rich men, captains, who are all great in a carnal sense. / The greatness of wisdom, which is nothing if it does not

---

[25] [Marion uses *charité* consistently, in accord with Pascal. We have replaced this with "love," since it is the more usual word in contemporary English, except where Marion is explicitly citing Pascal—Trans.]

come from God, is not visible to carnal or intellectual people. They are three orders differing in kind.... The infinite distance between body and mind symbolizes the infinitely more infinite distance between mind and charity, for charity is supernatural. / All the splendour of greatness lacks lustre for those engaged in pursuits of the mind. / The greatness of intellectual people is not visible to kings, rich men, captains, who are all great in a carnal sense. / The greatness of wisdom, which is nothing if it does not come from God, is not visible to carnal or intellectual people. They are three orders differing in kind.[26]

Thought therefore never begins to think in a (Christian) theological mode as long as it does not accede to what Jesus Christ puts in play: love.

And thought only accedes to this love if it manages to know it in a way that is suited to love itself, according to the modes of manifestation of the latter and following the rules of its logic—that are opposed to the rules of the logic of *cogitatio*, and therefore of the *metaphysica*. What Pascal equally brilliantly formulates is inscribed in a constant theological tradition:

I do not speak here of divine truths, which I shall take care not to comprise under the art of persuasion, because they are infinitely superior to nature: God alone can place them in the soul and in such a way as it pleases him. I know that he has desired that *they should enter from the heart into the mind, and not from the mind into the heart*, to humiliate that proud power of reasoning that claims the right to be the judge of the things that the will chooses; and to cure this infirm will which is wholly corrupted by its filthy attachments. And then it comes that while in speaking of human things, we say that it is necessary to know them before we can love them, which has passed into a proverb, the saints on the contrary say in speaking of divine things that it is necessary to love them in order to know them, and that we only enter truth through charity, from which they have made one of their most useful maxims.[27]

Philosophy knows perfectly the difficulty of moving from the first to the second order: to overcome this difficulty, it mobilizes uneasy, even extreme operations: doubt, the *epochē*, the conversion of the gaze, criticism, reversal (of values, of the natural attitude), the reduction, anxiety (or even boredom, responsibility, the call), and so on, but these

---

[26] Blaise Pascal, *Pensées*, trans. A.J. Krailsheimer (London: Penguin, 1995), 184, §308.
[27] Blaise Pascal, *The Art of Persuasion* (The Perfect Library, 1910), 355 (emphasis added) [trans. modified]. This is an implicit quote from Saint Augustine: "*Non intratur in veritatem, nisi per charitatem*" (*Contra Faustum*, XXIII, 18, PL 42, 507), which is based on Rom. 5:5, [a] thesis illustrated by, among others, Gregory the Great (*Moralia in Job*, VI, 37, PL 75, 762 sq.), Peter Lombard (In Sent. III, d. 24, c. 3), William of Saint-Thierry ("... non tam ratio voluntatem, quam voluntas trahere videtur rationem ad fidem," *Speculum fidei*, §25, éd. M.-M. Davy (Paris: Vrin, 1959), p. 46, Gilbert of Porres (*In Boethii de praedicationetrium personarum*, PL 64, 1303), A. de Halès (*Summa Theologiae*, Introd., q. 2, 3, 3), etc. The anti-thesis on "human things" corresponds to the definition of true judgment by Descartes (*Meditatio* IV, AT VII, p. 59). The opposition is cited by Heidegger (*Sein und Zeit*, §29, p. 139) who deflects its meaning or does not want to admit it. On all this, see Jean-Luc Marion, *D'ailleurs, Révélation* (Paris: Grasset, 2020), §§8–10.

operations, far from weakening the empire of the "spirit" over experience, strengthen it. To the contrary, when it is a matter of going from the second to the third order, not only does the operation cost infinitely more (we have to do henceforth with a conversion of the heart itself), but it requires getting rid of any empire and any influence, because it is not only a matter of loving (what we can eventually imagine we know how to do) but of being loved ourselves—what most of the time and at first glance we ignore (and therefore that we can hate). The dichotomy between the possible and the impossible fades, then, before an "infinitely more infinite" decision, that of loving or not loving. A logical, controllable, necessity is replaced by the uncontrollable adequacy of grace: a philosophical grammar, by a grammar of love; the love of wisdom by the wisdom of love.

Christian thought only begins as such by acceding to *agapē* and is only unfolded in outlining an independent and strong doctrine of love (let us not say in *constructing* it, because Christian thought finds itself instead constructed by this instance). Hence the imperative demand not to forsake the erotic phenomenon to the *metaphysica* (any more than to psychoanalysis, to the "mystical fable," still less to supposed spiritualities), but to think it to the depths, and thus from *agapē*, as performed "until the end" (John 13:1) by the Christ.[28] The task and the condition of possibility of Christian thought consists, above all and unconditionally, in having access to a conceptual—thus Trinitarian—thought of *agapē*. But, it must be admitted once and for all, this question is in no way one with that of metaphysics, or instead, it accuses the latter by showing its confusion: to be or not to be, such *is not* the question that arouses, identifies, and justifies Christian thought. On the contrary, as long as it remains on this metaphysical basis, it no longer thinks in a Christian way and no longer even *thinks* at all: it mimes, recovers, and repeats what remains foreign to it. For Christian thought it is never a question of thinking God metaphysically, nor of elaborating a "metaphysics of love"— to be sure, current formulas, but on reflection, contradictory or merely meaningless ones in principle. Doubling metaphysics therefore requires neither to forget it nor to criticize it, but to redouble this science "always sought and always missed" bearing on being [*l'étant*] as being [*l'étant*] by a conception of love accomplished as such (John 19, 28).[29] Between the two undertakings, there is neither competition nor alliance, neither conflict, nor compromise—for it is a question of two infinitely different orders. And the same thought should not venture to serve two masters [*ordres*] at the same time.

VI. Double metaphysics: make it serve a purpose other than its own

But what about the persistent *need* for reason? Indeed, it could be that reason cannot dispense with seeking (and finding) foundations for its objects, so that "we will always

---

[28] [See Jean-Luc Marion, *The Erotic Phenomenon*, trans. Stephen E. Lewis (Chicago: University of Chicago Press, 2007)—Trans.]

[29] See "Science always sought after and always missing," in Jean-Marc Narbonne and Luc Langlois, *La Métaphysique. Son histoire, sa critique, ses enjeux* (Paris/Quebec: Vrin, 1999).

return to metaphysics as to a loved person, with whom we fell out" (Kant).[30] But then, even if reason would achieve liberation from its longing and its metaphysical reflexes, philosophy after the *metaphysica* would be no less a legitimate requirement of thought. We have already identified these two undertakings, in themselves perfectly admissible: either a (neo-)-metaphysics, which is based on and leads to an ontology of the object (most often), or an ontology of being [*l'étant*], which would envisage it under another name, even in a revised form. However, these two enterprises—assuming that they were successful—would still not concern Christian thought, which is deployed starting from what called an "unthinkable (*ein Unvordenkliches*)," which comes to us from elsewhere like an irreducible (because given) *a posteriori: agapē* as its own foundation. In this sense, it takes the status of a theology directly focused on the third order, freed from any metaphysical standard, but following a norm that is Trinitarian *since* it is Christological. Thus there would be—or instead there are—two orders, which authorize and require two modes of thought and two irreducible logics: either the "spirit" (at the same time the *metaphysica*, metaphysics, and philosophy, eventually in a post-metaphysical form), or "love" (the logic of the erotic phenomenon, Christological and Trinitarian theology), which doubles metaphysics by redoubling the first two orders by the third.[31]

However, this caesura does not actually prohibit a return of "love" over the "spirit," which articulates between them these two orders. For Pascal explicitly maintains that, if each higher order remains invisible to the lower order (the second and third invisible to the first, the third invisible to the first two), each higher order sees and "judges" the one or those ones it dominates. This visibility, non-reciprocal but unilateral, which only works from top to bottom and never from bottom to top, actually makes it possible to overturn the point of view between orders, and to see, and thus to describe each lower order from the point of view of any higher order. Thus the "bodies" can be described and judged from the point of view of the "spirits" and "love," just like the "spirits" (and so the *metaphysica*, philosophy, the *Seinsfrage*, and so on) from the point view of "love." It therefore becomes conceivable to understand and interpret concepts of "spirit" starting from those of "love," or in other words, to submit them to an erotic reduction, in order, in the thread of hermeneutics which results from it, to review them (and to see what they could ultimately allow to be conceived there) in the light of *agapē*.[32] It is not a question of re-establishing *in fine* the slightest continuity between two infinitely incommensurable orders, but of noting the gap by discovering how the third order *does not see* the second like the second sees itself, and *sees there something other than what it shows*. The hermeneutics that the gaze of "love" deploys on the "spirit" does not see there what the "spirit" sees of itself, but discerns in it a symptom of love, a state of love which does not know itself. Instead of summoning the faculties to the court of reason, philosophy thus finds itself summoned to the court of *agapē*. Not that it is a

---

[30] Kant, *Kritik der reinen Vernunft*, A 850.
[31] [Pascal's term is translated by "spirit" but is also suggestive of "mind" as the second order is conceptual metaphysics. With regard to the ambiguity of terms of the three orders, see Janet Morgan, "Pascal's Three Orders," *Modern Language Review* 73, no.4 (1978): 755–66—Trans.]
[32] To see them in their true light, thus also recovering them, getting them back, in the familiar sense of bringing back a tool to its original condition and cleanliness by dint of a clean and polish.

matter of "introducing the class struggle in theory" (which would come back to judging the second order by the first, the superior by the inferior, the superstructure by the infrastructure, an approach that is characteristic of ideology, the antithesis of Pascal's model), but of introducing the *lux redarguens* of the third order in the field of the second order, which only admits the *veritas lucens*."[33]

Thus, by a privileged example, the *Seinsfrage* (and even metaphysics) can appear in a light that is not ontological, but—*sit venia verbo*—erotic. It is enough to question oneself about the equivalence between *ousia* and *parousia*, which presupposes that being [*l'être*] implies persistence in presence, therefore that being implies the possession of presence as a standing reserve to be appropriated; consequently the persistence of the appropriate standing reserve (*parousia, Beharrung*) is changed into perseverance (*conatus in suo esse perseverandi*), and therefore into the will to power as an exclusive self-will and a will of one's indefinite accumulation. (Ontic) nihilism then appears as an effect and a symptom of the denial of *agapē*, itself then reduced in the world to its kenotic figure.[34]

In this way the question of God is once again radically modified: there is a decentralization, or instead, a complete refocusing of the objectives of the philosophy of religion in its traditional sense. Because the question of being [*l'être*] has indeed little, if any, influence over the question of God, this question depends only on the decision of love—and this, in several ways. First, with regard to existence, since philosophy does not have (or no longer has) a concept of existence in general. Kant established it: existence offers no real perfection that could actually be described and that could enrich the definition of a thing or only qualify that thing. Existence is only the *de facto* position of the thing, a position that it is possible to produce or to acknowledge, but that it is impossible to explain and that *says* nothing about the thing. This unintelligibility of existence in general is even clearer in the case in which existence is applied to God: because we do not know if the *ens* (even the most real and perfect that we could conceive) offers enough dignity—and thus *divinity*—that we should be allowed to attribute it to God, as we attribute it to anything or everything in the world. That God is does not yet say anything of the divine, but is only an ontic almsgiving, a piece of small change that we will grant God easily because it costs us nothing, since everything—including the almost-nothing [*le presque rien*]—always receives it. Next, concerning essence: formally, supposing that God can be defined, God will be defined as the one who exceeds any definition—*id quo majus cogitari nequit*: it must thus be admitted that God escapes any concept of essence. Thomas Aquinas himself, quoting Denys the Areopagite, recalls that "we are joined to God as a stranger (*quasi ignoto*)," for "we know what God is not, but what God really is remains deeply unknown to us

---

[33] Saint Augustin, *Confessiones* X, 23, 34, BA 14, p. 202.
[34] See a sketch ("*Dieu et l'ambivalence d'être*," Inaugural conference of the "Dominique Dubarle Chair," *Transversalités*, n.125, Review of the Institut Catholique de Paris, January-March 2013) and a reading of the parable of the prodigal son (in *God Without Being*, trans. Thomas A. Carlson (Chicago: University of Chicago Press, 1982), chapter III, §4, and *Certitudes Négatives*, trans. Christina M. Gschwandtner (Paris, Grasset, 2010), chapter IV, §24. See also Jean-Luc Marion, *D'ailleurs, le Revelation*, §19 (Paris, Grasset, 2020).

(*quid vero sit, penitus manet incognitum*)."³⁵ *De jure*, the one who believes in God does not know more about the essence of God than the one who does not believe in God, and perhaps even *less*, for the believer knows why he or she knows nothing about Him—since "as divine virtue is infinite, no finite understanding can understand it, no more than its essence (*non potest aliquis creatus intellectus comprehendere, sicut nec essentiam ejus*)."³⁶ One can certainly aim for God as the pure actuality of being [*l'être*], precisely because God has no other essence than this actuality, but only in recognizing that we do not know fully what this *esse* means in itself: "*hoc intelligitur de esse, quo Deus in seipso subsistit, quod nobis quale sit ignotum est, sicut ejus essentia*."³⁷ Or, otherwise it will be said that the believer knows more than the unbeliever, because the believer knows why it is appropriate to know God only as unknown—so as not to substitute an idol for God, in the always finite measure of the spirit who imagines reaching God. Therefore, if neither existence nor essence is suitable for the knowledge of God, what is theological thought concerned with? It has to do with the access to "love," in which, alone—according to the Revelation of Christ—God is recognized. Love is reached only through love—one can only know God by loving God. The real debate, the only serious and rational one about God, consists in answering the question that the Risen One addresses to Peter: "Do you love me?" This question comes from a horizon infinitely foreign to metaphysics, which imagines that the question "Does God exist?" has the slightest relevance, when instead God reveals Godself as *agapē*. If a philosophy of religion undertook such a hermeneutics, it would allow thought to set under the light of *agapē* what would remain, otherwise, under its own sun, this sun under which everyone wants to set up their possession of essence in all injustice (Levinas, echoing Pascal). And this interpretive operation can be deployed in all domains, as well in literature as in political or economic analysis.

But in all cases, thought, specifically Christian thought, deals with its field of analysis just like, in the intelligence services, a case officer deals with a "source": it is a question of making the source say what he or she did not want to say at first, what he or she sometimes does not even know to know, of diverting the primary intention to reveal what would have remained otherwise hidden. In this way, you *double* an agent to make the agent a double agent. We could also say that Christian thought doubles what the "spirit" says, by making it speak the language of "love," when it thought it spoke only its own language. In the same way, we double an actor in a film, substituting another voice (or even another text) in the same language, or making the actor say the same thing in another language, diverted. It could be that philosophy, or even the *metaphysica* itself can, *in spite of itself*, teach us a lot more and much more than what it thinks it knows and expressly means. This is to allow it to *contra-dict* itself: certainly not making it speak counter-truths or pronounce incoherent statements, but *letting* it say something else, in the margins, or even in opposition to what it thinks it says and must say, *letting* it speak in a different, divergent or even contrary sense to what was intentionally meant at first.

---

³⁵ Saint Thomas d'Aquin, *Contra Gentes* III, c. 49.
³⁶ Saint Thomas d'Aquin, *Contra Gentes* III, c. 56 (see c. 55).
³⁷ Saint Thomas d'Aquin, *Contra Gentes* II, c. 12.

Christian thought does not need the *metaphysica*, but it can first double the metaphysical cape of the possible and the impossible, in order to redouble the first two orders by the order of "love" and open the proper field of theology, so that *in fine*, love can double any other rationality and submit everything to the one who submits all to the Father. This would then be anagogical to what happens, instead of analogical with what is.[38]

        Translated from the original French by Robyn Horner and Claude Romano

---

[38] I develop and correct here a first version of this text, published in Philippe Capelle-Dumont, ed., *Metaphysics et Christianisme* (Paris, Presses Universités de France, 2015) (reprinted in W. & A. Guimaraes Starnzynski Tadeu de Sores, ed., "Dossiê Marion," *Educacao e Filosofia*, vol. 30 [Uberlandia: Minas Gerais, 2016]). I thank my friend Philippe Capelle-Dumont for allowing me to do so.

Index of Names

Abensour, Miguel 38 nn.12–13, 39, 39 n.16
Agamben, Giorgio 81 n.2
Anders, Günther 93, 93 n.18, 95, 95 nn.25–8, 97
Arbib, Dan 177 n.57, 184 n.6
Arendt, Hannah 93
Aristophanes 123 n.3, 128 n.29
Aristotle 2 n.2, 36, 39, 39 n.20, 40, 106 n.7, 115, 128, 130 n.38, 160, 185
Aubenque, Pierre 133 n.62
Augustine, Saint 28, 65, 83, 153, 193 n.27
Austin, Lloyd James 46, 46 n.10

Bailly, Jean-Christophe 10, 19, 19 n.1, 21, 24
Balthasar, Hans Urs von 33, 33 n.9, 187
Banville, Théodore de 57
Barth, Karl 94, 98 n.35
Bataille, Georges 25, 99, 126
Baudelaire, Charles 43–7, 57
Baumgarten, Alexander Gottlieb 184, 186 n.8, 190 n.19
Beaufret, Jean 131 n.49
Beauvoir, Simone de 82, 125, 125 n.13, 128, 129 n.33
Bénichou, Paul 47 n.13, 49
Benoist, Jocelyn 136, 136 n.2, 139, 158, 164, 165, 165 n.7, 166, 167, 169, 170
Benson, Bruce Ellis 137 n.7, 164–5 n.6
Berger, Peter L. 3 n.3
Bergson, Henri 69
Blanchot, Maurice 99
Blanqui, Auguste 35
Bloechl, Jeffrey 10, 176 n.49
Boeve, Lieven 3 n.5
Bonaventure, Saint 100, 101 n.42, 185
Bossuet, Jacques-Bénigne 65
Bouillard, Henri 94
Boulnois, Olivier 184 n.6, 185 n.7
Brague, Rémi 187
Breda, H.-L. van 108 n.16
Breton, Stanislas 40, 40 n.26, 187

Brison, Susan 144 n.29
Büchner, Ludwig 51
Bush, Stephen 138, 138 n.13, 141, 141 n.24, 142
Byrne, Patrick H. 113 n.37, 115, 115 n.44, 115 n.46, 116 n.47

Cabestan, Philippe 13
Capelle-Dumont, Philippe 188 n.13, 198 n.38
Caputo, John D. 9, 10, 10 n.31, 152 n.8, 172, 172 n.30
Caquot, André 6 n.13
Carnot, Sadi 71
Caruth, Cathy 145 n.33
Casanova, José 3 n.3
Cau, Jean 133, 133 n.60
Cazalis, Henri 43, 44 n.4, 45, 53, 54, 54 n.34, 191 n.24
Chambon, Roger 155, 155 n.14
Chernyshevsky, Nikolay 51
Chidester, David 136 n.3
Clauberg, Johannes 186 n.8
Cohen-Solal, Annie 125 n.10
Collins, James 182 n.1
Comte, Auguste 123, 123 n.4, 124 n.5, 129, 149
Connell, Desmond 157 n.19
Conrad, Joseph 96, 96 n.30
Cox, Harvey 22

Dailey, Patricia 147, 147 n.38
Dawe, Bruce 15, 15 n.35
Dawkins, Richard 5, 5 n.11
Democritus 27 n.1
Derrida, Jacques 9, 9 n.26, 9 n.28, 12 n.33, 21, 39, 39 n.15, 81 n.2, 82, 82 n.4, 98, 98 n.36, 152 n.8, 153 n.11, 185, 187
Descartes, René 65, 73, 74, 91, 100, 127, 127 n.24, 149, 150, 152, 185, 191 n.23, 192, 193 n.27

Dickens, Charles 135, 135 n.1
Dieudonné, Manuel 101 n.43
Dostoyevsky, Fyodor 33 n.11, 83
Drummond, John J. 114 n.41
Dubarle, Dominique 91 n.8
Dumézil, Georges 67, 67 n.25
Dunn, Mary 136 n.5, 141, 141 n.22, 142
Duns Scotus, John 14, 184, 185
Dupuy, Jean-Pierre 95 n.29

Ellul, Jacques 11, 36–8, 39, 41, 41 n.28
Engels, Friedrich 68 n.29
Epicurus 73, 74, 123 n.3

Falque, Emmanuel 12, 91 n.7, 91 n.10, 93 n.19, 100 n.41, 101 n.42
Feiereis, Konrad 181
Feuerbach, Ludwig 6, 28
Fichte, Johann Gottlieb 184, 185, 186 n.8
Fink, Eugen 109 n.18
Foessel, Michaël 95 n.23, 99 n.38
Freud, Sigmund 79, 82, 84, 147
Freuler, Leo 51 n.25

Gauchet, Marcel 73, 124 n.7
Gilson, Étienne 186, 187, 187 n.10
Goldmann, Emma 35 n.1
Gouhier, Henri 91
Gramont, Jérôme de 100 n.41
Gregory of Nyssa, Saint 147, 147 n.39
Greisch, Jean 130 n.39, 130 n.41, 130 n.45, 181 n.1, 187
Gschwandtner, Christina M. 14

Haar, Michel 131 n.46, 131 n.51, 132 n.59, 133 nn.64–5
Halbwachs, Maurice 3, 3 n.6
Hart, James G. 111 n.29
Hart, Kevin 1 n.1
Hazard, Sonia 136 n.3
Heelas, Paul 3 n.5
Hegel, Georg W.F. 7, 7 n.16, 12, 21, 24, 80, 91, 92, 92 n.13, 128, 157, 182, 184
Heidegger, Martin 2, 9, 11, 36, 38, 39, 40, 40 n.23, 56, 87 n.1, 88, 89, 90, 90 n.6, 92, 92 n.12, 92 nn.14–15, 93, 93 nn.16, 17, 94, 94 n.20, 95, 98, 124, 124 n.9, 126, 129–34, 150, 150 n.3, 185, 186, 191, 191 n.24, 193 n.27

Heine, Heinrich 23
Henry, Michel 94, 99, 131 n.47
Herodotus 35
Hervieu-Léger, Danièle 3, 3 n.6
Hildebrand, Dietrich von 118 n.59
Hippocrates 104, 104 n.1
Hippon of Metapontion 2 n.2
Hirsch, Marianne 147
Hitchens, Christopher 5, 5 n.11
Holbach, Paul Heinrich Dietrich von (Baron) 51
Hölderlin, Friedrich 7, 49, 49 n.20, 52, 92, 93, 95, 131 n.48
Hollywood, Amy 146, 146 n.34, 146 nn.36–7
Hopkins, Gerard Manley 84, 85 n.6
Humbrecht, Thierry-Dominique 186 n.13
Hume, David 181 n.1, 185, 189, 189 n.15
Husserl, Edmund 2, 96, 96 n.32, 98–100, 105–9, 129, 129 nn.35–7, 133 n.63, 150, 150 n.2, 152–4 n.12, 159, 185

Ignatius Loyola, Saint 115, 115 n.45

James, William 6, 6 n.14, 136, 140
Janicaud, Dominique 22, 22 n.3, 131 n.47, 133, 133 n.63, 164 n.4
John Cassian, Saint 146
Jones, Tamsin 13, 170 n.21
Julian of Norwich, Saint 147

Kamtekar, Rachana 114 n.40
Kant, Immanuel 23, 99, 99 nn.39–40, 149, 150, 152, 184, 185, 186, 186 nn.8–9, 188 n.12, 190, 190 n.20, 195, 195 n.30, 196
Kearney, Richard 9, 10, 10 n.32, 11–12, 82 n.4, 83 n.5, 83 nn.6–8, 116, 116 n.49, 148, 148 n.42, 151, 151 n.4, 152 n.8
Keats, John 80
Keller, Catherine 81 n.2
Kierkegaard, Søren 80–1, 180 n.70, 185
Kolk, Bessel A. van der 144, 144 n.30, 147

Lacoste, Jean-Yves 94 n.21, 101 n.44, 180 n.70
Langlois, Luc 194 n.29
Largier, Nicholas 146 n.35
Latour, Bruno 65 n.13, 70 n.40, 72 n.46

Leconte de Lisle, Charles 44, 49, 49 n.18, 60
Leibniz, Gottfried W. 65, 73, 74, 75, 185
Léon-Dufour, Xavier 89 n.2
Lévi-Strauss, Claude 124, 124 n.8
Levinas, Emmanuel 11, 36, 37, 38–9, 41, 41 n.29, 81 n.2, 82, 98–100, 111, 116, 131 n.47, 137, 137 n.8, 151, 185, 187, 197
Locke, John 185
Lubac, Henri de 28, 28 n.2, 94
Luft, Sebastian 108 n.16
Luther, A.R. 111 n.27

Mackinlay, Shane 164 n.6, 170 n.24
Malabou, Catherine 11
Mallarmé, Stéphane 11, chapter 5 *passim*, 191, 191 n.24
Marcel, Gabriel 4, 4 n.8, 33, 33 n.10, 116, 116 nn.50–1
Marchal, Bertrand 43, 43 n.3, 44, 45 n.6, 54 n.33, 191 n.24
Marion, Jean-Luc 2, 5, 5 n.12, 7, 9, 9 n.27, 9 n.29, 13, 14, 32, 33 n.8, 89 n.5, 100, 131 n.47, 134 n.68, 136, 137, 137 n.9, 138 n.12, 139, 151, 152–3, 156, 156 n.17, chapter 13 *passim*, 182 n.2, 191 n.23, 192 n.25, 193 n.27, 194 n.28, 196 n.34, 198 n.38
Marx, Karl 6, 10, chapter 2 *passim*, 28, 18, 68 n.29, 79, 82, 93, 98, 98 n.36, 99, 128, 128 n.32, 182, 185.
Meillassoux, Quentin 11, 150, 150 n.1
Meister Eckhart 24, 131
Merleau-Ponty, Maurice 87 n.1, 98, 106, 106 n.10, 107, 157, 158 n.20
Montaigne, Michel de 24
Morgan, Janet 195 n.31
Mosès, Stéphane 6 n.13
Musset, Alfred de 46, 48, 49, 50 n.23

Nancy, Jean-Luc 2, 7, 7 n.17, 8, 8 nn.18–21, 23, 24, 9, 9 n.25, 9 n.27, 10
Narbonne, Jean-Marc 194 n.29
Nef, Frédéric 187 n.11
Nenon, Tom 108 n.16, 109 n.17
Nicholas of Cusa 190, 191 nn.22–3
Nietzsche, Friedrich 5, 7, 8, 11, 19, 22, 28, 43, 50–2, 74, 74 n.57, 79, 82, 95, 123, 123 nn.1–2, 126, 127 nn.21–3, 26, 27,
129 n.38, 131–2, 133, 133 n.64, 134, 182, 185, 187
Nizan, Paul 125
Novalis 48, 48 n.16, 49, 49 n.17, 49 n.19, 50, 60

Orsi, Robert 13, 136, 137 n.10, 139–42
Ortt, Felix 36
Otto, Rudolph 139

Pascal, Blaise 7, 7 n.16, 14, 85, 168 n.16, 181 n.1, 187, 192, 192 n.25, 193, 193 nn.26–7, 195, 195 n.31, 196, 197
Péguy, Charles 189, 189 n.16
Pichois, Claude 48 n.14
Poe, Edgar Allen 44, 44 n.4
Polacco, Michel 16, 66 n.21, 67 n.24, 67 n.26, 68 nn.27–8
Prinz, Jesse 114 n.40, 117 n.54
Protagoras 27
Proudhon, Pierre 11, 35–6, 37, 40, 41

Ricœur, Paul 4 n.7, 33 n.12, 81, 82, 82 n.3, 123, 151, 151 n.7, 167, 187
Riet, George van de 154 n.15
Robinson, Marilynne 10, 30, 30 n.1, 31, 31 nn.4–7, 32
Romano, Claude 134 nn.66–7, 136, 140 n.21, 142–3

Sade, Donatien Alphonse François Marquis de 23
Saint Aubert, Eugene de 87 n.1
Sartre, Jean-Paul 11, 43, 43 nn.1–2, 48, 48 n.15, chapter 10 *passim*
Scheler, Max 111 n.29, 112 n.52, 117, 117 nn.53–4, 118 n.58
Schelling, Friedrich 182, 182 n.3, 185, 195
Schürmann, Reiner 11, 31, 39–41
Serres, Michel chapter 6 *passim*
Sharf, Robert 137–9, 141, 142, 145, 148, 148 n.40
Shearson, William A. 155, 155 n.16
Simmons, Aaron J. 137 n.7
Smith, Jonathan Z. 136, 136 n.4
Snow, Nancy 117 n.54
Socrates 83
Sophocles 2 n.2, 6–7, 36, 63–4
Spinoza, Baruch 2, 181 n.1, 185

Steinbock, Anthony J. 12, 105 n.5, 106 n.7, 107 nn.11–13, 108 n.15, 110 nn.20–4, 111 nn.25–6, 30, 113 n.36, 113 n.38, 115 n.46, 117 nn.55–7, 164–5 n.6
Storchenau, Sigmund von 181, 181 n.1
Suarez, Francisco 14, 184, 184 n.5
Swanton, Christine 114 n.20

Taylor, Charles 3, 3 n.4
Taylor, Mark C. 137 nn.10–11, 148 n.40
Tegtmeyer, Henning 158
Teresa of Avila, Saint 115 n.46
Theobald, Christoph 96 n.31
Thomas Aquinas, Saint 66, 94, 127, 155 n.15, 160, 161, 161 n.22, 184, 185, 188 n.13, 196, 197 nn.35–7
Toner, Jules 116 n.52
Turgenev, Ivan 51

Veyne, Paul 7, 7 n.15
Vioulac, Jean 89 nn.3–5, 95 n.27, 98, 99 n.37
Vries, Hent de 12 n.33

Wallner, L. 181 n.1
Watkin, Christopher 7 n.17, 61 n.3, 63 n.9
Weber, Max 66, 66 n.22, 81, 124, 124 nn.6–7
Weil, Simone 33, 33 n.10, 189, 189 n.17
Wittgenstein, Ludwig 187
Wolff, Christian 186 n.8, 190 n.18
Woodhead, Linda 3 n.5

Xenophanes 27 n.1

Zarader, Marlène 164 n.6
Zyl, Liezl van 114 n.42

www.ingramcontent.com/pod-product-compliance
Lightning Source LLC
Chambersburg PA
CBHW061828300426
44115CB00013B/2290